ALSO BY LETTIE TEAGUE

Fear of Wine: An Introductory Guide to the Grape
(with Leslie Brenner)

EDUCATING PETER

ॐ

How Anybody Can Become an (Almost)
Instant Wine Expert

LETTIE TEAGUE

SCRIBNER
New York London Toronto Sydney

There are many people who have been of inspiration and assistance in the writing of this book, but there are three without whom it would never have existed at all: Peter Travers, Dana Cowin, and Alan Richman.

SCRIBNER
A Division of Simon & Schuster, Inc.
1230 Avenue of the Americas
New York, NY 10020

First Scribner trade paperback edition September 2008

SCRIBNER and design are registered trademarks of The Gale Group, Inc., used under license by Simon & Schuster, Inc., the publisher of this work.

For information about special discounts for bulk purchases, please contact Simon & Schuster Special Sales at 1-800-456-6798 or business@simonandschuster.com.

DESIGNED BY ERICH HOBBING
Text set in Stempel Garamond

Manufactured in the United States of America

1   3   5   7   9   10   8   6   4   2

The Library of Congress has cataloged the hardcover edition as follows:

Educating Peter: How I taught a famous movie critic the difference between cabernet and merlot, or how anybody can become an (almost) instant wine expert / by Lettie Teague.
Teague, Lettie.
p. cm.
1. Wine tasting—Amateurs' manuals. 2. Wine and wine making—Amateurs' manuals. 3. Peter I. Title.

TP548.5.A5T43 2007
641.2'2—dc22

2006037308

ISBN-13: 978-0-7432-8677-0
ISBN-10: 0-7432-8677-4
ISBN-13: 978-0-7432-8678-7 (Pbk)
ISBN-10: 0-7432-8678-2 (Pbk)

CONTENTS

OLD WORLD WINE

CONTENTS

New World Wine

Peter at Large in the Wine World, or Peter Goes Public

ACKNOWLEDGMENTS

Although Alan Richman likes to say, "Writing is the profession of unhappiness," his work has been an inspiration to me for decades; he is simply one of the best writers I know. Dana Cowin, my friend and boss and the editor-in-chief of *Food & Wine* magazine, is Alan's temperamental opposite; she is a perennial optimist, a great believer in ideas and people, and her belief in me has been an extraordinary gift. She is truly a great editor in chief. As for Peter Travers, I can't think of a more perfect pupil; Peter is funny and smart and relentlessly curious, though perhaps at times recklessly opinionated on the subject of Sauvignon Blanc.

The many other remarkable people who made this book possible include my deeply fabulous editor, Beth Wareham, and indefatigable agent, Alice Martell; *Food & Wine* executive "genius" editor Pam Kaufman, who has brilliantly, seamlessly, and oh so patiently edited my column, "Wine Matters," for the past seven years; *Food & Wine* managing editor Mary Ellen Ward, who provided both money and great music to aid in the writing of said column; Robyn Travers, who allowed her husband to spend nearly every Saturday and plenty of Sundays talking about and tasting wine; everyone in Napa who spent time with Peter and me but particularly Doug and Carolyn Smith, Bill Harlan, Pam Hunter, Carl Doumani, Beth Novak Milliken, Naoko Dalla Valle, Larry Stone, and Ed Sbragia; the entire staff of *Food & Wine* but especially assistant editor Megan Krigbaum, and Marcia Kiesel and Grace Parisi of the *F&W* test kitchen, who fed Peter and me from time to time.

Additional warm thoughts and heartfelt thanks go to my parents, Ed and Pat Teague; my sister, Arian Teague; my dear friends Kathy

ACKNOWLEDGMENTS

Levy, Willie Norkin, Louisa Hargrave, Victoria Worth, Kate Jones, Amy Cooper, Michele Repine, Bruce "Perfect Man" Arnot, Soula Jones, and Suzanne Ausnit; Robert M. Parker Jr., who is as much a great man and friend as he is a great wine critic; Joan Passman, who will always talk to me when Bob is out riding his bike; my travel pal Scott Manlin; Jeff Joseph, aka the Collector, who has shared many good bottles with me over the years (though no Pétrus as yet, alas); Linda and Park B. Smith, who is not only the honorary mayor of Châteauneuf-du-Pape but an enormously warm and generous man; Robert Bohr, wine director of Cru restaurant; retail guru Jeff Zacharia for teaching Peter a thing or two about Bordeaux and retail friends Roberta Morrell and Nikos Antonakeas; John Ragan, sommelier of Eleven Madison Park restaurant; and Dinex restaurant group wine director Daniel Johnnes who speaks French (almost) perfectly.

INTRODUCTION

The average wine book sets out to educate a few thousand readers; an ambitious book maybe tens of thousands. This book began with the transformation of just one: Peter Travers, the film critic of *Rolling Stone* and my friend of nine years.

As one who is regularly asked "What's the best way to learn about wine?" almost as often as "Can you recommend a great bottle under ten dollars?" I'd often wondered what it would be like to teach someone enough about wine that he or she would be able to read a restaurant wine list without fear, approach a wine merchant with confidence, and perhaps even score a few points off a wine-snob friend. I'm always happy to give specific advice (great $10 white: Argiolas Costamolino Vermentino; great cheap red: Morgante Nero d'Avola—both Italian), but I had in mind something more like the old Chinese proverb: Give a man a fish, you'll feed him for a day; teach a man to fish, you'll feed him for a lifetime. Or at least show him how to distinguish Cabernet from Merlot. In other words, I wanted to see if I could sufficiently equip someone for the wider world of wine—or, in Peter's case, inspire him to drink something other than what he called "fatty Chardonnay."

Peter was, in many ways, the perfect subject for such tutelage. As a film critic, he had already demonstrated a willingness to make bold pronouncements: "This movie stinks" could readily be translated to "This Cabernet tastes like a Merlot," while Peter's finely tuned visual sense of "The cinematography could be improved" could easily become "That wine is too white." As a frequent commentator on television, he projected complete confidence—particularly useful when it comes to dealing with sommeliers—and because he knew so many famous film people, he could, for example, report that Martin ("Marty") Scorsese's favorite wine was Chianti, another tactic for impressing those same sommeliers. But most important, Peter knew nothing about wine.

I met Peter for the first time many years ago in my own backyard. One of my neighbors had invited him to the cocktail party that my then husband, Alan, and I had held as a sort of reverse welcome party. We'd just moved into town, and in a fit of false courage or foolhardiness, we'd invited our neighbors over to check us out. Everyone was standing around drinking white wine when Peter and his wife, Robyn, arrived. We just happened to be serving Peter's favorite wine: Chardonnay. Peter admired it, and when I told him it was a Chardonnay, from Burgundy, France (a simple Mâcon-Villages), Peter mentioned he had some bottles of Burgundy too. "I was told they're quite valuable," he said.

In fact, Peter wondered if Alan and I could come over sometime and have a look at his bottles. Perhaps we could tell him what he had? It's a question that almost anyone in the wine business receives at one time or another, and almost inevitably the wines in question turn out to be bad—and usually they don't turn out to be Burgundy at all. Or they're wines that are way past their prime or have been stored in the worst possible conditions—such as the bottle of nonvintage Champagne one friend of mine kept in the refrigerator for over six years, waiting for "a special occasion" to arise. Never mind that the refrigerator is the worst place to keep a wine for any length of time (the complete lack of humidity eventually dries out the cork), it was even more depressing to think that nothing had happened to my friend in those six years that had warranted her opening a $30 bottle of wine. The famous wine critic Robert M. Parker Jr. once told me he thought that all nonvintage Champagne should be drunk "within fifteen minutes" of leaving the place it was made. And I have to say I think that he's right. Or that the truth lies somewhere between fifteen minutes and six years.

And yet, because Peter knew so many famous people, I thought that the Burgundies in his basement might actually be good. Famous people don't usually give out bad bottles of wine. Or so I naively believed at the time. So one Sunday Alan and I went over to have a look at Peter's wines. He led us down to his basement, which looked less like a suburban subterranean space and more like a Blockbuster Video store. Thousands of videos and DVDs lined the shelves of the laundry room, and almost as many movie titles were in the room next door. Peter's cinematic collection looked as if it began with *Birth of a Nation*. Just about, he admitted modestly. But where were the wines?

Peter led us over to the corner of the room and knelt down before a small space on the floor where he'd stacked a half dozen or so bottles. While it was certainly true that the wines were all white Burgundies, they were all from bad years. Some of the worst. "Bad vintages?" Peter repeated when I delivered the news. "What does that mean?"

"In Burgundy," I explained, "there is often bad weather. In fact, there is frequently hail, which can seriously damage vineyards and leave behind a poor quality crop."

"Hail in the vineyards?" "Peter was visibly distressed at the idea. "I've never heard of that in connection to wine." And so the education of Peter began.

How to Taste

Just as a would-be golfer is introduced to the game by first learning how to hold a club, so too did Peter need to learn how to hold a glass properly before he began tasting wine. While this may seem like a simple thing, it's surprising how few would-be oenophiles, and even some pros, know how it's properly done. When I first met Peter (who, by the way, doesn't golf), he clutched his wineglass so tightly it looked as if he expected it to be ripped from his hand. Where had he cultivated such a death grip on a glass stem? Were movie screenings such rough-and-tumble affairs that he needed to guard his glass of Chardonnay with two hands?

It wasn't just that Peter's grip looked particularly punishing, but that his hand position made the glass impossible to swirl. And swirling is key when it comes to releasing a wine's aromatic compounds, or "esters." I mentioned esters to Peter, knowing he would appreciate a technical term. Swirling increases the evaporation of a wine and lifts its aromas, its esters, above the rim of the glass. "But I'm left-handed," Peter protested, "I don't think I can do it"—as if swirling were something that southpaws weren't meant to do. "If a southpaw like Babe Ruth could pitch a fastball at ninety miles an hour, you can move a glass of wine around a few times," I said, though I knew that any baseball analogy was lost on Peter, unless it was couched in movie terms, specifically the 1948 classic based on the Bambino's life.

"You don't even have to swirl the glass in the air," I said, to reassure Peter, who was currently holding his glass uncertainly aloft. "You can just swirl it on the table a few times. In fact, plenty of professionals swirl their glasses on the table, not in the air." Peter looked skeptical but set his glass on the table and gave it a hard push or two. It was at least a movement in the right direction. "Now you're volatizing your esters," I said to him as he made a slow but complete 360-degree swirl with his glass. "I'm going to do that for Scorsese next time I see him," Peter declared. "I'll volatize my esters for him." This seemed like an odd way to entertain one of the greatest directors in film, but I figured Peter knew what Scorsese would like. He was the famous film critic, after all.

In fact, aroma is all-important when it comes to judging the nature and the character of a wine. The famous French enologist Émile Peynaud (the great Bordeaux guru and so-called father of modern winemaking) once posited that aroma is what gives a wine its personality. Some have even dared to put an exact figure to its importance, rating it a neat 80 percent of the overall impression of a wine. But whether a full 80 percent or otherwise, there is a great deal that can be learned about a wine from its aroma alone. For example, the aroma can tell you if a wine is dry or sweet, if it has lots of acidity or too much alcohol. Aromas also offer the first indication of trouble: a corked wine can smell like a damp basement or a pile of wet newspapers.

"Wet newspapers!" Peter exclaimed, putting his nose deep into the glass as if he were now smelling sodden headlines and type. "This wine isn't flawed," I reassured him. "You won't find those aromas." But Peter kept his nose plunged deep into the bowl, as if to be sure.

I asked him to take a good long whiff. "How long should the whiff be?" he replied, a stickler for detail. "Three or four seconds," I replied. Peter nodded, swirled his wine, and gave a sniff of exactly four seconds—his nose a few feet from the glass. (We'd have to work on glass position as well.)

"After I shake the glass, can I taste the wine?" Peter asked. Like most would-be oenophiles, Peter considered smelling the wine more of a ceremonial prelude to drinking than an end unto itself.

And yet a person can't taste anywhere near as much as he or she can smell; after all, only four things are detectable by taste: salty, sweet, bitter, and sour. (There is a fifth, umami, though I'm not exactly sure what it has to do with wine.) Other wine-specific characteristics that can be assessed by the taste buds include the presence (or lack) of tannin, acidity, and oak, as well as the weight and the length of the wine—how long it lasts—in the mouth. Just about everything else about a wine can be detected by its aromas—and there might be dozens of detectable aromas in a single wine.

"Should I be writing this all down?" Peter asked.

It's always a good idea to write down what you think are the most important or most interesting facts about a wine. Most people think they can remember all the specifics, and few actually do. The second-most common thing people say to me is "I wish I had written the name of the wine down." Yet no one has ever been able to explain to me why he did not. "Why don't you buy a notebook to write the names of the wines down in?" I said to Peter.

"What kind of notebook should it be?" Peter asked. "The kind you can paste labels inside?" I pictured Peter steaming the labels off bottles of fatty Chardonnay. Any kind would do, I assured him.

A notebook is a good place for anyone to jot down impressions, though for the exercise to be truly worthwhile, Peter first needed to learn a few tasting words. For example, the word *attack*, which is the wine's initial impression. "I like that word," Peter said, showing an unexpectedly pugilistic side. "I'll be using the word *attack* a lot."

But using a word over and over isn't the same as knowing how to use it properly when tasting a wine. And of course, you have to go beyond your initial impression of a wine and taste all of it. "If you only talk about an attack, it's like critiquing a movie based on the first five minutes," I said. Peter looked at me with a slightly raised brow, as if to ask how I dared raid his cinematic turf.

Once you're holding a fair amount of the wine in your mouth, you need to move it around so that it touches all the surfaces of your palate. That way you'll have the most complete impression possible of the wine. "Palate surfaces?" Peter balked at the words. "What palate surfaces? And who says I have them? And besides, what if mine aren't any good?"

In fact, Peter's palate surfaces are probably pretty much the same as those of everyone else, though some people, such as wine critic Robert Parker, have more sensitive palates. They are called supertasters, but I thought it better not to mention that to Peter lest he be further intimidated. Instead, I suggested that to find his palate surfaces—and get the full taste of the wine—Peter should keep his mouth open a bit while tasting. This is called retro-nasal breathing. "Draw the air over your tongue at the same time as you taste the wine. You can taste and smell the wine at the same time." I demonstrated while Peter watched. "That's disgusting," he said.

But still Peter gave it a try. I'd poured him a young New Zealand Sauvignon Blanc. "This wine has a really aggressive aroma," Peter remarked. "Even though there isn't much color at all." He studied his glass for a minute or two. I was intrigued that Peter expected the wine's aroma and color to be the same in terms of intensity. A wine's color, or its lack, has little to with its aroma. But it was an interesting observation. Some of the lightest-colored wines, in fact, are some of the most aromatic. Sauvignon Blanc is one example; Riesling and Pinot Noir are two others.

Few wine drinkers—even experienced ones—pay much attention to a wine's color. Yet color offers several immediate clues about a wine. Such as its age. The younger a white wine, the lighter the color. A white wine actually darkens with age. (And a white wine that's spent time in wood will always be darker than a white wine that hasn't.) With red wines, the opposite is true. Most young red wines start out fairly dark, sometimes almost purplish, and lighten, sometimes nearly to orange, as they age. Color can also be a clue about relative sweetness (dessert wines are comparatively darker than dry wines, and an old sweet wine can be dark gold).

As focused as Peter was on color, I wondered if he might turn out to be some sort of enological visual savant, in the way that some people turn out to be champion spitters or others possess a particularly good sense of smell. But Peter shrugged off the idea, saying, "I've just had a lot of practice looking at things. And besides, I don't think if I go to a restaurant and ask them to hold the bottles up to the light, they're going to like the idea."

AGE AND TEMPERATURE

Several things can affect the aroma and flavor of wine. The most obvious, and the most common, is temperature. When a wine is too warm, its flavors are easier to detect but its acidity, or backbone, is softened and the alcohol comes to the fore. Conversely, when a wine is too cold, everything, including its flavors and aromas, is compressed, tightly wound. When I gave Peter a glass of warm red and an ice-cold glass of white, he understood the problem right away. Though he vigorously volatized the cold wine, nothing happened. "There are no esters here," he declared. I assured him that he just had to wait until the wine was a bit warmer.

Peter was surprisingly untroubled by the too warm red wine. Even though it tasted mostly of alcohol and wood, he didn't complain. Was it, I wondered, because it reminded him of the wines he drank at home? Peter, like most people, stored his small collection of bottles (aside from the bad Burgundies) in the most convenient but hottest place in the house: a shelf directly over the kitchen stove.

To my mind, a too hot red wine is far worse than a white wine that's too cold. And although I've had some hot reds at Peter's house, the hottest wine I've ever had was a Cabernet Sauvignon at Peter Luger, the famous steak house in Brooklyn. Our waiter brought the wineglasses straight from the dishwasher. Or presumably, that was where they'd been scalded to a three-figure temperature. It was the first time I'd seen Cabernet Sauvignon practically bubbling in a glass.

A white wine served too cold is a more common, less painful experience and more easily remedied than one that's too hot. I showed Peter how the pros warm up a too cold wine quickly, cradling the glass between their open palms, rapidly passing it back and forth. Peter went one further, snuggling the Sauvignon to his chest like a kangaroo.

I've encountered a too cold white wine less often in better restaurants, where some sommeliers seem not to like to chill white wine at all. I've even been asked by a few if I would "actually like" to have my white wine chilled, as if I were someone with a particularly odd inclination. One sommelier (who did not ask me my temperature preference) even told me directly, "We only chill wine on request." What could be next? A waiter who asks if you want your wine in a glass?

Another, more insidious alteration of a wine's aroma and flavor occurs with age. Almost all (some say 95 percent) of the wine made in the world is meant to be drunk within a year or two of its release and few wines actually become more attractive as they age. A four-year-old Sauvignon Blanc, for example, is, with rare exceptions, pretty much over-the-hill. Other wines, such as Muscadet or Beaujolais nouveau, are meant to last for a season or two. "Like a summer-release movie," said Peter, who grasped the cinematic correlative immediately. "Nobody will want to see *The 40-Year-Old Virgin* six years after its release in August," he declared, naming the movie that stars Steve Carell that got a lot of attention on its release with the premise that the hero had never had sex until he was forty years old.

This seemed a good time to remind Peter about a good rule of thumb: namely, that just about any wine he finds on his local store shelf should be drunk within a year. (I knew, after all, where Peter shopped for wine.) And given that the bottle was stored above his stove, it would be better if he didn't wait more than six months.

To prove my point about wine that was over-the-hill, I produced a bottle that I'd found deep in my cellar: an eight-year-old bottle of white Sancerre. "This smells like a basement," Peter said after sniffing in disgust. Then I gave him the same wine from a current vintage. He refused to believe it was the same. "The aroma is so bright," he observed. Peter tended to describe scents in visual terms, which made him sound a bit like Barry Manilow, particularly when he described a Sauvignon Blanc as having a "lemon feeling."

"I thought an aged wine was a good thing," Peter protested after our exercise. "Not necessarily," I replied. In fact, given the pedigree (aka cheapness) of the Chardonnays he was drinking, an aged wine was likely to be a bad thing. Only an elite group of wines ever improve with age, and almost all of those are red (except, of course, white Burgundy, certain other whites, and dessert wines). And red was, of course, a color that Peter had yet to drink. But I had six wines for him to try next—each one made from a different noble grape—and three of them were red.

The Basic Six Grapes
and Beyond

Not only was Peter attached to only one grape, Chardonnay, but also a particular kind: California Chardonnays made with lots of oak. These were wines that Peter called "fatty"—to him an adjective of highest praise. And so my first challenge was not only to get Peter to consider adding a few other grapes to his repertoire, but also to try a few Chardonnays that weren't so "fat." The second part of this plan appealed to him more than the first. "Chardonnay just beats everything," he declared. The comparison was of course for him still the theoretical kind.

Plenty of people agree with Peter, including some knowledgeable types. Such as Burgundy winemakers, who make some of the greatest wines in the world from Chardonnay, such as the grand cru white Burgundy Montrachet, arguably the greatest white wine in the world. "That's not a wine I'm going to be tasting anytime soon, is it?" Peter replied, sounding surprisingly bitter for a man who didn't know it existed ten minutes ago.

But wines such as Montrachet are why Chardonnay is considered one of the noblest grapes in the world—along with about five or six other grapes. The small number of grapes so designated is made that much more dramatic by there being at least four thousand different grapes (aka varietals) in the world—many of which have more than one name. (The Malbec grape, for example, has thirty-four.) The greatest of all these grapes are called noble, and not many qualify; my list of noble grapes I wanted Peter to try included

11

Chardonnay, Riesling, and Sauvignon Blanc as well as Cabernet Sauvignon, Merlot, and Pinot Noir. (Syrah would have made the list too but I didn't want to scare Peter away.)

I pointed Peter to the six glasses on the table. This was five more than he was used to handling at any one time. "Are you sure this is the best way to go about it?" he asked nervously, eyeing the glass-ware. "You're spitting, not drinking," I reminded him. I'd tried demonstrating proper spitting technique to Peter a few minutes ear-lier. But he declared it "disgusting." In fact, spitting wine is some-thing amateurs often find hard to do. Sometimes even experienced amateurs. A friend of mine who lives outside San Francisco and travels to Napa at least once a month claims he simply cannot spit, and if tries to, then he can't taste the wine.

I called my friend Alex Bespaloff, the (late) famous wine writer and world champion spitter. Did Alex have any advice for Peter? Some saliva-related suggestion perhaps? Alex modestly eschewed the world champion title and claimed it was something he couldn't teach anyone else how to do; his perfect technique came naturally. He did, however, offer a story of his early spitting days. Many years ago, when Alex was visiting France and was still somewhat new to the wine trade and its rituals, he was particularly conscious not only of spitting correctly but also of spitting in just the right place. Several days into his tasting trip he stopped to see the director of a large Bordeaux wine company and was led to a warehouse. He found the director there—peeing against a wall. After that, Alex said he didn't worry so much about observing proper protocol.

I decided not to tell this story to Peter. If spitting appalled him, what might he say about wine professionals peeing on walls?

SAUVIGNON BLANC

Sauvignon Blanc is the lightest, and arguably the simplest, of the three noble white grapes. It is the only one that's regularly blended with another grape, Semillon, most notably in Bordeaux. (It's rare for a noble white grape to be part of a blend, while it's more common with the red. Riesling and Chardonnay are rarely blended, whereas Cabernet Sauvignon and Merlot are blended more often than not.)

"Who came up with the idea of blending first?" Peter asked, as if he expected me to offer a particular name. Like Einstein. I couldn't say. "I wonder when it was, if it was a man in Bordeaux," he mused. "I wonder if it was because of the weather—something like hail." Peter seemed to be increasingly obsessed with hail.

Sauvignon Blanc is grown everywhere in the world these days— from Uruguay to New Zealand and parts in between—though it actually originated in the Loire Valley of France. For Peter's first official Sauvignon Blanc experience, I'd chosen a wine from the star New Zealand winemaker Kim Crawford. The wine came from the same region—Marlborough—as the most famous New Zealand wine, Cloudy Bay, the wine that put New Zealand Sauvignon Blanc on the vinous world map.

"That's John Irving's favorite wine," Peter declared when I mentioned the Cloudy Bay–Marlborough connection. Peter had had dinner with the novelist at a film festival in Nantucket a few months earlier. Irving's book *A Widow for One Year* had been made into the movie *Door in the Floor,* which Peter had liked a lot. He'd liked Irving very much too—though not his taste in wine. Irving wasn't a fatty-Chardonnay man.

"Isn't this the wine they call cat's pee?" Peter asked, giving his glass of Sauvignon a cautious sniff, followed by a rather stiff-armed swirl. (It was clockwise rather than the customary counterclockwise, but at least Peter had gotten the proper motions down.) Had John Irving alerted him to that particular smell?

In fact, cat's pee is an aroma often ascribed to certain Sauvignon Blancs, particularly the more herbaceous ones. In New Zealand, they get even more site-specific: "Cat's pee on a gooseberry bush," I told Peter.

"Well, I must have a different kind of cat at home, because I'm not getting anything like that with this wine," Peter replied.

One of the most notable attributes of Sauvignon Blanc is its aroma, which can range from herbal (grassy or even green bean) to citrus (limes and lemons) depending on where it's grown. It's much more likely to be herbaceous in New Zealand than the Loire Valley, owing to the difference in climate and viticultural conditions. It's also a wine that's fairly high in acidity, which its fans find refreshing. Peter simply said, "Ouch."

"*Ouch* isn't an accepted wine-tasting word. You should use one of the words from the tasting-vocabulary sheet that I gave you," I told Peter. "But it hurts," Peter protested. He would feel differently when he drank it with food, I assured him. Acidity is what makes a wine refreshing and lively and creates a sort of backbone for wine; without it the wine would be flabby and lifeless. But Peter, accustomed as he was to a vinous diet of butter and oak, seemed unmoved by the argument. I tried a populist appeal. "A lot of people like Sauvignon Blanc," I said encouragingly. "And more and more winemakers are planting it—more than ever before. In fact, a lot of people are choosing to drink Sauvignon Blanc rather than Chardonnay."

"This wine is actually getting more popular?" Peter repeated in disbelief. He tasted it again. "Maybe it's because there's so little to it. People probably just think it's less fattening than Chardonnay."

RIESLING

There is arguably no greater white grape in the world than Riesling. And that's not just the opinion of winemakers in Austria and Germany and Alsace in France—who make some of the best Rieslings in the world. It's not even just the opinion of American restaurant sommeliers, who have made Riesling their personal varietal cause, as it goes so well with so many different kinds of food. As sommeliers know, a great Riesling can also age longer than many great red wines and develop even more interesting qualities as it ages, not the least of which is aromatic—transitioning from floral and citrus to mineral and steel and even petrol.

"Petrol!" Peter interjected. "Are you saying old Riesling smells like a gas station?"

"No, but we'll have an old Riesling and you'll see what I mean," I replied.

Because Riesling almost never spends even a moment in oak (and if it did, it would be time misspent), Riesling also possesses an incredible transparency of flavor—there's little else but the grape in the glass. In this regard, Riesling is a lot like Pinot Noir in that it can clearly reflect the place where it's made. This is a great attribute when it's grown in just the right place (the steep hills of Germany's Rhine or Moselle rivers, for example), but a terrible thing when the place is wrong (e.g., the Napa Valley floor). "You mean winemakers don't know where to plant it by now?" Peter interjected. "Haven't they been making Riesling for thousands of years?"

That was true, though not necessarily all over the world. In Australia, for example, they've only been making Riesling a few decades, although some Australian Rieslings are very good.

"Why don't they put Riesling in oak?" Peter wondered. The simple answer was that oak would pretty well obliterate the flavor of the grape. Unlike the way a less-than-perfect Chardonnay can be fixed up with a longer bout in oak, there's not a whole lot that can be done about a less-than-perfect Riesling, except perhaps to add a bit of sugar. (Riesling is grown in a lot of iffy climates where it doesn't necessarily attain high sugar levels.) But, of course, the addition of sugar masks the flavor too.

"Riesling is like a filmmaker who has to depend on a good story and good character development instead of big names or theatrical flourishes," Peter declared.

Because Riesling is so different from Chardonnay in character and flavor, I didn't expect Peter to care much for the 2004 Pike Riesling from Clare Valley, Australia, I gave him. (Certain parts of Australia, particularly the Clare and Eden valleys in South Australia, can produce wonderfully dry and minerally Rieslings.) And yet, the first time he tasted it, or rather inhaled it, Peter practically swooned. "It's the aroma," he said, sounding a bit dazed. "It jumps up to meet me," he added, making Riesling sound more like a Labrador retriever than a wine. But Peter was right about the aroma, which was intensely floral. And that it had evoked an emotional response from him seemed like good progress.

CHARDONNAY

When our lessons began, Peter only cared about one grape: Chardonnay. And yet, in many ways, his feelings for the grape had less to do with the wine than the winemaker, as Chardonnay is as much a winemaker's idea as it is a wine. That is to say, it's eminently malleable, perhaps more so than any other grape. Thick-skinned, gold-colored, and relatively aroma-free, Chardonnay is also an important grape in the viticultural world. It's the white grape of Burgundy and a key component in Champagne. It's actually grown in just about every viable kind of vineyard around the world; in fact, Chardonnay, the most planted grape in the world, could probably be grown in a terrarium, if the need arose.

Chardonnay is also, of course, responsible for some of the worst wines in the world, and its generous proportions have made it the source of a lot of bad (wine writer) clichés: it's the "busty blonde" of the wine world, the "bombshell" and the "ingenue." Was Peter put in mind of some kind of B-level actress, I wondered, when drinking his favorite wine? Seemingly put off by such a suggestion, he refused to reply.

The Chardonnay that I gave Peter to taste was a lavishly oaked but still a clearly delineated wine, a sort of thinking man's bombshell (the 2002 Vine Cliff Bien Nacido Chardonnay, an excellent New World Chardonnay). Made from grapes grown in the famed Bien Nacido vineyard in the Santa Maria Valley near Santa Barbara, it's an oak-aged wine that isn't dominated by oak like so many California Chardonnays but showing instead sweet, delicious fruit—apple and pear with a mineral edge. "I'm not spitting this, I'm swallowing this," Peter declared. I couldn't disagree.

PINOT NOIR

There probably aren't enough words to describe the difficulties inherent in growing and making Pinot Noir. In fact, there are probably more words to describe it in the world of psychoanalysis than there are in the winemaking world. The impulse that drives wine-makers to try their hand at Pinot Noir is probably better described in psychology texts than wine books. It's a thin-skinned, tempera-mental grape, almost guaranteed to disappoint as often as it pleases, both its producers and its fans. *The Heartbreak Grape* was the title of a book, and an apt one, about Pinot Noir. Even that moniker probably seems like an understatement to winemakers attempting to make something great from this grape, since Pinot Noir has just about every bad quality you could name from a viticultural perspec-tive: it requires a specific climate, rots easily, propagates slowly, and isn't much good unless it's harvested in small quantities. In other words, it's not exactly a cash crop.

"Well, what can you tell me about Pinot Noir that's good?" asked Peter.

Pinot Noir is the grape of all the great reds of Burgundy, and like Chardonnay it's important in Champagne. Pinot Noir is also found everywhere—from Tasmania (the only place in Australia cool enough for Pinot to grow properly) to New York State (where it's actually too cool for Pinot Noir to get fully ripe). And yet every winemaker in the world, at one point or another, seems convinced he or she can make something memorable, if not ethereal, from the grape. And if not, well, then the winemaker's name can be added to a long list of (other) noble Pinot Noir failures.

One reason Pinot Noir is so compelling is its aroma—one of the most beguiling in the world. While its primary aromas and flavors are those of red fruits such as strawberries and cherries, there are also more elusive elements such as minerals, soil, and earth. And in the mouth, Pinot Noir can be delicate but also possess a firm, refreshing acidity, which means it goes well with food. Indeed, much has been written about the food-friendly qualities of Pinot Noir, and even when it fails to thrill on its own, Pinot Noir can still work pretty well with food.

Peter listened carefully as I described this to him, then declared, with the satisfaction of someone who has grasped the most salient fact, "Pinot Noir is the grape of *Sideways*." Peter, like most Americans, believed that the 2004 movie *Sideways* (and its poetically Pinot Noir–obsessed character, Miles) had single-handedly changed the fortunes of Pinot Noir and its growers. (I didn't want to disillusion Peter with the nonromantic, noncinematic fact that there has been a growing interest in Pinot Noir for nearly ten years, not just in California but all over the world—in other words, long before *Sideways,* the nonselling novel, became *Sideways,* the hit film.) In fact, there's so much Pinot Noir planted in New Zealand, it's said to be enough for every man, woman, and child in that country to drink a bottle a week for the rest of their lives (as some zealous New Zealand winemaker once proudly informed me). The Pinot Noir I gave Peter was a 2002 Roumier Bourgogne, a basic red Burgundy from a great vintage and a leading young Burgundian vigneron, Christophe Roumier.

Peter stuck his nose so far into the glass I started to worry. "I like that," Peter finally said of the wine's aroma. After a brief pause, he declared, "This is exactly what I want." He inhaled for well over four seconds—maybe even three times that long, though, alas, his happiness didn't extend much beyond aroma. "It's kind of disappointing," he remarked after tasting the wine. "It doesn't taste like it smells." And with that, Peter experienced the frustration that Burgundy drinkers have encountered for years (and with a lot better wines than basic Bourgogne). That's the problem with Pinot Noir. Even $600 bottles of it can be disappointing, or worse.

MERLOT

Merlot is equal to Chardonnay as the most easily pronounceable grape and the most culturally maligned. And yet it's not a simple grape; like Chardonnay, it too is capable of producing great wine. It's not as hard to grow as Pinot Noir, but Merlot is not without its own viticultural challenges. Merlot is even more difficult to grow properly than, say, Cabernet Sauvignon—which most wine drinkers (and even some winemakers) don't realize. Many seem to believe that a wine such as Merlot, with its softer fruit and more supple tannins, is somehow easy to make. But this isn't true. Merlot can be a hard grape to control. For example, in Washington State—my favorite place in the United States for Merlot—the Merlots are so big and so structured that several winemakers there told me that they need to blend Cabernet into their Merlot to make it softer and more palatable.

"I just can't picture that," Peter replied. "Most Merlots that I have had are soft and boring." In fact, he seemed skeptical that Merlot was a noble grape at all. "Where else is it grown besides California?" Peter asked me in a challenging tone. I gave him a fast global rundown: California, of course, but also Washington State (which produces some good, structured Merlots) and Chile (where a lot of Merlots are actually the grape Carmenère, a Merlot doppelgänger that until recently was thought to actually be Merlot). Merlot is also grown with success in Italy, Argentina, South Africa, and, of course, most famously, the Right Bank of Bordeaux, the home of Pétrus, probably the most famous Bordeaux in the world made entirely from Merlot.

"Pétrus is Alexander Payne's favorite wine," Peter remarked, naming the director of *Sideways*. "He likes the 1982 vintage." How could that be? The entire movie *Sideways* was a rant against Merlot! "That wasn't Alexander's idea," Peter replied authoritatively. "It was the author of the *Sideways* book who hated Merlot."

Peter seemed lost in contemplation of Merlot's geographic spread. But in fact he was thinking of something else: "Will we taste Pétrus at some point? I think it's important that I taste the best Merlot in the world."

Instead, I opened a bottle of the 2001 Duckhorn Napa Valley Merlot, which at $45 a bottle was about $500 cheaper than the comparable vintage of Pétrus and a pretty delicious wine. Duckhorn was one of the California wineries that made Merlot famous; although it went through a period of producing mediocre, overpriced wines, it was now producing some impressive bottles. "I like this wine, it tasted like a grape that I bit into," Peter commented. "It seemed like it was doing the job but doing a little extra. There was a little surprise." In other words, it was Merlot with texture and substance.

CABERNET SAUVIGNON

"I can't see through this" was the first thing Peter said when faced with a glass of Cabernet Sauvignon. This summed up his feelings about the grape. In fact, Cabernet's character was as impenetrable to him as its color. Peter's Cabernet knowledge was pretty much limited to this single fact: "Men drink it in steak houses." While he had been in lots of steak houses in New York (Michael Jordan's was his favorite), Peter was just as happy to drink a Chardonnay with his porterhouse (as I've seen him do more than once). When I told Peter that Kevin Zraly, the famous wine educator, had actually once declared Chardonnay and steak a perfect match because "Chardonnay acts like a red wine," it was the happiest I'd seen Peter since the day he had had lunch with Marty Scorsese and treated the famous director to a volatized ester show.

In fact, Cabernet Sauvignon has a great deal in common with Chardonnay: they are both big, structured wines that are easier to make than thin-skinned varietals such as Pinot Noir or temperamental varietals such as Sauvignon Blanc. In many ways Cabernet is much easier to grow. It's the most important grape on the Left Bank of Bordeaux, the primary component in such world-class wines as Château Lafite and Château Latour. It's planted just about everywhere in the world—from France to California to Australia, Chile, and Argentina. In fact, Cabernet may be the most prolific grape of the noble six and the easiest from which to make a decent wine.

Peter didn't seem impressed by this information. Instead, he was nervously contemplating his dark glass of 2001 Hartwell Napa Valley Cabernet. There wasn't much aroma, he reported. And he was right. In fact, I've rarely found a young Napa Cabernet with much of a nose—it takes years for most California Cabernets to develop an aroma (and some never do). But Peter was surprised by how soft it was in his mouth. "It's almost sweet," he reported. And almost soft. Or at least the tannins were softer than he expected.

The grapes got very ripe in Napa in 2001, I explained, and as a result many of the wines were softer and more approachable in their youth. It's also the style of winemaking currently in fashion in much of the world, whereby grapes are harvested later and later—at maximum ripeness. Peter nodded. The wine had been a much better experience than he'd imagined. He expected Cabernet to be harsh, impossibly tannic. Maybe he'd like to take it home, perhaps have it with dinner? The wine would go well with steak. At least as well as the Chardonnay he favored. Peter shook his head. He wasn't ready for that. "Maybe I should be ashamed, but I really liked the Chardonnay. And even the Merlot. I'll take both of those wines with me."

Peter's
Tasting Vocabulary

To truly understand a subject as complex as wine, one must acquire a vocabulary or at least learn a few key words and tasting terms. Peter, for example, had a lot of good instincts and some interesting ideas, but lacked the right words to properly describe (to himself and others) what he found in a wine. He needed to develop a wine vocabulary. (For example, the word *ouch* is not considered a valid tasting term—although it was one of Peter's favorites and seemed to sum up his feelings about certain wines.)

Aroma—*Aroma* and *bouquet* are often used interchangeably to describe the nose of a wine, but in fact only a young wine has an aroma—that is, scents of primary fruit and oak—whereas a bouquet develops over time as the wine develops secondary aromas such as truffles and mushrooms and earth. "That's fascinating," remarked Peter. "I might have to obsess over that for a while."

Barrique—These are small, fashionable French oak barrels used by producers all over the world. You'll see them mentioned on the back labels of many expensive wines. The tighter-grained French barriques impart a much more subtle flavor than most (wider-grained) American oak barrels.

Beefy—A beefy wine has lots of everything—tannin, fruit, structure—in an unsubtle way.

Body—Wines with body are wines of substance, of fullness and generosity in the mouth. A wine with a "good body" is as much to be admired as a person similarly endowed.

Breathe—When people open a bottle and say, "I want the wine to breathe," they forget that they're just giving the wine a one-inch-diameter bit of air. To truly enable a wine to "breathe," it's best to decant it. This softens the tannins of a young, tight wine and also helps to open up its aromas.

Chewy—A chewy wine has lots of texture and fairly strong, though not necessarily astringent, tannins.

Claret—This is a British term for Bordeaux, though more and more California winemakers are making wines they call Claret, which are mostly Cabernet-dominant blends. Francis Ford Coppola was one of the first in Napa to call his Cabernet-based wine Claret.

Closed—A wine that has no aroma is often referred to as closed. This is usually because the wine is still quite young. "I think I've had a lot of closed wines," Peter remarked. I didn't have the heart to tell him that the $7 wines he was drinking probably weren't closed as much as they were just . . . cheap and lacking in aroma—and a whole lot else besides.

Corked—If a wine is infected with something called TCA and smells like wet newspapers or a wet basement, it is said to be "corked." Or if a wine is lightly corked it can simply have no flavor at all.

Ester—"My favorite word!" Peter says. These are the compounds that contribute to the aroma of a wine.

Extracted—This word is (now commonly) used to describe a big, concentrated wine. It is what is left when all the possible solubles are removed in the making of a wine, reducing it to its core, "extracted" element: wine in its most concentrated form.

Finish—This is the way that a wine lingers on your tongue. Some tasters even time the length of a finish, but I didn't want to get Peter started with a stopwatch. A notebook was all he could handle right now.

Firm—A wine that has lots of structure and tannin, such as Cabernet Sauvignon or Syrah, is often described as "firm."

Flabby—This word describes a wine that lacks acidity and lacks a refreshing quality. Just as no person would want to be described thus, no winemaker would be proud of having produced a flabby wine.

Fresh—*Fresh* is just as it sounds: a wine that is bright and invigorating.

Fruity—People too often equate fruitiness with sweetness. A fruity wine is simply a wine with a lot of exuberant, primary fruit character.

Green—A green wine is often made from underripe, or "green," fruit.

Hard—The tannins are excessive and obtrusive in a hard wine.

Hollow—A hollow wine simply has nothing in the middle; it may have a beginning, or "attack," as Peter liked to say, and an end or "finish," but there's nothing in between.

Hot—A hot wine has an excess of alcohol. "It's interesting that *hot* should mean too alcoholic," Peter observed. "It sounds like a positive thing. Or something Paris Hilton would say, like 'This wine is so hot!'"

Length—This refers to the length of time that a wine lingers in your mouth. "Is that always going to be a big fat wine like Chardonnay?" Peter asked. Not necessarily, I said. A wine with good length can also be something as streamlined as a Riesling or Sauvignon Blanc.

Middle palate—A great wine always has a good beginning, middle, and end. When wine tasters talk about a wine's "midpalate," they mean the collective sensations that tie the start and the finish of a wine together.

Mouth feel—A high-quality wine has a good "mouth feel," that is, its texture is pleasurable, and its elements—fruit, tannin, and acidity—are in balance.

Nose—This word serves as both a noun and a verb in the world of wine tasting. This was good news for Peter, who liked nothing better than talk about noses and "nosing."

Oxidized—A wine that has been exposed to excessive amounts of oxygen and frequently smells like a bottle of Sherry that's been left open on the sideboard for a long time. "I've been in houses where people have bottles like that," remarked Peter.

Rich—This means pretty much what it sounds like—a rich wine has lots of intensity, in both body and flavor.

Round—This is a pretty self-explanatory term, used to describe a wine that is pleasant, easy to drink.

Soft—This can be a good thing, i.e., the wine is not overly tannic, or too much of a good thing, that is, the wine lacks definition, but it depends on whether the wine has enough balancing acidity. If a wine is soft in a bad way, it lacks acidity.

Tears—These are the drops of wine that stream down the inside of the glass after the wine has been poured; they are alternately referred to as tears or legs. A wine that is big and rich, aka more viscous, will always have longer tears. Many people believe (incorrectly) that tears indicate a high-quality wine, but it has more to do with the type of wine than anything else. For example, a full-bodied Chardonnay will have longer, and longer-lasting, tears than a lighter, leaner Riesling.

Texture—The texture of a wine is the way that it feels in the mouth (aka its mouth feel). Words commonly used to describe wine texture include *smooth, creamy, thin,* or *coarse.*

Tight—A tight wine is generally one that is young and therefore inaccessible, i.e., its tannins or acidity are more pronounced, often masking its fruit. When a tight wine (more often red wines are described as tight than white) begins to open up and to reveal itself (either through time or exposure to air), it is said to "unwind."

SOME FREQUENTLY ENCOUNTERED WINE TERMS

Appellation—The French were the first to create an appellation system (Appellation d'Origine Contrôlée) for their wines, in 1935, as a means of identifying a wine of a particular grape or grapes, made in a particular place. The French appellation system has served as a model for wine classification systems all over the world, including the United States. The French model, however, remains the most rigorous (and detractors would say "rigid") of all. There are more than five hundred appellations in France, although only 15 percent of French wines are actually AOC-designated wines.

Château—This is simply the name given to an estate where wine is made, most famously in Bordeaux.

Commune—A commune is a recognizable subregion of a more important region. For example, Pauillac is a commune of Bordeaux.

Cru—This term is used in both Bordeaux and Burgundy to recognize the most important châteaux (Bordeaux) and vineyards (Burgundy), which are ranked either "premier" or "grand" cru.

Growth—This term was first used in Bordeaux in the Médoc classification of 1855 to recognize that region's most important wines. In that classification system, the wines were ranked first through fifth "classified growths."

Négociant—A négociant is a broker, one who sells wine or grapes, as opposed to one who owns vineyards. (Although négociants such as Drouhin may own vineyards as well.)

What Makes a Wine Great?

After our first few tasting sessions, Peter posed a question that people have been asking for hundreds of years: "What makes a wine great?"

What had made Peter ask? Was it something he'd read? Or a wine he'd tasted? Peter shook his head: neither. He just wanted to know more than what he called "the ingredients" of a wine—its flavors and aromas. Not just "basic stuff." Peter wanted to know what else he should be looking for—and how to recognize it when he found it. "Just in case I accidentally taste something great," he said.

For a man still obsessed with oaky, aka fatty, Chardonnay, it was a good, albeit complex, inquiry. Perhaps the answer was the same as it was for movies? Peter replied he could see parallels between the two.

"Both wine and movies are totally volatile," Peter opined. Movies were volatile? I was surprised. I'd thought movies were static. After all, they're preserved on film. Peter shook his head and said, "It's not that the movie changes. It's our attitudes about the movie that change. For example, someone will see something different in a movie long after its makers are dead." Wasn't that like a wine that someone might not understand for decades to come?

For example, Peter offered, "A movie like *It's a Wonderful Life* was a huge failure when it was released. Nobody cared about it at the time. Now, of course, it's played over and over on television every year at Christmastime."

I realized that Peter had grasped an important fact in a short time. There are legions of stories of overlooked vintages, underestimated wines, and wine innovators denounced for what were once thought to be wild ideas. The man who is now widely heralded as the father of New York State winemaking, Dr. Konstantin Frank, was practically institutionalized back in the 1950s when he insisted that Riesling could grow in cold regions such as the Finger Lakes in upstate New York. The powers that be in the state's viticultural elite said he was crazy; it was too cold, and only hardy crosses of native Labrusca grapes could thrive in such weather. And yet, when a cold winter came and all the Labrusca vines died, the Riesling survived. Riesling is the grape that has now made the Finger Lakes famous in the world of wine. "But are Finger Lakes Rieslings great?" Peter wanted to know. "And if not, what qualities do great wines have to have?"

Well, like anything else, a great wine must have the ability to endure. A wine that is at its best in the first year or two—and granted, that's almost all of the world's wines—wouldn't qualify as great. A great wine needs to be capable of developing over time. And that means that the wine has to be perfectly made—in perfect balance, with equal amounts of oak and fruit, even at an early age. My friend Robert M. Parker Jr., the famous wine critic, has five criteria that a wine must meet to be considered great:

1. It must have enough interesting qualities to hold a taster's interest.
2. It must grow better over time.
3. It must be a wine with a particular personality made in a particular place. A great wine can't come from just anywhere.
4. The wine needs to have been treated right (in the vineyard) from the start. It must come from a low-yielding, properly managed vineyard, one whose vines are canopied and trellised according to its particular grape type.
5. And finally, a great wine should reflect an individual's (the winemaker's) point of view. For example, the famous winemaking consultant Michel Rolland makes wine all over the world (France, California, Chile, India, etc.), and though each of his wines necessarily tastes of the place where it is made, each one also bears the signature of a Rolland-influenced wine.

Peter nodded and announced he was going to talk it over with Francis Ford Coppola, whom he planned to see the following week. "After all," reasoned Peter, "he's one person who does both. He has created great movies and makes a great wine in Napa. Or at least I'm told it's great. But Coppola is the only one I know who has continued this wine business all the way through moviemaking. And when you make movies like *Apocalypse Now* and *The Godfather,* you're great. I just don't know if his wines are great because I haven't tasted them. But perhaps I will?" Peter asked hopefully.

Bottle Colors, Shapes, and Sizes

Although it may seem superficial, it's always useful to know something about bottle shapes, sizes, and colors. They not only provide preliminary information about a wine but are also more consistently informative than an actual label, as a label's information may vary widely from country to country. In Germany, for example, the labels are painstakingly precise. In Italy, they're almost information-free. I figured someone as visually oriented as Peter would appreciate such clues.

BOTTLE SHAPES AND COLORS

Bottle shapes evolved for practical, traditional, and stylistic reasons. The Italians, unsurprisingly, have embraced the third category the most, creating whimsical bottle shapes that have no meaning outside the winery or even to the designers who conceive them. For example, Fazi Battaglia, an Italian white wine made from the Verdicchio grape, was once packaged in an urn-shaped bottle, a choice that long confused me. Why would a producer package his wine in a sort of funeral urn, thereby reminding drinkers of death while they were consuming the wine? (Perhaps Fazi Battaglia finally realized this wasn't a good thing; they've since switched to more conventional packaging.)

But there are still plenty of stylistic holdouts around. For example, one of my favorite Italian producers, Ceretto, produces a slightly sparkling, delightfully fresh Moscato in an awkward triangular bottle. When I showed this to Peter, he called it "dangerous." (I'd thought it was snazzy.) But the fact is, wine retailers don't like odd-shaped bottles either. They don't stack well or fit easily on shelves.

Of all the conventional bottle shapes, the Bordeaux bottle is probably the most common. Designed sometime in the eighteenth century, this bottle has square, slightly tapering shoulders, theoretically to catch the wine's sediment. "How does it do that?" Peter asked, squinting at the bottle and turning it in his hand, looking for the cache of captured sediment at the bottom. But there was nothing to see since the bottle held a young California Cabernet. (Sediment, which precipitates out as a wine ages, is rarely found in a young Cabernet.) "Then why do they use this bottle at all?" Peter replied sensibly. It's the style, I replied, and it shows the wine is capable of aging. "But why are Bordeaux bottles dark green?" Peter continued, trying to peer through the glass of the Cabernet bottle. "I don't like it when I can't see the wine. I just want to see how red the wine is. That might sound ridiculous, but it's what I want."

The darkness of the bottle glass is another sign that a wine can be aged; the dark glass is protection against light. (Exposure to light hastens aging in a wine, as it does with film or, for that matter, painting.) A clear glass bottle signals a wine that should be drunk immediately. (I suspected Peter had a lot of clear bottles in his wine-drinking past.)

The second-most common bottle shape is the Burgundy bottle. Used for both red and white wines all over the world (the Bordeaux bottle is most often, though not exclusively, used for red), a classic Burgundy bottle has roundish, sloping shoulders. This shape implies that the wine will be softer, rounder, and less likely to require extended aging. That means there's no need for a design that will catch sediment (which doesn't often occur in less tannic grapes such as Pinot Noir).

The Burgundy bottle is used far beyond the borders of Burgundy, in just about every country of the world for almost every grape except Bordeaux varietals such as Cabernet, Sauvignon Blanc, and Merlot . . . although there are always exceptions to the rule.

"Exceptions! What good is a rule if there are exceptions?" Peter exclaimed hotly.

The third-most common bottle shape is the tapered bottle of Germany and Alsace, France. This bottle is most often used for such grapes as Riesling and Gewürztraminer. The shape signals that an aromatic wine is inside, and it is to me a perfect example of how the shape of a bottle can indicate a wine's qualities. Peter nodded and looked a bit bored. "Is there really any reason to know what these bottle shapes mean?" he asked somewhat impatiently. "I can't imagine people really go to a restaurant and order a wine with the expectation it will come in a certain bottle." I admitted this was probably true.

"And even if they did," Peter continued, pressing his advantage, "what would they do? Would they send back a bottle of Chardonnay because it was in a Bordeaux bottle? Would you?"

I would wonder what the departure from convention meant, I replied. It might signal a different style of wine. For example, some unoaked Australian Chardonnays come in Bordeaux bottles because they are crisp and dry rather than rich and full. But Peter was clearly unconvinced that bottle facts were useful. "I'm not sure if I like knowing that Cabernet should come in a Bordeaux-style bottle," he said. "I might not have been bothered by that fact and know it could be a problem. For example, if I saw Cabernet in a Riesling bottle, I might start screaming, 'That Cabernet looks like perfume to me!'"

I should have realized that Peter, with his visual fixation, would be capable of taking such facts to an extreme. Now he was fretting aloud about a bottle of white wine he had received from Francis Ford Coppola. It had come in what Peter called "a square-shaped" Bordeaux bottle. But what did that signify? Peter didn't know. "Perhaps it's Sauvignon Blanc or Semillon?" I prompted. They are, after all, the two white grapes of Bordeaux. "I don't know," Peter confessed. "I was afraid to look under the paper."

BOTTLE SIZES

A standard wine bottle holds 750 ml and a half bottle half that amount. A few wineries are experimenting with an in-between size, 500 ml, which seems like the perfect amount for two people having dinner, but it hasn't really caught on to any practical degree.

But the perfect bottle size, according to serious collectors and true lovers of wine, is the magnum, which holds two regular bottles' worth of wine. The magnum, with its larger dimension and smaller ratio of bottle opening to the liquid inside, is considered the perfect (slower) way to age wine.

"How many magnums do you have in your cellar?" Peter asked me in a challenging tone. Less than a dozen, I confessed. But those bottles give me great pleasure; they promise future dinner parties and good times with friends. In fact, people with magnums always seem to share their wine with friends. "Well, what else are they going to do with a bottle that big?" Peter replied practically.

I have a good friend, Park B. Smith, who embodies the true spirit of the magnum lover. Park, the owner of a highly successful home-furnishings company (which bears his name) and an equally success-ful New York City restaurant, Veritas, has one of the greatest wine collections I know of. Park also has more magnums than anyone else I know of—about sixty thousand bottles or so. I don't think I've ever been to Park's house or out to dinner with Park and his wife, Linda, when he hasn't brought a magnum or two along. Park carries his double bottles the way other people do business cards. "I think I should meet this fellow Park," Peter said.

HOW WINE IS MADE

A favorite saying among winemakers has been repeated so often it's become a cliché: a great wine is made in the vineyard. This is meant to imply a more natural state of winemaking with an emphasis on good viticultural habits rather than winemaking tricks. Peter, who'd never heard this saying before, liked it a lot. He nodded. It made perfect sense. "In fact," Peter said, "it's a lot like the movies. Directors will say the movie is made in the editing room, but it's not. It's made a long time before that, starting when the film is cast. For example, if you cast an actor like Mark Wahlberg in a Shakespearean play, you know he is going to be bad and the film will be bad."

Peter's analogy held true to a point. A good wine has to come from a good vineyard where the soil is of a particular sort suited to the particular grapes, which must in turn be planted in just the right site and trellised and canopied in just the right way.

"That makes a vineyard sound more like the editing room," observed Peter. Trellising grapes? Managing vine canopies? That sounded a lot like manipulation to him. *Manipulation* is a pretty strong word, I replied. Certainly, some vineyard techniques can increase or decrease grape yields and correspondingly increase or decrease the ripeness of fruit (e.g., pruning the vine canopy to allow more or less sun on the grapes). That wasn't manipulation but more of a maximization of the quality of the grapes. Peter considered this. "Maybe vineyard management is more like the shooting of the movie," he conceded. "And making wine is more like the editing room—the place where you have to fix things that didn't go right."

Once the issue of manipulation seemed to be settled, I described what took place in a vineyard over a year. Vines are dormant in the winter. In February or March a preliminary pruning reduces the number of buds that will appear in the spring. A few months later, bud break occurs. Grape clusters emerge in June or July, and the ripening process begins shortly after that. Grape ripening is also known as veraison, when the skins begin to change color and the sugar and the acid in the grapes increase dramatically. Then, depending on the region and the grape variety, harvest generally takes place between August and November. Peter looked a bit dazed. Perhaps a field trip would help make the process a bit clearer.

Although the suburbs of New York City are hardly "wine country," I did have a neighbor with a vineyard or at least a few Pinot Noir vines in his yard. In fact, I'd seen them from afar: eight or nine rows of vines on a gently sloping hillside that ran down to a small creek that ran into Long Island Sound. The Côtes de Nuits it was not, but it wasn't a bad location, all things considered: a hillside slope (good drainage) and a maritime influence (moderating cool winds). "Maritime? Don't you think that's going a little too far?" Peter said skeptically. "Let's just sneak over and have a look," I replied.

It was early August; the grapes had probably just gone through veraison. The change in color would be a dramatic thing to see, I promised Peter, who looked dubious. "Isn't that still trespassing?" he said.

"Anyone who's trying to grow Pinot Noir in Westchester would want us to bear witness to their achievement," I insisted. "Besides, we'll just explain it's for educational purposes. And if that doesn't work, we can just plead the influence of *Sideways*."

Peter grumbled but followed along. We cut through several neighboring yards until we reached a tiny vineyard on a slight rise of a hill. But as we drew closer, I realized something was terribly wrong. Instead of an accomplished suburban vineyard, we found a study in viticultural neglect, if not downright disaster. Some terrible, wasting disease had struck, and only a few grapes, tiny and shriveled, hung from the vines. The leaves were curled and pimpled with what looked like warts. "Something's wrong here," I said, in a great understatement. I looked around, almost hoping my neighbor might appear, to explain what had happened. "Let's get out of here," replied Peter, unnerved by the sight of the desiccated grapes.

Safely back at my house, Peter was drawn to the topic of vine disease. "I'm curious about all the things that can go wrong," he said. The vineyard scene, Peter said, had reminded him of the movie *Parrish*, starring Troy Donahue. "It's a film about people in the tobacco business whose fortune hangs on the well-being of the tobacco plants. If there's a tiny speck on the plant, they have to rip the whole thing out." It sounded riveting, I muttered sarcastically. "What did you say?" Peter replied.

"That sounds a lot like phylloxera," I replied.

Phylloxera is a tiny insect related to the aphid and a native of North America that can destroy entire vineyards, if not wine regions. It was responsible for the devastation of nearly all of Bordeaux in the late nineteenth century. By the time the Bordelais had figured out what had happened, almost nothing was left of their vines. "Phylloxera sounds a lot like what happens when Jerry Bruckheimer gets involved in a movie," commented Peter.

WINEMAKING

Peter doesn't write much about the actual making of movies in his reviews—the type of cameras, the editing techniques—but nevertheless he knows a lot about how a film is made. And I thought it was just as important for Peter to know how wine is made—if only for conversational fodder at his next cocktail party. In fact, two weeks after our vineyard discussion, I overheard Peter at a party telling a seemingly enthralled woman, "You know, the wine isn't made in the winery. It's made in the vineyard." (Peter could make fresh the most hackneyed winemaking cliché.)

Wine is made by the conversion of sugar into alcohol. It's that simple. At the same time, it is much more complex. The initial alcohol conversion takes place during the fermentation of the grapes. Then, in most cases, a second fermentation, called malolactic, takes place. This is the conversion of hard (malo) acids to softer (lactic) acids, which lower the wine's acidity, making it softer and rounder. "Mal-o-lactic," repeated Peter, making the process sound like some appliance that's sold on late-night television, the kind that slices and dices vegetables and fruit "in a jiffy."

Almost all red wines in the world go through malolactic fermentation, as do some white wines such as Chardonnay and Semillon. The whites that don't are generally wines with naturally high acidity such as Riesling and Sauvignon Blanc, which their winemakers actually want to maintain (softening the acidity in these wines would turn them flabby). These are generally the same grapes that winemakers don't age in oak either but in neutral stainless steel, as the oak could impart too much flavor. For example, Peter would never see an oak-aged Riesling. Or a grape such as Pinot Grigio,

38

whose delicate character would likely be overwhelmed or smothered by oak.

Sauvignon Blanc is another example of a wine that is not usually aged in oak, although for a long time winemakers in California used to do exactly that, treating it as if it were a sort of Chardonnay stepchild—they gave these wines lot of oak and called them *fumé blanc*. (This name arose from a marketing vision as much as a winemaking technique. It's generally attributed to Robert Mondavi, who wanted his wood-aged Sauvignon to have a classy French sound.) But Sauvignon Blanc isn't much aged in wood in California these days—one reason there aren't many California Sauvignons called *Fumé* anymore.

The discussion of oak reminded Peter of the movie *Mondovino*, by Jonathan Nossiter, which had come out the year before. "I thought the movie spent a lot of time chastising American winemakers for using too much oak and manipulating their wines," Peter recounted. "That guy Michel Rolland [a famous Bordeaux winemaking consultant shown over and over in the film] kept saying 'microoxidize' wine. I have no idea what that term means, but he sounded like a cigar-chomping studio executive, asking for more explosions and car crashes."

THE IMPORTANCE OF OAK

Oak is to winemakers what love is to poets, a universal and evergreen topic. But, like any subject discussed to an extreme, it can soon become tedious. "It's not tedious to me," Peter replied. I wasn't sure if Peter was referring to oak or to love, until he added, "After all, my initial attraction to Chardonnay was the oak." And besides, Peter wondered, "Since winemakers spent so much money on oak, why not make wine where you could taste it?"

Peter wasn't so far off the mark. A lot of winemakers (and not all of them are in California) feel their lumber source should shine as much as their grapes. Considering that a single French oak barrel (barrique) can cost over $800, this viewpoint was in some ways not hard to understand. Yet the idea of putting a wine in wood, either for fermenting or aging or both, isn't merely to get the taste of the barrel but to use the wood as a frame, supporting the fruit but also serving as a background flavor, rather than the dominant note. The fruit of a wine is the painting, and if the only impression you have of a wine is the oak, then you can't see the picture for the frame. "Well, maybe if you're drinking rotgut wine, you'd rather taste oak than fruit," said Peter practically. (With some of the cheap Chardonnays Peter drank I thought he might have a point.) Actually, some winemakers don't use oak at all but oak flavoring or oak chips, I said. "Oak chips?" Peter repeated, professing shock. "What do you mean? I've never seen a chip in any glass of my wine."

FRENCH VS. AMERICAN OAK

The two most common oak barrels used in winemaking are French and American. Others are made in such countries as Russia, Slovenia, and Hungary, but the French and Americans have pretty much cornered the world's wine-barrel business. The difference between the two is distinct: the flavors of American oak are much more dominant. And perhaps as befits anything American, there's just a lot more of everything with American oak: more aromas, more flavors, more wood. In other words, American oak can really pack a punch. "That doesn't seem so bad," said Peter, who in fact thought it sounded pretty good.

Actually, it can be too much of a good thing: a winemaker might not want the flavor of the oak to compete with or overwhelm the fruit in a wine. Sometimes the oak is too intense, overwhelming all the other flavors. "A wine like California Cabernet, can't it take something like American oak?" Peter asked, naming what to him was the world's most powerful wine. In fact, most California Cabernets are aged in small French oak barrels, which tend to be more neutral and less overt. French oak barrels are tighter grained than American; that means their flavors aren't as pronounced. (A good rule of thumb regarding oak: the tighter the grain, the more flavor-restrained.) That's why most great wine producers use French rather than American oak; they want to showcase their high-quality fruit rather than the wood. "But who's left for American oak producers to sell to?" Peter wanted to know.

I reassured Peter that plenty of wine producers use American oak, especially in Spain. Australian winemakers are big American proponents, as are the winemakers of Chile, especially when it comes to grapes like Carmenère. And plenty of American producers use both American and French oak, especially with Zinfandel. And as long as an American oak barrel only costs half as much as its French counterpart, Peter would not have to worry about French barrel makers putting American barrel makers out of business anytime soon.

OLD WORLD WINE

❧

FRANCE

Probably no chapter of this book was more eagerly awaited and simultaneously dreaded by Peter than the one accorded to the wines of France. "There's so much I don't know and can't pronounce from France," Peter said. "And while all of it scares me, there's nowhere more terrifying to me than the wines of Bordeaux." So that's where we started.

BORDEAUX

"Do you know what Bordeaux means to me?" Peter asked, the day of our first Bordeaux tasting. This was of course a rhetorical question.

Peter described a scene from the movie *Prime,* in which Uma Thurman plays a woman dating a much younger man. Uma is also a patient of a Jewish shrink, played by Meryl Streep. Uma tells her all about the guy she is dating, who turns out to be Meryl Streep's son, although she doesn't find that out until much later in the movie. After she does find out, however, Meryl invites Uma to her house for a Passover seder. Uma brings a bottle of Bordeaux to Meryl's house. (And, no, Peter couldn't see the label of the wine in the film.) Meryl takes the wine from Uma and puts it into the refrigerator, saying, "We could have it with dinner if it gets cold in time." And, Peter reported, the whole screening room convulsed into laughter.

"I don't get it," I replied. "What was so funny?"

"The point," Peter explained, "was that the Bordeaux showed, in shorthand, how sophisticated Uma Thurman was and how unsophisticated Meryl Streep was, for putting the wine into the refrigerator."

I still didn't get it. "Couldn't it have been a white Bordeaux?"

Peter shook his head. "I never thought of that. I guess the whole screening room assumed all Bordeaux was red.

"But isn't all Bordeaux a crock?" Peter continued. "Isn't Bordeaux kind of overhyped and mediocre anyway? Wasn't it all just marketing?" After all, Peter had never had any great Bordeaux—in fact, he couldn't recall any Bordeaux he'd ever had that wasn't anything "beyond your basic rotgut."

Given that Peter rarely spent more than $10 a bottle, it wasn't hard to understand how he'd reached this conclusion. If there's one wine that's particularly elusive, it's a good cheap Bordeaux. Beyond that, there are a lot of great Bordeaux, I told Peter; it's not all marketing and hype. But you do need to have a lot of money to spend.

And this generally means the great "first growths" of Bordeaux, the five châteaux whose names (Mouton, Lafite, Margaux, Haut-Brion, and Latour) even someone like Peter knew. "What are growths?" Peter asked. "It sounds like some sort of condition you'd consult a podiatrist about."

In fact, the five first "growths," or classes, refer to the Médoc châteaux that were ranked in the famous Bordeaux classification system of 1855. This system divided the wines of Bordeaux's Médoc region into five different growths according to their value, prestige, and presumably quality. The classification was actually supposed to be temporary—only for the duration of the World's Fair in Paris that year—but it has endured a good 150 years and beyond. Considering that it was the work of some Bordeaux wine brokers who ranked the properties according to the prices that each could command, it is amazing that the system has stuck.

Just imagine a bunch of liquor salesmen in America being given that kind of say over Napa Valley Cabernet! I said to Peter, who seemed unsurprised. In fact, he just shook his head. He'd already decided Bordeaux was corrupt.

The only thing worse to Peter than the possible corruption of Bordeaux was that it was rife with Cabernet Sauvignon, the principal grape of the Left Bank of Bordeaux. After all, there was no grape Peter liked less than Cabernet.

Never mind it happens to be the principal grape of every first growth and the chief reason those wines age so well. "I just don't like what Cabernet does to my mouth," Peter said. "But then I've never had a first growth Bordeaux."

"Age-ability is one of the chief reasons Bordeaux isn't a 'crock,'" I told Peter. "The greatest Bordeaux age better and more consistently than almost any other wine in the world." For example, I'd recently attended a Bordeaux tasting in Beverly Hills put together by Bipin Desai, a world-famous wine collector and bon vivant. The featured wine had been the famed Bordeaux second growth Château Cos d'Estournel, and the vintages went all the way back to 1928. "That wine was spectacular," I said to Peter of the '28, and so were the '59 and the '61 vintages; in fact, they were almost all vibrant and full of life, showing how beautifully great Bordeaux can age. Peter still looked skeptical. "Run the numbers," he replied. "How many of the sixty-first first through fifth growths are really producing top wines? How many wines are we really talking about?"

It was true that great Bordeaux was a pretty finite universe, I conceded, but that is true of just about any wine region in the world.

"Yes, but in Bordeaux, they act like everyone makes great wine, and we know that's not true," Peter insisted. It wasn't that Peter did not have a point, but then the same could be said of, say, Burgundy. Or Napa or any other famous wine-producing region in the world.

The truth is, Peter is far from alone in having bad feelings about Bordeaux. In fact, unbeknownst to him, a Bordeaux backlash has been building for years, and producers of the cheap wines have particularly been affected, facing stiff competition in the world marketplace against the (even) cheaper and fruitier wines of Australia and Spain. In the past couple of years (2005–6) Bordeaux producers have been forced to turn thousands of gallons of their unsold wine into industrial alcohol.

"I think I drank some of those wines," Peter replied when I told him this.

But Bordeaux has always been more vulnerable, more dependent, on the whims of the foreign market than any other region in France. In fact, its history is less purely French than that of any other wine-producing region in the country. The English fought over it for decades and once even totally controlled it (in the seventeenth century) and have owned some of its best châteaux. The Dutch and the Irish have as well—including Château Lynch Bages and Château Dillon. The English even bottled their own Bordeaux for quite a long time, buying wine in casks and shipping it home to be bottled in London.

"So you're saying this so-called classic wine is a mutt?" Peter replied. "I mean, let's recap: Bordeaux is a wine made from a bunch of different grapes by a bunch of different guys from a bunch of different countries. It doesn't sound very noble to me."

"That's not the complete history," I said to Peter. "What I'd been trying to say was that the history of Bordeaux isn't as straightforward or as insular as, say, Burgundy or the Loire."

"You don't have to get all defensive."

A BORDEAUX FIELD TRIP . . . TO SCARSDALE, NEW YORK

Peter seemed so hostile to the wines of Bordeaux that I decided an intervention was in order. Perhaps he needed to talk to someone, sort through his anger at the wines. In short, he needed to talk to someone who truly, deeply loved Bordeaux. I thought of my friend Jeff Zacharia, the owner of Zachys wineshop in Scarsdale, who had been obsessed with Bordeaux for at least twenty years and had built Zachys into a veritable temple to its wines. Maybe Jeff, in his Bordeaux-fueled passion, could convince Peter of its many virtues.

I called Jeff and told him briefly about Peter's hostility toward the wines of Bordeaux. Jeff said he'd do what he could and suggested Peter and I meet him the next Saturday morning at his store. But when Peter and I arrived at the appointed hour, Jeff wasn't there. While we waited, an eager young salesman approached us. Could he help us find a wine?

"We're here to see Jeff," Peter replied, in the tone of a man about to visit the dentist. Well, while were we waiting, might we be interested in looking at some wine? the salesman persisted. "We're here for Bordeaux," Peter said, in a monotone.

The salesman nodded and said, "Of course." After all, we were in a wine store whose fortune was largely built on the sale of Bordeaux. But in the meantime, could he interest us in something else? "I have a terrific 2003 Vacqueyras, from the southern Rhône," the young salesman said, pointing to a case that was directly behind us. "Not only is it a delicious wine, but there is an intriguing story behind it as well."

"What's that?" Peter replied.

"Well, the winemaker had just finished making the wine, and shortly thereafter he fell off a ladder and died."

Peter and I gave the salesman the same blank stare. "I think it's good to have a story behind every wine," said the oblivious salesman. Was this a sales tip? I wondered.

"I think that would be a wine I'd be too sad to drink," Peter finally said to the salesman. Fortunately, Jeff soon appeared and swept us off toward the Bordeaux section, where presumably no château owners had fallen off ladders and died tragic deaths.

Jeff asked Peter a few warm-up questions to get a sense of his knowledge of Bordeaux. Did Peter know that Bordeaux was divided by the Gironde estuary into two banks, left and right? He did. I'd told Peter to "think of the two banks as the same of Paris, except reversed. The old guard is on the Left Bank and the upstarts, the Bohemians, are on the Right." Jeff looked puzzled by the idea but continued his lecture, undeterred. "On the Left Bank," said Jeff, "you'll find the Cabernet-dominated wines—Lafite, Latour—and all the other major châteaux, while on the Right Bank are the Merlot and Cabernet Franc blended wines. There aren't any impressive châteaux on the Right Bank like there are on the Left, but there are still many legendary wines made there—like Cheval Blanc, Pétrus, and Ausone."

Peter didn't see much point in talking about the Left Bank. "I don't feel like I can ever enter the Left Bank," he said to Jeff.

"Why?" Jeff replied.

"It sticks in mind as the place where everything that scares me about Bordeaux comes from," replied Peter. Jeff didn't, of course, realize Peter was talking about Cabernet. "Besides," added Peter, "they're all wines that I know I can't afford."

"How can you say that?" Jeff replied, immediately ready to leap to the defense of one of his beloved banks. "Don't you realize that a first growth Bordeaux can be cheaper than a Mondavi Reserve Cabernet?"

"Well, then I can't afford that wine either," Peter replied.

Jeff wasn't willing to let it go. He told Peter that all would-be Bordeaux drinkers needed to start on the Left Bank because, as he said, the wines were "more consistent" than those of the Right Bank. "And besides, you really need to start with some classic wines to really understand Bordeaux," he added. According to Jeff, the Right Bank had "higher peaks of greatness" but wasn't as consistent as the Left, year in and year out.

"But what are the peaks of greatness?" Peter replied. "Where can those wines be found?"

Jeff looked momentarily flummoxed. "Well, I guess that would have to be Château d'Yquem," he finally replied, naming the legendary dessert wine from the Graves region of Bordeaux.

"I haven't had that wine," Peter replied.

"Although there are a lot of great wines in Bordeaux, I get excited when I can still make discoveries," said Jeff, who travels to Bordeaux "at least" two times a year. "Like I was when I rediscovered a lot of the wines from the 1996 vintage were overlooked because the 1995 wines were so good."

Peter nodded. He understood the point that Jeff was trying to make, in cinematic terms. "That's like the movie *Network*," Peter replied. "When it first came out, everyone ignored it or said it was too exaggerated. Then ten years later, everything happened that the movie said would, and people decided it was genius filmmaking."

Then Peter asked Jeff to point out a few more Bordeaux that he considered discoveries, wines that were affordably priced. Jeff led Peter over to the front of the store.

"You cannot find a better deal for twelve dollars than this 2001 Château Duplessy," Jeff said, just as a woman came up and grabbed six bottles of the wine—as if on cue.

"People always want to know what the best deals are," said Jeff, who insisted that, contrary to what Peter believed, values could be found in Bordeaux. Jeff named two more, including the 2001 Château Les Trois Croix ($18), which "is owned by the winemaker of Mouton Rothschild." Peter finally looked intrigued.

What Jeff encountered was much like what happened to Peter at the Sundance Film Festival. "I come back from Sundance and people don't want to know about the big names; they want to know what the best movie is that they've never heard of," Peter remarked.

Things seemed to be going well between Peter and Jeff, so I left them alone while I went to another part of the store to buy some Bordeaux.

TASTING BORDEAUX

Peter proved enthusiastic when it was time to taste the wines that I'd bought. In fact, he even claimed he'd changed his mind on the classification system ever since his conversation with Jeff. Now Peter decided that the Bordelais (aka Bordeaux winemakers) were "brilliant" at creating a system that has endured through changes of taste and time. In fact, he thought it was a system that could be applied to film.

"*Citizen Kane* is like a first growth film. It's stayed great from one decade to the next because it created an entirely new genre of film," Peter opined. "*Citizen Kane* set a new standard of filmmaking. Orson Welles used techniques like deep-focus photography that no one had thought of using before." (Deep-focus photography imitates the human eye; that is, everything is photographed in focus, from the foreground all the way back.)

Peter had, in fact, decided that the entire Bordeaux classification was a piece of cake. "Once you learn it, that's it," he declared. What could be more simple than memorizing the names of châteaux and their ranking of growths one through five? (When I mentioned to Peter he'd actually have to memorize over fifty Bordeaux names, he wondered if he could "only worry" about first and second growths and maybe skip growths three through five.) But some of Bordeaux's best bargains are from the lesser growths, I protested. "Well, I could also learn about a few of the cheaper wines," Peter conceded, "since those are the wines I can actually afford."

Peter could do that, but he would still have to learn about Bordeaux vintages, because in Bordeaux, more than almost any other place in the world, vintage matters a lot. And that had to do with the region's bad weather.

"Hail?" Peter asked hopefully. Not really. The biggest problem in Bordeaux is rain.

There can be a lot of rain in Bordeaux, as the climate is maritime—some thirty miles from the Atlantic Ocean—and too much rain means rot in a vineyard. The greatest Bordeaux vintages—most recently 1982, 1990, 2000, and 2005—have all been hot years in Bordeaux. "Maybe what I need is a Bordeaux weather report," Peter replied.

I decided to start our Bordeaux tasting with the Right Bank of Bordeaux and the regions of Pomerol and St. Émilion, as the wines made there contain more Merlot than they do Cabernet Sauvignon. The wines tend to be softer and more approachable. (Although in St. Émilion, there is a good bit of Cabernet Franc, a sort of poor cousin to Cabernet Sauvignon, with a personality that's a little less assertive, a little less tannic.)

Now that Peter was a professed fan of the Bordeaux classification system, I had to break it to him that it didn't actually apply to all of Bordeaux. In fact, the system didn't apply to the Right Bank at all: Pomerol wines are unclassified, while St. Émilion wines are classified different from the famous 1855 system. And the St. Émilion classification is much more recent; it didn't even exist until 1959.

POMEROL

Pomerol is a rustic region, even today. There are no great châteaux in Pomerol, at least not in the architectural sense. I've ridden on horseback through Pomerol, and it looks more or less like nice farmland. It's hard to believe great wines are made there.

The most important grape in Pomerol is Merlot, which does best in Pomerol's clay soils. The second-most important Pomerol grape is Cabernet Franc rather than Cabernet Sauvignon, and therefore the wines tend to be softer and rounder than those from the Left Bank. One family owns just about every château of note in Pomerol — the Mouiex family, owners of the legendary Château Pétrus and Château Trotanoy, among many others. But Peter wasn't interested in the details of the Mouiex empire. He wanted to know when we'd be tasting Château Pétrus.

Alas, Pétrus was not in the budget. Instead, I'd chosen a wine from just outside Pomerol, in one of the region's so-called satellite regions, Lalande de Pomerol. The wines produced there are stylistically similar to those of Pomerol though priced more attractively.

"I like this a lot; it's really grapy," Peter pronounced about the soft and supple 2001 Lafleur Pomerol ($20 a bottle). "This wine doesn't require any food to taste good," he declared, his highest form of praise.

A few great Pomerol châteaux: Pétrus, Trotanoy, l'Évangile.

ST. ÉMILION

St. Émilion is the other major Right Bank Bordeaux region. But while Pomerol is rustic and undeveloped, St. Émilion, especially the town of St. Émilion, is undeniably cute. A little too cute, some might say — a picture-perfect French town. As a result, quite a few tourists throng the streets of St. Émilion. "It sounds kind of like a place where they'd rip you off," Peter remarked.

St. Émilion may be the most dynamic region in Bordeaux right now. It's home to some of the most ambitious winemakers of the past twenty years, many of whom do not own vineyards but buy grapes instead, making some untraditional but highly praised wines — in their garages. (Hence the derivation of their name: *garagistes*.)

The classification system of St. Émilion is interesting; unlike the 1855 Médoc system, it calls for the wines of St. Émilion to be reviewed every ten years. And much like a Michelin-star restaurant, a St. Émilion château can be demoted or raised up. But though it may seem like a more enlightened system than that of the Médoc, it isn't well known outside Bordeaux, and its categories are less readily identifiable than those of the Médoc first through fifth growths.

For example, at the top of the St. Émilion system are the "A" premier grand cru class wines, including such famous names as Cheval Blanc and Château Ausone. Next are the "B" premier grand cru producers—Pavie, Beau-Séjour Bécot, Trotanoy. After these first two groups are the grands crus, which are more of a mixed bag. While some of these wines can be very good, some are classed in this group because the grower has political clout. But Peter liked the idea that the wines could be promoted or demoted after review. "It sounds very American," he commented approvingly.

"I like the idea that the châteaux have the potential to move up," Peter added. "But maybe they should try rating them with one to four stars, like they do the movies."

The grands crus of St. Émilion can be excellent value. The wine we were tasting, the 2001 Bellefont Bellcier, was a good example; although it was a grand cru wine, it only cost about $25. "That's a still a lot of money to me," Peter pointed out.

Peter didn't like the Bellefont as much as he had the Lafleur Pomerol, which he pronounced easier to love. And he was right; the Bellefont, like most St. Émilion wines, had a lot more Cabernet Franc in it than Merlot, and consequently it was a more tannic and structured wine.

"Structure is harder to love," Peter observed.

A few great St. Émilion châteaux: Ausone, Angélus, Cheval Blanc.

St. Estèphe

St. Estèphe is the most northerly region of the Médoc and is generally regarded as the least compelling, or the least sexy, of the Left Bank subregions (aka communes). If Peter found the Bellefont hard to love, it was unlikely he'd find St. Estèphe wines more appealing, as they are notoriously hard, austere, and unyielding in their youth.

St. Estèphe is also problematic in terms of promotion, as the commune lacks star power; there are no first growths in St. Estèphe—did the St. Estèphe growers lack political clout when the big prizes were handed out in 1855? However, St. Estèphe is home to what's called a "super second" château, Cos d'Estournel, which many believe should be rated a first growth.

Jeff had recommended that Peter try the second-label wine of Cos, called Les Pagodes de Cos ($40), from the 1996 vintage. "Second-label wines are important for most all of the big châteaux. They are a sort of bridge line," Jeff had said, meaning that they enable wine drinkers who may not have a lot of money to get a taste of the real thing. At the same time they provide the château with some ready cash (they are on the market sooner than the first, primary wine). As I might have predicted, Peter didn't love the fairly tannic Pagodes either, although he did grant it a begrudging respect.

"At least now I have a name for what I don't love: structure," Peter said. "If someone asks, I'll just say, 'This wine is too structured for me.' At least that way I can sound intelligent when I don't like a wine."

A few first-rate St. Estèphe châteaux: Cos d'Estournel, Montrose, Calon-Ségur.

PAUILLAC

Pauillac is the superstar subregion (commune) of Bordeaux; three of the five first growths are located in Pauillac, and unsurprisingly, some of the biggest, most tannic and structured wines are made there. Pauillac is also the home of other highly rated châteaux, including Château Lynch Bages, a respected fifth growth. This was the wine I'd chosen for Peter. Predictably enough, Peter turned out not to be a Pauillac man.

"This wine is ashy," he complained of the 2001 Lynch Bages. "Are all wines from Pauillac this ashy? I'm not a fan of ashy wines." I wouldn't call it ashy, I'd call it big, tannic, and backward, I said to

Peter. It wasn't showing much in the way of fruit—pretty typical of a young Pauillac.

"Well, I call it ashy," Peter replied stubbornly, examining the label. "You say this is a fifth growth, but the château looks pretty nice. Doesn't a nice château mean this wine should rank a little higher than a fifth growth?"

In fact, a lesser Bordeaux might often have a fancier château on its label than a first growth. Impressive real estate doesn't necessarily translate into a great wine. For example, Château Latour's label isn't fancy; there's just a squat tower on the front. Peter wasn't comforted by this fact. "Now I'm going to be skeptical when I look at the label," he said. "Now I'll think if it's a great-looking château, they're making a crummy wine."

A few famous Pauillac châteaux: Mouton Rothschild, Lafite Rothschild, Latour Rothschild.

St. Julien

The commune of St. Julien is home to more second growths than any other commune on Bordeaux's Left Bank. Some are so good they're also called super seconds. Wines from St. Julien tend to be more approachable than many other Left Bank wines, somewhere between the structured wines of Pauillac and the softer, more accessible wines from Margaux, the commune nearby. St. Julien wines are also considered good-value wines, consistent, and often easy to appreciate when young. They also have some of the easiest names to remember and pronounce: Château Gloria, Château Talbot, and fourth growth Château Beychevelle. The latter may be St. Julien's most recognizable wine, thanks to the sailing ship on its label. I bought the 2001 Beychevelle for Peter, as it's generally one of St. Julien's most accessible wines—supple and smooth. "This is so smooth it's hard to believe it's Cabernet," Peter remarked—his highest form of praise. "But what's with the boat?"

A few excellent St. Julien châteaux: Talbot, Ducru-Beaucaillou, Léoville–Las Cases.

MARGAUX

Margaux is the largest of the important Médoc communes and is home to wines that are sometimes referred to as "feminine," mostly because they have the most beguiling aromatics, but not necessarily because they are any softer or more accessible than other Left Bank wines. For example, first growth wine Château Margaux contains about as much Cabernet (75 percent) as a Pauillac wine.

I chose the 2001 Château Giscours for Peter to taste. This third growth Margaux château has made a comeback in recent years (there were some charges of fraudulent winemaking leveled against the château in the late 1990s—something I thought best not to tell Peter, prejudiced as he already was against the "corrupt" Bordelais). The wine was still quite young and tannic, but the fruit was dense and richly appealing. Peter, however, contended he had to "fight through the tannin to get at the wine."

Again, I reminded Peter, what he was encountering was structure, the fruit tannins and the oak tannins, all of which would make the wine last—longer than, say, the Lafleur from Lalande de Pomerol, which I made him go back and taste, to see if he still loved it as much as he had the first time. (Peter tried it again and admitted it seemed simple by comparison, "almost like Beaujolais," compared to the Giscours—sweeter and softer, less interesting.)

"Perhaps," Peter reasoned, "structure isn't an altogether bad thing."

Some top Margaux châteaux: Margaux, Palmer, Rausan-Ségla.

GRAVES

This commune is a bit of an anomaly in Bordeaux; that is, it's just as famous for its white as its red wines; in fact, the commune's most famous château, the first growth Château Haut-Brion, does both colors equally well. (As does its rival and equally brilliant neighboring producer, La Mission Haut-Brion.) Alas, our budget didn't allow for these wines. (The wines of Haut-Brion and La Mission, both red and white, cost well into three figures in a good vintage.) But I did have a red and a white Graves for Peter to taste so that he might have some sense of the Graves style, which is lighter and more aromatic than that of other Médoc wines.

Graves (the name is literally translated to "gravel") is actually further divided into two regions: Graves and Pessac-Léognan. The latter is the more prestigious of the two, and it's the location of all the better châteaux, including the one that I'd chosen for Peter: the 2001 Château de Fieuzal, a château with no official rating but whose wines, both red and white, are considered good buys. (In fact, this is probably true of the wines of the region overall.) "I'd almost call this wine pretty," Peter commented of the attractive and rather light but fragrant Cabernet Sauvignon–dominant red. "But that doesn't sound like a very Bordeaux-like thing to say. I mean, how much will anyone pay for a 'pretty' Bordeaux?" Peter had a point, but *pretty* can be an accurate characterization of a charming Pessac-Léognan wine.

The white wine I'd chosen was the 2004 Château Bouscaut, a property owned by Sophie Lurton, whose family is one of the most famous in Bordeaux. (The Lurtons own properties all over the region—from unrated châteaux in lesser Bordeaux regions such as Entre deux Mers to classified Bordeaux growths. The Lurtons are to the Médoc what the Mouiex family are to Pomerol.) The white wines of Graves and Pessac-Léognan are some of the best bargains in Bordeaux, and the Bouscaut, at $15, is one of the best. It's made from a blend of Sauvignon Blanc and Semillon, the two grapes of white Bordeaux. Peter had, of course, tried and declared himself a less-than-ardent fan of Sauvignon Blanc, but when it was blended with the rich, almost waxy white grape Semillon, Peter found much to admire.

"I love this wine!" Peter declared. "It's so fresh and delicious, I wouldn't have thought it was Bordeaux at all." Though the Lurtons may not have recognized it as such, this was, from Peter, the highest form of praise.

Some top Pessac-Léognan châteaux: Haut-Brion, La Mission Haut-Brion, Pape Clément.

BARSAC AND SAUTERNES

Although the vast majority of Bordeaux wines are dry, its sweet wines from Barsac and Sauternes, made from late-harvested grapes afflicted with botrytis (or "noble rot"), are some of the most legendary in the world of wine.

"*Afflicted* isn't a word I like to hear associated with wine" was all Peter said.

The most famous such afflicted wine is made in Sauternes—at Château d'Yquem—a wine that is both literally and figuratively in a class by itself. (Château d'Yquem was the only sweet wine recognized in the famous 1855 Médoc classification.) Even Peter had heard of Yquem (which he initially mispronounced, as many do, by leading with the *d'*, which is actually silent).

"Say EEE-kem," I said to Peter, who replied, somewhat bitterly, "What does it matter? If it's as famous as Pétrus, I won't be tasting it either."

BURGUNDY

Peter was looking forward to the Burgundy chapter the most, or, as he put it, "It's my greatest chance to appear stupid." Whether or not this would actually end up being the case, Peter could at least be comforted by being far from alone in being baffled by Burgundy. It's the most complicated wine region in France and possibly the world.

For starters, Burgundy comprises five subregions, each with a very different identity. In its extreme north, there's Chablis, home to famous white wines of the same name (and which looks on a map as if it might well be part of Champagne rather than Burgundy). Second, southward, is the Côte d'Or, the smallest but most important region in Burgundy, where the region's most famous red and white wines are made. Just below the Côte d'Or is the Côte Chalonnais, where some of the best "bargains" of Burgundy, both red and white, can be found. Below that is the Mâconnais, most famously home to the ubiquitous restaurant wine Mâcon-Villages. Finally, there's Beaujolais, so far south it's actually geographically considered part of the Rhône.

The two key grapes of Burgundy are Chardonnay and Pinot Noir, although in Beaujolais, the grape is Gamay. "You said that last grape with a strange tone to your voice," observed Peter. "Are people in Burgundy ashamed of Gamay?"

Gamay is a lesser grape than Chardonnay and Pinot Noir, and the wines produced from it are rarely complex, though it can produce some good wine in Beaujolais (and in Oregon too).

CÔTE D'OR

The Côte d'Or (or "golden slope") region of Burgundy is remarkably small. Most people on a first visit there find it hard to believe that so many of the world's greatest wines are made in such a small place. They might even say, as Peter did while looking at a map of the thirty-mile-long region, "Is this really all there is?" But for Peter, its diminutive proportions were reassuring. Maybe this won't be so hard, he said hopefully.

Of course he was wrong.

Burgundy may have more complications per square mile or perhaps even square meter than any other wine region in the world. There is a tremendous amount of detail to consider—as the most casual glance at a Burgundy bottle will reveal. For example, there are hundreds of premier and grand cru vineyards in Burgundy, whose names appear on dozens of producers' labels because many vineyards are carved into tiny parcels that belong to several different families. Winemakers may own a piece of a grand cru or a premier cru vineyard and make a radically better (or worse) wine from the same plot of land than someone else. (This all happened as a result of the Napoleonic Code, which mandated equal inheritance for every family member, which means an already small vineyard might be divided many, many times.)

There are more than thirty grand cru vineyards in Burgundy; theoretically they are where the greatest wines of Burgundy are from, although some are more famous than others (La Tâche, Le Montrachet, Corton) and some grands crus are greater than others. In fact, some select premier cru vineyards can produce better wines than some grand cru vineyards, depending, of course, on the producer.

There are hundreds of premier cru vineyards, and their quality is even more various than the grands crus, though theoretically a premier cru wine is the second-best wine produced in Burgundy, after a grand cru. After the premier crus come the hundreds of wines made from vineyards that aren't officially recognized but can be of good quality; these unofficial vineyards are called *lieux dits,* or "place names."

Next are the village wines, made from vineyards within a certain radius of a specific Côte d'Or village. These wines generally carry the name of the village along with the name of its most famous neighboring vineyard. For example, the village wine Gevrey-Chambertin combines the name of the village, Gevrey, with that of its neighboring grand cru vineyard, Chambertin.

Every village produces wines of a particular style. For example, the wines of Gevrey-Chambertin and Pommard tend to be (comparatively) big and robust, while Chambolle-Musigny and Volnay wines tend to be more nuanced and delicate. Being able to identify and appreciate the subtle differences of each village (not to mention each vineyard) is an important part of a Burgundy lover's life.

After village wines (in descending order of quality) are regional wines. These wines may be made from a certain area of the Côte d'Or, such as the Côte de Nuits, which means the wine could come from anywhere in that region. (A wine labeled simply Côte de Nuits could come from anywhere in the northern half of the Côte d'Or. Likewise, a Côte de Beaune wine could come anywhere from the southern half of the Côte d'Or.) At the very bottom of the

Burgundy wine hierarchy is basic Bourgogne, a wine that could come from anywhere in Burgundy. "I think that's all that I can afford," Peter said.

Yet the Burgundy that Peter remembered best was a grand cru white Burgundy, Bienvenues-Bâtard-Montrachet. He had tried it in a wine bar on West Fifty-fifth Street in Manhattan some twenty years ago.

"I said to the guy behind the bar that I wanted to taste something really good even if it was incredibly expensive," Peter recalled. "And when he gave me that Bienvenues, I bashed my head on the table I loved it so much." Peter got a far-off look in his eyes.

"Did you ever have the wine again?" I asked.

"No! It was way too expensive—maybe twenty dollars a glass— and even then it just seemed ridiculous to me," Peter replied. "But it was the first time that I realized that there was something out there that was out of my reach but that was worth reaching for. And yet I never learned anything about it. Now I want to know everything."

THE BEST OF TIMES IN BURGUNDY

I had both good and bad news for Peter regarding his newfound Burgundy zeal. The good news was that there has never been so much good Burgundy as there is today, with more and more producers making great wines. And there have been a string of good vintages (2002, 2004, and 2005). The bad news was that Burgundy has never been so expensive. A simple Bourgogne can cost $20 a bottle, and a grand cru Chablis as much as $150 a bottle, while a Le Montrachet wine can easily run to the four figures.

"Chablis is expensive?" Peter was incredulous. "I had no idea. Whenever I go to Mary Higgins Clark's house in Cape Cod, it's Chablis all around. She says, 'Get me a glass of ice-cold Chablis.' It's the only thing I drink when I'm with her."

A real Chablis (as opposed to California "mountain Chablis") from a grand cru Chablis vineyard is actually one of the most sought-after wines today. Great Chablis is consistently one of the most expensive wines at auction, almost impossible to acquire without paying a high price. Everyone seems to be collecting Chablis from producers such as Raveneau and Dauvissat. Peter looked at me in disbelief. He had no idea Mary Higgins Clark was so cutting-edge.

I had a bottle of 2002 William Fèvre Chablis for Peter to taste. Not only is Fèvre an excellent producer, but 2002 was a great year in Chablis. It was also a pretty affordable wine ($22). Did it taste like what Peter drank with Mary Higgins Clark?

"This wine tastes like steel," Peter replied, "and the wine at her house tastes like steel too."

Steel is one of the characteristic flavors of true Chablis thanks to its minerally soils (though if the wine is served "ice-cold" as it purportedly was at Mary Higgins Clark's house, then the steel Peter was tasting might have been the coldness of the wine). No great Chablis should be drunk in such a glacial condition. And with tens of millions of books in print, I was sure Mary Higgins Clark drank the real deal.

A few great Chablis producers: Dauvissat, Raveneau, William Fèvre.

Meanwhile, Peter, having perhaps had too much Chablis with Mary Higgins Clark on the Cape, was eager to try other white Burgundies. So we went on to taste wines from the Côte de Beaune. This is the southern half of the Côte d'Or, where all the great white Burgundies are made—although a fair amount of red wine is produced there as well. The three most famous Côte de Beaune towns all lend their names to the great white wines: Meursault, Chassagne, and Puligny. (The latter two append the name of the region's most famous grand cru vineyard, Le Montrachet, to their name—e.g., Puligny-Montrachet.)

Although the villages are within a few miles of one another, the wine produced in each has a different and particular character. Open and somewhat flowery, Meursault may be the easiest of all to appreciate. So that's where Peter and I started—with a couple of 2002 Meursaults by Jadot, a leading Burgundian négociant. (A négociant buys grapes rather than owns vineyards, although some, such as Drouhin and Jadot, do both.) The first wine was a village bottling (simply "Meursault"), while the second was a premier cru, Meursault-Genevrières (there are no grand, only premier, cru vineyards in Meursault). The first wine Peter found "just right—not sweet or cloying or too oaky," while the premier cru was "much more complex" and tasted "like nuts." (In fact, nutty-almond flavors are characteristic of Meursault.)

The next wine, Chassagne-Montrachet, is somewhere between Meursault and Puligny-Montrachet in terms of style, though a young Chassagne tends to taste more like the latter than the former—that is, more open and accessible. Unlike in Meursault, there are both premier and grand cru vineyards in Chassagne-Montrachet. Peter found the 2002 Jadot Chassagne-Montrachet "steely," by comparison to the Meursault, and the 2002 Jadot Puligny-Montrachet even more so.

"This wine almost hurts my teeth," Peter reported. "It's like I'm chewing on rocks." Indeed, Puligny is the most austere and minerally of all three white Burgundies, and its soil is quite stony. It takes the longest to evolve, while Meursault is the easiest to appreciate. I figured this was why Peter, a fatty Chardonnay lover, liked it best.

"*Beguiling* is exactly the word for Meursault," Peter declared. "I'm beguiled by this wine. It sounds like a song. But what about Montrachet? I know that's the greatest white Burgundy of all."

Peter knew about Montrachet thanks to Sean Connery. Several years ago, Sean Connery was filming a movie in New York and had kindly allowed Peter's son, Alex, then a teenager, to visit the set. Connery even posed for a picture with Alex (which became a much-sought-after Travers family Christmas card). Peter had wanted to thank Sean Connery and had asked the actor how he might show his appreciation. Connery's reply was specific. Peter could send him a case of 1986 DRC Montrachet. Peter sent a card instead.

A few great white Burgundy producers: Domaine Lafond, Coche-Dury, Ramonet, Roulot.

OTHER WHITE BURGUNDIES

Pouilly-Fuissé is a sort of bridge wine between Mâcon-Villages and the white Burgundies of the Côte de Beaune. It was quite fashionable about thirty years ago and consequently became overproduced and overpriced. (Not to mention wrongly pronounced: say Poo-ey Foosay. Both *l*'s are silent.) Now Pouilly-Fuissé is closer in price to what it's worth, and some are quite good (Château Fuissé Vieilles Vignes), although they aren't as complex or as elegant as a Côte d'Or wine.

Mâcon Villages, on the other hand, is a serviceable wine: bright, attractive, though rarely very interesting or intense. But it's generally well priced and it's a particularly good buy in ripe vintages, as it's a simple wine meant to be drunk in its youth. (There are some exceptions, such as the wines of Olivier Merlin, whose Mâcons are of such clarity and purity that he could be making wine in the Côte d'Or.) Peter actually liked the 2002 Olivier Merlin Mâcon La Roche Vineuse Vieilles Vignes better than he did the 2002 Pouilly-Fuissé, which he actually thought had spent "too much time" in an oak barrel. This was a novel accusation, one I'd never heard from Peter before. Did it augur a change in taste or was it just a wine Peter didn't particularly like?

RED BURGUNDY

The great red grape of Burgundy is, of course, Pinot Noir, the grape Peter (and everyone else) fell in love with thanks to a certain low-budget film whose name I had forbidden Peter to mention more than six times (he was already on mention number four).

"I'm really excited about this tasting," said Peter. "And I promise to mention some other movie than the One You Expect Me To."

I'd decided to start with a couple basic red Bourgognes. These wines can be great deals, particularly in good vintages. The two Bourgognes I bought were from négociant Joseph Drouhin and

Domaine Roulot—Jean-Marc Roulot is a favorite producer of mine. He's so good that even his most basic Bourgogne is a well-made, good-value wine.

"Even better than Drouhin?" Peter wanted to know. Drouhin is also a good producer, I assured Peter. The Drouhin name is old and famous; they have been making wine for over 125 years.

"Then they must be tired," quipped Peter.

Peter admired the color of both wines and the aromas of the Roulot, but professed himself disappointed with the actual taste of both, which he reported was "nothing at all. It just tastes like wine." In other words, they lacked intensity.

"And yet when you say Burgundy, people expect to be impressed," Peter complained.

Unfortunately, Peter would have to spend a little more money to be truly impressed. In fact, he'd have to spend a lot of money. And because it's Burgundy, there were no guarantees—even with wines that cost hundreds of dollars.

"I think I'm getting the picture about Burgundy," Peter replied. "And it's a screen full of dollar signs."

After the disappointing Bourgognes, I gave Peter a new wine to try, Marsannay. This wine is made in the northernmost part of the Côte d'Or (practically in the suburbs of Dijon), and while it's a lesser appellation (it just received DOC [Denominazione di Origine Controllata or denomination of controlled origin] status), there are some solid Marsannays around. I gave Peter a glass of 2002 Domaine Trapet Marsannay, thinking he would like it because it had lots of lush fruit and a bit of oak. "There isn't excessive oak," I warned him.

"Who said I like excess?" Peter replied defensively. "I don't necessarily always like excess. Take, for example, a movie like *The Family Stone*, with Sarah Jessica Parker and Diane Keaton—the mother is dying and yet that isn't even enough, they have to add in a hundred other sentimental things. It's excessive. I guess you'd say it's oaky. And I don't like an oaky movie. It just says one thing over and over again."

Our next wine, the 2002 Jadot Nuits St. Georges, came from a region not far from Marsannay, but the taste was completely different.

"It has a lot of concentration, it's a lot stronger," commented Peter, "and it has a better color too." A great color was one of Peter's highest forms of praise.

The next wine I gave Peter provided an even more vivid contrast: the 2002 Pommard Jadot Clos de Commanderie premier cru. (Pommard was long the favorite Burgundy region of English-speaking oenophiles because it was so easy to pronounce.)

"That's spectacular," Peter raved after tasting the wine. "The nose is really good, it has acidity and complexity, and yet it doesn't say to me, 'I'm stronger than you are.'"

What did he mean? That it had more power and concentration? Peter nodded. "It may not be immediately beguiling like the Meursault, but it is impressive. It helps me to understand why people love Burgundy so much. When it's good, there's nothing else like it in the world.

"I'm going to drink a lot more Burgundy, both red and white," Peter resolved. "When I make a lot more money, that is. The wines of Burgundy remind me of the films of the late Jean Renoir, who I think is the most sensual movie director in France. Everything glows in a Renoir film. I think I can get that glow from these wines too—I just may have to take out a bank loan to do so."

Some great red Burgundy producers: Domaine de la Romanée Conti, Michel Lafarge, Domaine du Comte de Vogüé, Domaine Georges Mugneret, Domaine Leroy, Méo-Camuzet, Marquis d'Angerville.

Great recent Burgundy vintages: red, 2003, 2002, 1999, 1997, 1990; white, 2005, 2002, 1999, 1996, 1995, 1992, 1989.

Principal Côte d'Or Burgundy appellations (north to south):

Côte de Nuits: Gevrey-Chambertin, Morey St. Denis, Vougeot, Chambolle-Musigny, Vosne-Romanée, Nuits St. Georges.

Côte de Beaune: Aloxe-Corton, Savigny-lès-Beaune, Volnay, Beaune, Pommard, Meursault, Puligny-Montrachet, Chassagne-Montrachet.

Peter Meets His First Famous Burgundian, or Dinner with Laurent Drouhin

When I found out that a member of the famous Drouhin family, Laurent Drouhin, had moved from Beaune to my hometown, Mamaroneck, New York, I asked if we could have dinner together — Laurent, Peter, and me. Laurent and his wife graciously agreed.

Although Laurent had been to New York City many times before moving to one of its suburbs, it soon became clear he'd never encountered a man such as Peter.

"Did you move to Mamaroneck just to have dinner with us?" Peter asked Laurent by way of an opener. Laurent blanched a bit but recovered seamlessly. He was French, after all. "Absolutely," he replied. In fact, Laurent, a tall, well-groomed man, and his blond, well-groomed wife, Beatrice, told us they would be living in Mamaroneck "for at least three more years" as Laurent took charge of the export division of the business.

We met at a local restaurant, Le Provençal; Laurent was already there with a dozen bottles nearby when Peter and I arrived. The first wine Laurent poured was the basic 2004 Drouhin Chablis. He described the fermentation process and the location of the vineyards to Peter, who nodded knowledgeably and leaned over to offer Laurent this confidence: "There was a time when I would lick the oak off of a barrel. But now I've learned some restraint." Laurent nodded, no doubt wondering how long it was before he could get back to Beaune.

"I read in a book the other day that white Burgundy is decanted but never red. Is that true?" Peter asked Laurent.

There are no rules, Laurent replied, though I was sure he wished there were — especially when it came to conversations with certain film critics.

"I love rules," Peter said.

"Then I will give you a rule," Laurent replied. "If the wine is over ten years old, do not decant it. Open it half an hour beforehand and let it breathe in your glass."

"I read that the sommelier of Guy Savoy in Paris decants everything," Peter offered. Laurent simply nodded; he was clearly done with the topic.

"I've been trying to read all that I can about Burgundy," Peter said to Laurent, who was now pouring his next wine, a white wine called Véro. This was an entirely new wine, Laurent told Peter. "It's a blend of village-level wines from all over Burgundy—Chablis, Meursault, Puligny-Montrachet."

"Isn't that kind of an odd idea?" Peter replied. "I just learned that the best wines in Burgundy come from one particular place."

But Laurent simply nodded and didn't reply. Instead, he intoned, "The closer you get to wine, the closer you get to Burgundy."

While this answer did nothing to resolve Peter's question, it seemed to please the two men, and they nodded in mutual satisfaction while I silently considered what a peculiar wine Véro actually was—a bunch of valuable place names subverted into a generic blend.

The next wine Laurent poured was a Beaune Clos des Mouches. This premier cru vineyard (which produces both red and white wine in equal amount) is synonymous with the Drouhin name—they own most of it after all. And if it's not their best, it's certainly their most famous wine. Laurent had brought two vintages of the red Beaune Clos des Mouches for Peter to taste—the 2000 and the 2002 (never mind the white is the more famous wine). The 2000 was soft and pretty, while the 2002 had the richness and depth of the much better vintage. I was curious what Peter would say. Of the 2002 he practically waxed rhapsodic: "This wine has a finish on it that says it is a wine for an occasion." The assessment clearly impressed Laurent Drouhin—as I discovered when Peter called to tell me he'd gotten a nice e-mail from Laurent the very next day. What did it say?

Peter forwarded the e-mail to me. *It was a great pleasure to meet you,* Laurent wrote. *You talk about your ignorance—what ignorance? You are a wine lover with a great palate and an elegant sense of humor. That's what it's about when it comes to wine.*

"What did Laurent write to you?" Peter asked.

"Nothing," I replied. "Not a word. Obviously he wasn't as impressed with my palate as yours."

"Well, Laurent did say something about wanting to go to a screening with me sometime," Peter replied.

ALSACE

Although any wine region in France, if not the world, was bound to suffer by comparison to Burgundy for Peter, I hoped he might fall in love with Alsace too—even if it's not an easy wine region to understand or, for that matter, to visit. (There are no direct flights from the United States.)

But Alsace is one of my favorite wine regions in France. I like it as a tourist (the towns are still quaint and small, the houses painted bright colors) and also as a wine professional. It's where some of the world's best Riesling is made—not to mention some world-class Gewürztraminer, a grape that's even harder than Riesling to get right.

Peter had had a few Alsace wines before: "I've ordered Alsace Gewürztraminers in restaurants before, but they're always so sweet." This, in a sentence, sums up the principal problem of Alsace today: the wines are often too sweet.

Not that many winemakers in Alsace will admit this. In fact, if you ask an Alsace vigneron why his wine is too sweet, the first thing he'll do is deny it. Then maybe he'll say it's because the weather has been warm and the grapes were very ripe. But the real answer is that Alsace wine styles have changed. When I visited Alsace a year and a half ago, producer Jean Trimbach (one of the few Alsace winemakers to make dry wines) told me he thinks only a handful of producers in Alsace are making truly dry wines.

The wines of Alsace, unlike any others in France, are varietally labeled. That is, the grape is given marquee treatment and the producer and vineyard are subordinated to the grape. This seems like a good reason Alsace wines would be popular among Americans. But alas, there are some obstacles. One problem is that the bottles look more German than they do French, from the typescript of their labels to their names. Alsace, after all, changed hands between the

French and the Germans over centuries before finally ending up with the French—which means a lot of producers have Germanic-sounding names. Then there is the shape of the bottles—long and tapered like those of German wines. (A friend of mine calls them "needle-nose" bottles.)

"I like the idea of the grape names, but I don't like the look of the bottles," said Peter. "I like Riesling and Gewürztraminer, but I don't like not knowing if the wines are going to be dry or sweet. Can't they put some sort of code on the back of the bottle?" One Alsace producer, Domaine Zind-Humbrecht, has actually done this, numbering their wines with codes of one through five according to their level of sweetness. But you would have to know it—there is no explanation of the numbers on the labels.

I gave Peter a glass of Trimbach's simplest Riesling (an excellent value at $15 a bottle, although Trimbach makes a wide range of wines at various prices, including one of the absolute greatest Rieslings in the world, the grand cru Clos Ste. Hune). Peter professed himself pleased. "It's wonderfully dry," he remarked. "Why can't all Alsace wines be like this?"

It was a good question. And it's not to say there are not many great sweet wines in Alsace, deliberately made. The wines of Domaine Weinbach, which often incorporate small lots of botrytised grapes (the noble rot of Sauternes), are often quite sweet—but at the same time are quite well-balanced, with a firm thread of acidity. Domaine Weinbach is run by two of the most beautiful women in Alsace, Laurence and her sister, Catherine. I didn't mention this to Peter, as I was afraid he might ask to stay in their house as well.

I gave Peter one of the most lauded of the Domaine Weinbach wines, the 2002 Grand Cru Schlossberg Cuvée Ste. Catherine l'Inedit Riesling. It was, to me, the perfect example of the Domaine Weinbach style—incredibly opulent but at the same time beautifully balanced.

"This is amazing," Peter said. "It's so rich and intense, I can't imagine drinking it with anything. This wine would be too good to waste on food."

A few great Alsace producers: Hugel, Trimbach (particularly its flagship Riesling, Clos Ste. Hune), Domaine Weinbach, Kreyden-weiss, Albert Boxler.

THE LOIRE VALLEY

I was surprised by how much Peter loved the wines of the Loire, especially since they have so much acidity—the one quality Peter usually found so off-putting. In fact, most of the grapes grown in the Loire—Sauvignon Blanc, Chenin Blanc, and Cabernet Franc—are notable for high acid levels. This means they tend to go well with food, but in less-than-great years their acidity can be off-puttingly high.

A high-acid wine can also be off-putting to someone without something to eat. Or at least it was to Peter, who found many of the wines to be, well, oppressive without food. Even an excellent Sancerre, such as the 2004 Château de Sancerre, made him complain that he couldn't "get past" the acidity. He said the same of the fresh and lively 2004 Domaine de la Pepiere Muscadet, which is such a good Muscadet and such a good deal ($10) that it even has a cult following in the States—not something that can be said of many $10 wines. Peter found this hard to believe, though he conceded it did have some of the "steely" qualities he admired in Chablis, but again, "too much acidity" as well.

I soon realized that the only way I could convince Peter of the virtues of Loire wines was to pair them with food. So I brought along a Vouvray from Huet, one of my favorite Loire producers, the next time Peter and I had dinner. Huet makes Vouvray (from the Chenin Blanc grape) in both sweet and dry versions and is probably the greatest Vouvray producer in France. Huet is also a great example of how versatile Loire producers can be—making a range of wines that are sweet and dry and sometimes sparkling too.

"Is it that hard to make a buck in the Loire that they have to do so many different wines?" was all Peter said.

The wine I brought to Peter's house was the 2002 Huet Le Mont Sec Vouvray (a great deal at about $30 a bottle—another virtue of

Loire wines is that they tend to be well priced). "This is amazing," Peter commented. "It goes on and on, and yet even though I'm sure it has a lot of acidity, because it's from the Loire, you really can't tell." Peter offered me a deal: feed me and I'll be happy to drink wines from the Loire.

OUR FAVORITE BARGAIN LOIRE WINES

Muscadet—It's arguably the simplest white wine in the world, but a good, crisp Muscadet (drink it as young as possible) is also a great bargain. Look for Domaine de la Pepière and Domaine de la Tourmaline wines.

Vouvray—These are possibly the single most versatile (and diverse) white wines of the Loire. Made from the Chenin Blanc grape, Vouvray ranges from sweet to dry and from sparkling to still. Domaine Huet makes them all and makes the best, but producers Champalou and Naudin are also good.

Chinon—This light, juicy red is made from Cabernet Franc grapes; Chinon is the most popular wine of the bistros of Paris. The best producers are Olga Raffault and Joguet.

Menetou Salon—This Sauvignon Blanc wine is the better-priced alternative to Sancerre (which it greatly resembles and which is just down the road). Domaine Chatenoy is a producer worth looking for.

Samur—Although both sparkling and still wines are made in Samur, it's the sparkling wines that are some of the best bargains from this Loire appellation. Gratien & Meyer (of the Alfred Gratien Champagne house) makes a particularly good wine.

THE RHÔNE VALLEY

The people I know who drink Rhône wines don't just drink them, they obsess over them—sometimes to the exclusion of all else. Take, for example, my friend the magnum lover, Park B. Smith. While his profession is home furnishings (Park B. Smith is also his company's name), Park's personal obsession is Châteauneuf-du-Pape, the most famous wine of the southern Rhône. And his obsession finds its expression in some pretty big numbers: Park has twenty thousand bottles of Châteauneuf-du-Pape; half of those bottles are magnums. Park may have the largest collection of Châteauneuf outside of France, or outside the Rhône Valley for that matter. Park was even named an honorary mayor of the town of Châteauneuf-du-Pape some years back and was presented with keys to the city (something no other American besides Robert Parker can claim). And Park is a great ambassador: every time I've been to his home, he's opened at least three or four magnums of Châteauneuf-du-Pape. "Do you think I could get an invitation to his house?" Peter asked. "I think it would be useful for me."

First, I suggested, Peter should learn something about the wine. Châteauneuf-du-Pape ("the new house of the pope"), as every student of European history knows, was named after Pope Clement V, who created his court in Avignon, and his successor, John XXII, who created a summer palace nearby in an old castle in Châteauneuf. It's the most important appellation in the southern Rhône Valley; in fact, it was where the French appellation system was created in the early 1920s.

Châteauneuf-du-Pape is one of the most blended wines in the world—with up to thirteen grapes, both red and white, permissible in the making of the wine (French wine laws dictate that certain grapes can be grown in certain regions). The most important of the thirteen grapes are Grenache, Mourvèdre, Syrah, and Cinsault, with the exact blend left up to the individual producer (French law does at least allow for a bit of winemaking freedom in this regard). There are also white Châteauneuf-du-Papes, wines made from blends of several grapes, though the most important are Grenache Blanc and Roussanne. But white Châteauneuf is rarely as good or as long-lived as the red (although the white produced by the legendary Château de Beaucastel does come close in some vintages).

THE SOUTHERN RHÔNE

Other notable southern Rhône reds include Côtes du Rhône (which covers an enormous territory) and Gigondas, a Grenache-dominant wine that's fairly close in character to Châteauneuf; in fact, it's considered a sort of poor man's Châteauneuf. (I've never seen a bottle of Gigondas in my friend Park's house.) But the Côtes du Rhône is, in terms of volume, the most important wine of the southern Rhône, as it accounts for a good 70 percent of the region's production. Both are good values, though Gigondas is probably the most undervalued wine.

"Probably because it's so hard to say," commented Peter.

Châteauneuf-du-Pape, on the other hand, is not the great value it once was, since it's become so fashionable in the past several years. This is due in part to a string of great vintages—beginning in 1998 and continuing all the way through 2004 (with the exception of the disastrously wet 2002). It's also thanks to wine critic and Rhône fan Robert Parker, who was one of the first to recognize and champion up-and-coming Rhône producers (of both the north and the south). As a result, prices have risen dramatically in just a few years. Now a top Châteauneuf-du-Pape, such as one of my favorites, Domaine de la Janasse Vieilles Vignes, can cost over $100 a bottle.

Peter looked cross and complained, "Why doesn't this guy Parker just shut up about them?"

Yet, when we began tasting, Peter understood why Parker couldn't "shut up" about the wines. We started with a Côtes du Rhône, the 2003 Chapoutier, which to Peter was "pretty good," probably the highest praise a Côtes du Rhône attains. But the 2003 Les Espalines

Cuvée Les Tendrelles Gigondas from Patrick LeSec, a blend of Grenache and Syrah, was even more impressive, with a terrific nose of herbs and spice, and in the mouth it felt rich and textured.

"This wine has a wonderful taste," Peter reported. "And it has a lot more going on than the Côtes du Rhône." The wine was also fairly soft, thanks to a fairly generous amount of Grenache. "Whatever Grenache is, it's a grape I could love," Peter noted, and proceeded to drink, not taste, the rest of the Gigondas.

Grenache is one of the most important—and widely planted—grapes in the world (it's the second-most-planted red grape of all). It's especially important in southern France and Spain, although the Australians have made pretty good use of it too. Its chief characteristics are a certain rusticity (i.e., lack of polish), soft tannins, and sweet fruit. But most all, Grenache wines don't age particularly well—hence the necessity of often blending it with other grapes. (Although there is always an exception that proves the rule, as in the case of Château Rayas, a Châteauneuf-du-Pape that is 100 percent Grenache.)

As much as Peter appreciated the Gigondas, it was the 2001 Château Beaurenard Châteauneuf-du-Pape that impressed him the most, beginning with the classic earthy-spicy aromas that fairly billowed from the glass when Peter poured the wine—so vigorously it actually sloshed audibly in the bottle. "You're never supposed to hear the wine when you pour it, are you?" Peter asked nervously—a possible violation of protocol.

"Seductive!" Peter and I both declared almost simultaneously upon tasting the wine. Park Smith was right. The wine had a powerful spicy aroma coupled with rich, warm flavors in the mouth. Peter asked how much the wine cost—the second-best way of telling when he liked a wine. (The best was when he drank all the wine in his glass.) I'd paid about $40 for the bottle, which put it out of Peter's category of everyday wine. I was surprised when he declared the Gigondas, at $27, to be a good everyday drink.

"It's a better value than the Côtes du Rhône," Peter asserted. How dramatically Peter's "number"—not to mention grape choice—had changed. It was hard to believe it wasn't so long ago that he'd been content with a $9 Chardonnay.

A few great Châteauneuf-du-Pape producers: Château de Beau-castel, Domaine de Marcoux, Henri Bonneau, Domaine Charvin, Clos des Papes.

THE NORTHERN RHÔNE

Although it's considered part of the same wine region as the southern Rhône, the northern Rhône has little in common with its southern counterpart, starting with the style of its wines (big, rich, and tannic, and mostly unblended), as well as the grapes that go into them (Syrah for the red, and three grapes for the white: Viognier, Marsanne, and Roussanne). The most famous northern Rhône wine, Hermitage, is correspondingly opposite to the most famous wine of the south, Châteauneuf-du-Pape.

Considered the "manliest wine in the world" (or at least until the advent of blockbuster Australian Syrahs and Napa cult Cabernets), Hermitage is an enormously rich, tannic Syrah-based wine that can take several years or decades to show its true character. The Hermitage Peter and I tasted came from the difficult (aka wet and rainy) 2002 vintage, and it wasn't as masculine as I'd hoped.

As Peter said, "This wine seems more boyish than manly to me." It was, at least, a good illustration of how important vintage can be—with the best wines and producers.

In fact, our next wine, the less manly Crozes-Hermitage, was from a good vintage and seemed, by contrast to the Hermitage, downright intense. (It also offered a good illustration of how a lesser wine of a great vintage can trump a theoretically better wine from a bad year.)

Crozes-Hermitage and St. Joseph are two Syrah-based reds along the model of Hermitage (they're located nearby), though the two are softer and fruitier than Hermitage and styled to be drunk fairly young. I'd chosen the 2001 Jaboulet Domaine de Thalabert Jaboluet Crozes-Hermitage for Peter. Jaboulet is one of the most reliable names in the northern Rhône; their La Chapelle Hermitage is a much-collected, much-sought wine.

"This wine is really slapping me around—but I mean that in a good way," Peter reported about the Crozes-Hermitage as he took a whiff. This, I soon learned, was Peter's way of describing Syrah.

The last northern Rhône red we tasted was the 1999 Bernard Burgaud Côte Rôtie, easily the biggest, most intense wine of all. "This wine is going to put hair on my chest," Peter declared. Côte Rôtie (the name means "roasted slope") was always considered second-class to Hermitage until Marcel Guigal began making his single-vineyard wines—La Mouline, La Turque, La Landonne—back in the seventies. They're now some of the most coveted and expensive wines in the world.

"Are they the Pétrus of the Rhône?" Peter wanted to know.

In a way they were. And my friend, a lawyer, whom I call the Collector (Peter would meet him later), loved them nearly as much as my friend Park Smith did the wines of Châteauneuf-du-Pape, though his cellar falls short of Park's twenty-thousand-bottle mark.

"The wines of the Rhône are amazing," Peter reported at the end of the Rhône chapter, "especially the Châteauneuf-du-Pape. And even if Robert Parker has driven up the prices, I'd probably pay whatever it costs. I'd pay forty dollars for that Côte Rôtie in a second. I'd probably buy the Châteauneuf-du-Pape too. In fact, I'd buy them all."

Could this really be true? The same man who once feared Cabernet was now embracing manly Syrah? Or was it all just a ploy to get invited to Park's house?

A few great northern Rhône producers: Guigal (Côte Rôtie), Clape (Cornas), Verset (Cornas), Jaboulet (Hermitage).

CHAMPAGNE

"I've never actually even looked at the Champagne selection on a wine list," confessed Peter. "It would never occur to me to order a bottle of Champagne in a restaurant unless I was celebrating something."

The last time I saw Peter drink Champagne was when his son, Alex, turned twenty-one: Alex had specifically requested Louis

Roederer Cristal, a fancy *tête du cuvée* (or top-of-the-line) Champagne with a following chiefly composed of rappers, rock stars, and certain underworld types. (Cristal costs about $175 a bottle.)

Peter often mentioned Cristal as one of his favorite wine memories, though it seemed to have more to do with the occasion than the wine. This wasn't surprising, considering Champagne is so closely tied to particular events (birthdays, weddings, anniversaries). And yet because there's only so much celebrating that can take place in a person's life (presumably at least), not many people drink a lot of Champagne. Or, like Peter, even look at it on a wine list. (Champagne prices on a wine list, by the way, are an excellent way to find out if the list is overpriced, as the retail price of Champagne is pretty common knowledge. For example, nonvintage Veuve Clicquot is about $40, so if it's $110 a bottle on a wine list, you're likely being gouged other places on that wine list as well.)

Since Peter, like most everyone else, only drank Champagne on special occasions and lacked knowledge of a few basics as to its proper handling (how to open a bottle), I decided to start our Champagne lesson there.

Peter thought that a Champagne bottle should be opened with great ceremony, that is to say, by showering and exploding bubbles all over the floor. This was the method he'd seen in the movies after all. I had to break it to him that this was in fact the least desirable method of all, an anathema to anyone who knew anything about Champagne.

The cork should only give a small whisper when it leaves the bottle, I told Peter, demonstrating with a bottle of Mumm's. You should ease the cork out almost as if you're coaxing it to leave the bottle.

Peter was unimpressed. "Isn't the explosion part of the point? The signal to celebrate?"

There's as much pressure inside a bottle of Champagne as there is in a city bus tire, I told Peter. Would he want to explode a bus tire in his living room? Or on his dining room table?

Peter appeared taken aback but also intrigued by this danger. "A bus tire!" he exclaimed. "Now, that's exciting."

Peter observed, "Champagne is the most movie-oriented wine. Take a James Bond film—it's all about the Champagne."

"Bollinger, right?"

"No," Peter corrected me. "Dom Pérignon. But that could change. They'll have to change everything now that Pierce Brosnan is gone, including Bond's brand of Champagne." But we needed to talk about more than just cinematic Champagne (though my favorite Champagne movie moment is the seemingly bottomless half bottle of Mumm's in *Moonstruck*).

Champagne, for all its frivolous associations, is a tremendously complex wine, and its creation is expensive and time-consuming, beginning with its blending. Most Champagne is a blend, or cuvée, of three grapes: Chardonnay, Pinot Noir, and Pinot Meunier. Occasionally a few other grapes might be used or omitted (for example, in a blanc de blancs Champagne, there is only Chardonnay). These grapes come from vineyards all over the region of Champagne (located less than two hours from Paris), although some parts of Champagne are more famous for certain grapes than others. For example, the subregion Côtes du Blancs is famous for its Chardonnay grapes, while the Montagne de Rheims is better suited and famous for Pinot Noir.

The best vineyards are rated premier and grand cru, though oddly enough it's the town that receives the rating, not the vineyards themselves. The vineyards of the town of Cuis, for example, are all rated premier cru. This isn't something many wine drinkers know or keep track of, as they do vineyards of Burgundy and Bordeaux.

When it comes to making the wine, different vineyard parcels are usually fermented individually. A Champagne maker may have up to fifty different tanks or barrels (or "lots") of wine to blend together, some from different years. This is another distinctive aspect of Champagne: even the most basic nonvintage cuvée may be the creation of several years' worth of wine (the newest vintage plus one or two earlier ones, to lend depth and complexity). It's how a Champagne house such as Moët & Chandon or Veuve Clicquot creates its own style—coming up with a blend they can reproduce year after year.

"Making Champagne sounds a lot like making a Steven Spielberg movie," Peter observed. "Spielberg will come in and put his name on movies like *Gremlins* and *Goonies*—it will be 'Steven Spielberg presents'—even though he may have nothing to do with directing the actual movie."

But Peter's analogy wasn't entirely apt. A Champagne house has a director, a winemaker, a master blender who is in charge of all the components. He or she is not just standing by, watching someone else make it. The blend was the signature of the house after all. Maybe the final wine wouldn't have the mark of a specific vineyard or a region, but it would have the imprint of the Champagne house itself.

"Just like a Spielberg production," Peter insisted.

I decided to change the subject to weather—a perennial point of interest for Peter. Champagne is the most northern winemaking region in France and is frequently subject to bad weather, including hail.

"Hail!" exclaimed Peter, immediately distracted and pleased.

But Peter was still more interested in practical matters. "What do you actually do with a glass of Champagne?" he asked, looking at the glass I'd just poured. Should it be swirled or not? Did Champagne have esters that should be volatized, or should Peter "just leave it alone in the glass"?

It's never a bad idea to swirl a glass of Champagne, as it has an aroma, like any other wine. But it's more compressed, as Champagne is served at a much colder temperature than nonsparkling wine. That may be why people tend to remark more on Champagne's appearance, especially the size of the bubbles and how they look foaming up in the glass. Bubbles are, of course, important in Champagne, and as a general rule the finer or smaller the bubble, the better the wine. A big, fat bubble is a clue to a coarse wine, while a lack of bubbles may mean that the Champagne is flat or simply old, although some Champagne makers actually try to limit the bubbles. When I visited Champagne producer Francis Egly of Egly-Ouriet, he told me he wanted the bubbles "anchored to the wine," that is to say, invisible.

"Who would have ever guessed there was so much to know just about bubbles alone?" Peter remarked. Meanwhile, he was having a hard time spitting out the Champagne. "It's a lot harder to spit out wine with bubbles than it is flat wine," Peter remarked. Don't say *bubbles,* say *bead,* I reminded Peter. And the collection of bubbles that forms on the top of the glass is a *mousse,* not a *head,* by the way.

I'd poured glasses of the Mumm nonvintage Champagne as well as its California sparkling-wine counterpart, Mumm Napa Valley Cuvée. Though the latter wasn't Champagne but a sparkling wine made in the Champagne method, I thought it would provide a good illustration of how much climate can influence a wine. Both were made from the same grapes and pretty much the same technology, but Champagne is cold whereas Napa is warm. The Mumm Napa sparkling wine was noticeably fruitier and sweeter with bigger bubbles, while the Mumm nonvintage Champagne was more austere with more acidity.

"I'm having trouble smelling the wine because of the bubbles," Peter reported. "I just get a noseful of carbonation."

In fact, some Champagnes may be a bit more carbonated than others, depending on the style of the wine and the Champagne house. The 1996 Bollinger RD that we tasted is a rich vintage Champagne that's almost more like a wine than a Champagne, thanks to a combination of additional aging and house style. The initials *RD* stand for "recently disgorged," which means the wine is given extended aging in the bottle and on its lees (aka its sediment) before it's given the final dosage (a mixture of Champagne and sugar) and recorked. It's radically different to the taste, but is that also because it's from a particular year? Peter wondered. And is it a good thing that it's from one year or another?

The theory behind vintage Champagne is that a Champagne house will only make it in the best of years—showcasing the attributes of a particular year (as opposed to the nonvintage cuvée, which showcases the style of the Champagne house). Of course, some less-than-scrupulous producers will produce a vintage Champagne in less-than-stellar years because they can charge more money for a vintage than a nonvintage wine. Peter seemed surprised by this. But wasn't it true of movie directors too—that they might make movies that weren't as good as their other pictures, and they wouldn't charge any less for admission than they would for their better efforts?

HOW CHAMPAGNE IS MADE

After the final blend of wines is chosen (this is called the assemblage), the wine is given a small bit of sugar, wine, and yeast, bottled, and topped with a metal cap. This combination creates the secondary fermentation that results in trapped carbon dioxide gases that give Champagne its bubbles. These bottles are turned by hand or by machine for weeks or months, and shortly before they are ready to be released, the temporary cap is replaced and a sugar syrup is added (dosage) to add a bit of sweetness. (Some Champagnes are not "dosed" in this manner, but they are uncommon, not to mention very, very dry. It's fashionable among certain small producers not to "dose" their wines or to do so at extremely small, almost imperceptible levels.)

Types of Champagne

Sweetness	Style
Brut—dry	Blanc de blancs—white wine of white grapes
Sec—off dry	Blanc de noir—white wine of red grapes
Demi-sec—sweet	Rosé—blend of red and white wines

"I'm very taken with the tradition and the ritual of Champagne," said Peter. "I feel there's a real form to it—like learning to dance. It reminds me of when I went to Vienna and didn't know how to dance, a woman told me, 'It's a sin not to dance.' Champagne feels like it has a real form to it. But there's also a recklessness about it that I like. I mean, I wouldn't be reckless with a Pinot Noir, but I might be reckless with a bottle of Champagne."

Big Champagne Houses
and Small Champagne Growers

Peter had never had a Champagne made by a small grower; he'd only
had big-name Champagne from the houses Moët & Chandon and
Veuve Clicquot (aka grands marques). (Champagne growers are
known as *récoltants manipulants* and designated *RM* in tiny type on
the front or back of Champagne labels.) These wines from smaller
growers are harder to find, but usually less expensive and often
better than many of the grand marque Champagnes. Peter liked the
idea of independent growers. "Indie Champagne!" he declared.
"They're like the Sundance of Champagne."

Some top Champagne houses: Bollinger, Deutz, Pol Roger, Tait-
tinger, Krug, Moët & Chandon (Dom Pérignon).

A few great Champagne growers (*récoltants manipulants*): Egly-
Ouriet, Vilmart, Pierre Gimonnet, Guy Charlemagne.

ITALY

Because Peter values order and predictability, I was afraid of how he'd react when we began tasting and talking about Italian wines. After all, there probably isn't a country more anarchical than Italy when it comes to wine (though as anyone who's ever driven a car in Italy can attest, it's an outlook that's not specific to wine).

Every Italian province produces wine, and every province's wines are different, sometimes radically so, from those of the province next door. The wines of Lombardy, for example, bear little resemblance to the wines of Piedmont, which in turn have little in common with those of neighboring Valle d'Aosta. Furthermore, within each of these regions there are wildly divergent wine styles, with some producers making modern wines while others are quite traditional. Some have planted international varieties such as Chardonnay and Cabernet, while others are focusing on indigenous grapes such as Aglianico and Erbaluce. Peter looked more and more grim as I described the current viticultural scenario in Italy.

"It certainly doesn't sound like France," he declared. "In France they seemed to have done a good job of figuring everything out."

Well, that was true to some extent but it wasn't the whole truth. Maybe Italian winemakers aren't as closely regulated as the French (their appellation system is still slight by comparison, and there's no meaningful hierarchy of the wines), but as a result the Italians are freer to experiment than the French and they're making some terrific and terrifically unexpected wines. This is good winemaking, but it can be difficult for a consumer. It's just hard to know, sometimes, what's actually in a bottle of Italian wine, let alone where it's from or who made it.

"That's my problem," exclaimed Peter. "I look at an Italian label and I have no idea what the wine inside could be. Sometimes there's just a single name and I don't know if it's the grape name, the wine name, or the name of the winery or the name of someone's brother-in-law. The only Italian wine I can consistently identify is Chianti, but I don't want to just drink Chianti the rest of my life—even if it is one of Marty Scorsese's favorite wines. It just seems like Italian winemakers don't care if you know what their wines are or not. Are they selling so much wine that they don't need to make themselves understood?"

Peter was correct in guessing that Italian winemakers are having a successful time of it these days—a lot more people buy Italian wine now than ten or fifteen years ago, when people thought of Italian wine as strictly Barolo or Chianti. I was actually selling—or trying to sell—Italian wine back then. And it wasn't easy. Fifteen years ago the idea of a $25 Italian Chardonnay was so unusual it was almost ludicrous, and even if the wines were good, not many people took Italian wine seriously, outside of Barolo, Barbaresco, and Chianti. They didn't want serious white wine from Italy or, for that matter, red wines from places like Umbria and Emilia-Romagna.

As a result, I regularly failed to meet my monthly sales quota. (One restaurant owner I met years after my sales career ended told me it had taken him years to sell the five cases of Moscato d'Asti he'd bought from me. "It was a permanent part of my inventory," he said.) Now, of course, people drink all kinds of once unfamiliar Italian wines—Sicilian Nero d'Avola and Primitivo from Puglia—they're all now mainstream enough to be sold in Costco alongside bottles of $10 Mondavi Woodbridge Chardonnay.

TUSCANY

Tuscany is probably the best place to start when it comes to understanding the changes that have taken place with Italian wine. It's where some of the biggest changes in the past twenty years have occurred—though in many ways it has remained a very traditional region. After all, Tuscany is the home of Chianti, Italy's (still) most traditional wine. And yet there have been changes with Chianti too. Though it was once made only from Sangiovese (the most planted red grape in Italy, and Tuscany's star) and other native grapes (including a white grape, Trebbiano), today Chianti Classico can even contain a percentage of international grapes such as Cabernet and Merlot.

This is a fairly recent development, although it's been part of an overall trend in Tuscany over the past couple of decades. Twenty years ago, any wines made in Tuscany from nonrecognized, aka international, grapes could only be labeled *vino da tavola*—the lowest level of officially sanctioned wine. But by 1992, the government decided to recognize the high quality of the wines made with such nonofficial grapes by granting them a special category, IGT, or Indicazione Geographica Tipica. By then these nontraditional wines, called Super Tuscans, had become some of the most sought-after Italian wines in the world.

The first Super Tuscan was Sassicaia, a Cabernet Sauvigon blend created in 1948 by Marchese Incisia della Rocchetta in the then obscure Tuscan coastal region of Maremma. Other Super Tuscans followed, including, most famously, Tignanello, another Cabernet blend, created in 1971 by another marchese, famed Florentine nobleman Piero Antinori, whose younger brother Ludovico Antinori created his own Super Tuscan, Ornellaia and Masseto, an all-Merlot wine that's considered by many to be the Italian answer to Pétrus and one of the best Merlots in the world.

And as it turned out, Peter had the opportunity to taste all of these big names, thanks to his new friend Jeff Zacharia. Peter and I were invited to a fancy tasting that Zachys had put together in New York featuring "the best wines in the world." Peter made a beeline for the Sassicaia table, where he immediately introduced himself to the marchese's son, announcing he was "a student of great Super Tuscan wines." The young Marchese Incisia della Rochetta appeared charmed; he immediately poured Peter a generous glass of wine. And as an afterthought, he poured me a little bit too.

I said a few words about the wine (which seemed softer, fleshier, and more forward than some previous vintages of Sassicaia I'd had), then moved on to taste the Massetto, a truly impressive wine, a big, rich, and substantial Merlot (with a substantial price tag too: about $250 a bottle—the most expensive of almost all Super Tuscans). Peter hung back; he and the young marchese were having an important chat. Ten minutes later, he was still there. Ten minutes more and I returned to drag him away (a small crowd had gathered behind Peter, trying to get a taste of the wine).

"The marchese says that in order to really understand their wines, I should come visit him in Italy. He said I could stay as long as I liked—and to come anytime." Peter brandished the marchese's business card as proof.

Peter attempted much the same thing with Marchese Piero Antinori, who stood behind the table pouring his own Super Tuscan, the 2001 Tignanello. Piero Antinori is, of course, the most famous wine name in Italy and the most famous Italian wine name in the world. "He looks more like a prince than a winemaker," Peter commented, gazing at the marchese. "He looks like he belongs on the front of a coin." I guessed the marchese probably was—or one of his ancestors had likely been; after all, the Antinoris have been in Florence for over five hundred years.

"Are Super Tuscans always better than Chianti?" Peter wanted to know. Certainly they were meant to be better than basic Chianti, I replied, but not necessarily better than a Chianti *riserva*, which was a winery's traditional wine. Almost all Super Tuscans were made by Chianti producers, whose reputation was first established by their Chiantis, so it would be unwise to neglect those wines in favor of their Super Tuscans. And besides, I said to Peter, some producers were more famous for their Chiantis than for their Super Tuscans.

Take, for example, the producer Felsina, whose Chianti Classico I gave Peter to try. Felsina, one of the greatest Chianti producers, also makes a Super Tuscan, Fontalloro, an all-Sangiovese wine. While it's good and well made, Fontalloro is mostly overshadowed by Felsina's Chiantis, particularly their Chianti Riserva Cru Ranchia. Even their basic Chianti is good—a classic wine with notes of red cherry and spice, firm but without excessive tannins and with good acidity—the latter an attribute of a good Chianti.

The other famous wine of Tuscany is Brunello di Montalcino, another Sangiovese wine. The first Brunello, created in the mid-nine-teenth century, was also the creation of a noble-born Tuscan, Fer-rucci Santi of Biondi Santi. It was originally styled as a fairly tannic and austere red. The "new" Brunellos are more accessible and lush. Traditional Brunellos are still around too—from such producers as Lisini and Biondi Santi—but both types are pretty expensive. A good Brunello can cost $50 and more. There have been a string of good vintages of Brunello—1998 through 2000—driving the price even higher.

The Brunello I gave Peter was the 1998 Brunello di Montalcino Casanova della Cerbaie. It was decidedly the modern kind. "This is delicious," said Peter, "but the name is too long. Why do they need all these names anyway? Why can't they just call this wine San-giovese?" I explained that Montalcino was the town where the Brunello came from; the rest was the producer's name. "Is this the way it is for every Italian label?" Peter wanted to know. "Because if I know that the grape comes first, followed by the place, then the winemaker, then I'll be all set."

Alas, I had to break it to Peter that this wasn't always true with Italian wines. Sometimes there might just be one name on the label and no way to know if it was a grape, a producer, or a place. Remember, for example, Sassicaia? It's the name of wine and also the name of a place. (Sassicaia actually has its own DOC.)

"This is getting ridiculous," Peter huffed. But Italian movies could be pretty obscure too, I ventured. For example, I found some Fellini movies completely impossible to understand. Such as *Juliet of the Spirits*. What is that movie about?

"It's just Fellini," Peter replied.

Some top Tuscan producers: Castello di Rampolla, Fontodi, Felsina, Antinori, Biondi Santi, Tenuta della Ornellaia, Tua Rita.

PIEDMONT

The only other wine Italian wine region as famous as Tuscany is Piedmont, home of Italy's two most noble wines: Barolo and Barbaresco (also the names of the towns where both wines are made). Indeed, if wine were the only criterion, Piedmont would probably be the most famous wine region in Italy. But it lacks the tourist infrastructure of Tuscany (no museums, no fancy hotels). It's also more diverse than Tuscany—lots of other less famous wines are made in Piedmont, red wines such as Dolcetto and Barbera and whites such as Gavi di Gavi, Arneis, and Moscato. While many of these other wines can be good, the fame of the region rests on Barolo and Barbaresco—the greatest wines in the world and among the most expensive Italian wines.

"Isn't there some sort of classification system that rates these wines?" Peter asked. "How do you really know they're the best in the world? Or, for that matter, which ones are best?"

Clearly his time talking about Bordeaux with Jeff Zacharia had been well spent; Peter seemed to be completely converted to the Bordeaux classification mind-set.

Unfortunately for Peter and everyone else confused by Italian wine, there are no formal rankings as such of Barolo and Barbaresco. It's more a matter of accomplishment over time and critics' ratings as to which wines and producers are best. Some producers, such as Altare, Clerico, and Bruno Giacosa, have been making great Barolos and Barbarescos for years, and still do so, in a traditional style—rather tannic, austere wines that take a long time to come around. Other producers, such as Paolo Scavino, make Barolos that are more fruit-forward—they spend less time in oak barrels— more approachable in their youth, and thus more modern in style. Then there's Angelo Gaja, the man who is credited with the creation of modern Barbaresco and who brought Piedmont international acclaim with his single-vineyard Barbarescos. He has his own style. "So you just have to know these things?" Peter asked, perplexed. I was afraid that was true.

One of the largest estates in Piedmont is owned by Michele Chiarlo, who makes Barolo and Barbaresco as well as several other wines, including La Court Barbera, which is a well-made wine and a good buy. I gave Peter a glass of Chiarlo's 2000 Barolo. This wine was from a famous vintage, one of the most famous in modern times (in fact, some critics have declared it "perfect"). In terms of modern versus traditional winemaking, Chiarlo is somewhere between the two—his wines generally have lots of ripe, generous fruit (modern), but they can finish a bit austere (a hallmark of the more traditional wines).

"Is Sangiovese the grape of Barolo and Barbaresco too?" Peter asked, examining the back label of the Chiarlo wine, where he noted with displeasure that he found no mention of a grape. The grape of both Barolo and Barbaresco is Nebbiolo, which has been compared to Pinot Noir because of its fragrance (roses and tar are the classic aromas of Barolo, especially those with some bottle age) and structure, though sometimes Barolos can seem so big, so tannic, they are more like Cabernet. *Nebbiolo* comes from the Italian word *nebbia,* which means "fog." There's a lot of fog in the vineyards during the winter months in Piedmont.

"I like that," Peter said. "I always like it when there's weather involved with the wine. Of course, I'd prefer it if they'd put the name of the grape on the bottle too.

"This is pretty aggressive," Peter remarked upon tasting the wine—this was his code word for tannin. "And I'm not getting either tar or roses."

Just to confuse matters more, two other important Piedmont red wines, Dolcetto and Barbera, aren't the names of places but grapes. I mentioned this as I pulled out a bottle of Dolcetto. "Oh, that's really helpful," Peter replied sarcastically. "How am I supposed to keep track of them? Couldn't these producers agree on whether they should use a place name or a grape name? Are Piedmont wine-makers that political?"

I speculated that it might be because Barolo and Barbaresco were historically important wines, and like the producers in Burgundy, Italian producers wanted their towns to be identified with their wines—whereas in the case of simple wines such as Dolcetto or Barbera, there wasn't much prestige in any association.

"It may not be prestigious, but I like this Dolcetto," Peter remarked of the 2003 Andrea Oberto Dolcetto we tasted. "It's nice and fruity but it's also very dry. When you told me the name means 'sweet,' I expected it to be at least fruitier. But it has a lot of acidity, so I know it's a good wine with food."

A few great Barolo producers: Bruno Giacosa, Paolo Scavino, Ceretto.

A few great Barbaresco producers: Angelo Gaja, Produttori del Barbaresco, Rivetti.

SOUTHERN ITALIAN WINE REGIONS

If famous and relatively well-regulated wine regions such as Piedmont and Tuscany seemed chaotic to Peter, I was afraid of what he'd think of wines from the Italian south—wines made in such regions as Puglia, Campania, and Abruzzi—which have, until recently, been well outside the modern winemaking, not to mention regulatory, scene.

But some exciting winemaking developments have occurred in southern Italy in the past decade or so, thanks to investment from northern Italian producers and the realization by southern Italian producers that there was more money in selling their wines abroad than down the road to their neighbors (as far as most southern Italian wines went not so long ago). These changes meant adapting, at least in part, to global tastes. Hence, new wineries such as Planeta in Sicily began planting grapes like Merlot and Chardonnay. But it also meant improving native varietals such as Aglianico and Nero d'Avola by limiting yields and using French oak barrels—in short, making them taste more like international wines.

As a result, some of the best values in Italian wines now come from grapes and places that no one had heard of ten or even five years ago. Who, for example, could have guessed there would be such a strong market for Sicilian Nero d'Avola? Or Primitivo from Apulia?

Or Sardinian Vermentino? "I hadn't noticed," said Peter skeptically. Hadn't he noticed all the cases of Nero d'Avola in the front of Zachys when we visited the store? Peter hadn't. "I only had eyes for Bordeaux," he replied.

Remember you called cheap Bordeaux "a bunch of rotgut"? I reminded him. Well, the inexpensive wines of southern Italy are what people are buying now instead of that cheap "rotgut" Bordeaux. They're a lot more enjoyable (fruitier, softer tannins) and a lot better value.

"What does Nero d'Avola taste like?" Peter wanted to know. It's a bit like a southern Italian version of Malbec, the star red grape of Argentina that Peter had seen on wine lists before: rich and deeply flavored with moderate structure and soft tannins.

The most important red grape in southern Italy is Aglianico (Ah-lee-on-ico), which has been called "the Nebbiolo of the south" because some winemakers believe it can produce wines that are nearly as good as Barolo and Barbaresco (and consequently price their Aglianicos almost as expensively). Some of the best Aglianicos are made by Feudi di San Gregorio, a producer in Campania that also makes great white wines from native grapes such as Falanghina and Greco di Tufo too. But their star wine is a red called Serpico—a 100 percent Aglianico made in small French oak barrels. (No relation to the Al Pacino movie of the same name.) I had a bottle of the 2001 Serpico that I poured for Peter. Smooth and richly textured, the wine has the body and weight and structure of a Cabernet Sauvignon but a bit of wildness, a bit of earthy, spicy notes that is pure Aglianico.

"I don't get any Al Pacino in this wine at all," Peter said.

A few good southern Italian producers: Argiolas (Sardinia), Feudi di San Gregorio (Campania), Planeta (Sicily), Taurino (Apulia), Tasca d'Almerita Regaleali (Sicily).

ITALIAN WHITE WINES

Happily for Peter, Italian white wine is a lot easier to understand than red. Italian whites are usually identified by grape name and not the place where they're made. There are some exceptions, of course, such as Soave and Gavi (both place names), but by and large, Italian whites sport the name of the grape from which they're made, e.g., Pinot Grigio, Falanghina, Pinot Bianco, and Vermentino.

"You didn't mention Chardonnay. What about Chardonnay? Isn't there any Chardonnay in Italy?" Peter asked. Some Chardonnay is planted in northern and southern Italy, but it's become less and less important as more and more wineries are emphasizing native grapes such as Falanghina over international grapes like Chardonnay.

There are exceptions, of course. For example, Planeta, the Sicilian producer, makes a big, wood-aged Chardonnay, and Marchese Piero Antinori makes Chardonnay in Umbria at Castello della Sala. (Antinori was actually one of the first to make Chardonnay in Italy.) But right now there's more interest in native varietals.

"I have no trouble with that," said Peter, "as long as they put the grape names on the label."

I like several Italian whites, and one of my favorites is Soave, made by producers such as Pieropan, Anselmi, and Gini. Peter seemed shocked to hear that Soave was actually a desirable wine. He was one of many who still think of Soave as a cheap seventies Bolla-made wine. (In fact, even Bolla Soave has gotten a lot better since then.)

"This has a kind of creaminess," remarked Peter of the 2004 Pieropan Soave. "It doesn't taste like Soave at all—even though I don't even know what I mean when I say that. I guess I mean it has a taste and I don't expect Soave to taste like anything."

Pieropan's Soaves have an intense mineral finish, and unlike most Soaves, indeed, unlike most Italian white wines, Pieropan wines can age well—several years or more. "But don't expect this to be true of many other Italian whites," I warned Peter. "Almost all of them are best drunk very young—no more than a year or two old."

This is especially true of a wine like Pinot Grigio, that ubiquitous Italian white and a staple in Peter's home. "It's not that I'm a big Pinot Grigio fan," Peter said, correcting me. "I don't even like the stuff. It's just the only wine my friend Anne Martin will drink. When she visits our house, we always have to have a bottle of Santa Margherita Pinot Grigio on hand. And do you know how much that stuff costs?" he continued in an outraged tone. "It's twenty-five dollars a bottle and it doesn't even taste like anything! And you know something strange? I think that's what Anne Martin likes about it!"

That was probably true of most Pinot Grigio fans. But for the rest, there are interesting Italian Pinot Grigios around, wines that actually have flavor. Most come from the northern regions of Friuli and Alto Adige, where they tend to be made by small producers in small amounts. In fact, all kinds of interesting white wines besides Pinot Grigio are made in Friuli and Alto Adige, from grapes such as Sauvignon Blanc, Riesling, Pinot Bianco, and Gewürztraminer. The Hofstatter Gewürztraminer of Alto Adige is one of my favorite Gewürztraminers in the world—a big, flavorful wine that unlike most Alsace Gewürztraminers is bone-dry. Hofstatter also makes a great Pinot Grigio for less than $15 a bottle.

"Remember I'm not a big Pinot Grigio fan," Peter warned me when I gave him a glass of the Hofstatter wine. But upon tasting it, his expression changed. "This is great—it's minerally and dry and has actual flavors. It even has a finish. I might get Anne Martin this instead of the Santa Margharita next time—although it has so much flavor she might not think it's Pinot Grigio at all."

THREE ITALIAN WHITE WINES PETER AND I LOVE

Pieropan Soave—Veneto

Made from the Garganega grape, "which sounds like a character in a horror movie," said Peter, Soave is the most common wine made in Veneto. The quality is highly variable—ranging from characterless wines made by cooperatives (essentially wine factories) to those from serious producers such as Inama, Anselmi, and Pieropan, all of whom turn out rich and minerally wines.

Argiolas Vermentino Costamolino — Sardinia

Vermentino is a wonderfully aromatic white grape grown in Sardinia, Liguria, and Corsica. Argiolas is a top producer in Sardinia, and their Vermentino is one of the best: bright and juicy with exotic fruit notes. It's also a great bargain — about $14 a bottle. "Maybe I can get Anne Martin to drink this instead of her usual Pinot Grigio," said Peter, who seemed to spend an awful lot of time plotting alternative wines for Anne Martin.

Abbazia di Novecella Kerner — Alto Adige

The Kerner grape, created in Germany, is similar to Riesling. In fact, it's a cross between Riesling and the native Alto Adige grape Schiava ("Another grape name that sounds like a horror movie," commented Peter). Kerner has the same bright acidity and mineral notes of Riesling, and the abbey where this wine is made is one of the most important landmarks in Alto Adige. "I like this wine, but what I really like is the name. It's so easy to pronounce. Why aren't there more Kerners around?" Peter asked.

PETER'S (CONFLICTED) CONCLUSIONS ABOUT ITALIAN WINE

"As much as I love Italy, I think I'm scared of it," said Peter. "There are something like eight hundred varietals and they all have different names. And there really don't seem to be any regulations. It's such a free-for-all, so different from France. And the wines are so different too — they've got all that acidity. You tell me that makes them good with food, and yet I don't like many of them on their own."

But, Peter added, "Italian movies and film directors are some of my absolute favorites—directors like Rossellini, Scorsese, Antonioni, Fellini. They revolutionized the way Americans thought of foreign films. I mean, movies like *La Dolce Vita* and *Paisan* really opened people's eyes to another world.

"Was the same thing true of Italian wine?" Peter wondered, though in the same breath he complained, "Nothing about them seems simple. Even the ones you tell me are great value wines and that are pretty simple have such complicated, three-part names—like Nero d'Avola, which, by the way, I wouldn't even know was a grape because the Italians wouldn't tell me. I guess that's revolutionary in a way, that Italian winemakers don't really care if I understand or not. But to really understand Italy, I have a lot more studying to do."

ITALIAN GRAPES PETER NEEDED TO KNOW

Aglianico—This red grape produces dark and powerful reds in southern Italy.

Barbera—This high-acid red grape of Piedmont produces intense and flavorful though sometimes a bit rustic (i.e., unpolished) wines, depending on the producer.

Dolcetto—The name may mean "sweet," but the wines this red grape produces are dry, fruity, and lively in Piedmont.

Falanghina—This aromatic white grape of southern Italy can produce interesting dry wines in the hands of careful producers such as Feudi di San Gregorio.

Nebbiolo—This is the most important red grape of Piedmont; it's the grape of Barolo and Barbaresco, which produces intense, long-lived, generally high-acid, and distinctly aromatic wines. (A well-aged Barolo is said to be redolent of "tar and roses.")

Nero d'Avola—This is the most important red grape of Sicily; it produces richly textured and full-bodied wines.

Pinot Grigio—Although it's become synonymous with neutrality, this grape can produce distinctive, minerally dry white wines in northern Italian regions such as Alto Adige and Friuli.

Vermentino—This aromatic white grape is grown all over Italy—from Liguria to Tuscany (notably in Maremma) all the way to Sardinia, where some say it does best of all.

SPAIN

If Peter had thought Italian wine was complicated, how was I going to explain the wines of Spain? The largest wine-producing country in the world, Spain is also probably the most complex. So much is happening in Spain—new wines being made, new wineries being built, old regions revitalized, and old vineyards rediscovered. And most of these changes have taken place in a short time—mostly in the past decade or so.

"Is there maybe one winemaker leading Spain right now?" Peter asked. "Someone like Pedro Almodóvar? If so, maybe you could use him to explain all of Spain to me." (To Peter, Almodóvar was Spain's only director of consequence, the one filmmaking original.)

There are actually several winemaking superstars in Spain right now, though in terms of influence all over the world, there are three superstars: Telmo Rodríguez, who makes wine in many regions in Spain; Álvaro Palacios, who makes wine in several places too but is chiefly famous for the wines he makes in Priorat, a region near Barcelona; and Peter Sisseck, who created the first cult Spanish wine, Pingus, in Ribera del Duero, though he isn't even Spanish but Danish. And all three winemakers just happen to look like movie stars.

Telmo Rodríguez is probably the most photogenic of the trio (think a young Davy Jones of the Monkees) as well as the best exemplar of the new Spain. Rodríguez's family owns a traditional winery in Rioja, Bodegas Remelluri, where Rodríguez first made wine (after graduating from school in Bordeaux), but he left the family business after just a few years. Rodríguez wanted to make lots of different types of wine, in lots of different places, preferably from great vineyards that had been overlooked or forgotten, vineyards that could be "recuperated," as Rodríguez said.

When I first met Rodríguez, or Telmo, as I later called him when we became friends (I spent five days traveling around with him by car), his avowed ambition was to make "a great eight-dollar wine." (Which he does in several places in Spain.) This isn't an ambition many American winemakers probably have. But lots of other Spanish winemakers seem to share this goal, which helps to explain why Spanish wines can be such great values too.

Rioja

Rioja is (still) the best-known, most traditional winemaking region in Spain, although many of its wines have become quite modern over the years. There are actually two winemaking factions in Rioja, divided between modern-style winemakers such as Telmo and more traditional producers, who believe in aging their wines for a long time in barrel and bottle. Telmo's wines are more international, more "fruit-forward." And unlike old-style Rioja producers, who age their wines in American oak, newer producers tend to choose French oak, preferring the flavors it produces. Telmo's 2001 Altos de Lanzaga is one such wine.

"This is incredibly dense and rich," Peter commented after tasting the Lanzaga. "It's almost like a Cabernet to me. It's got a lot of Cabernet-like tannins."

One of the arguments of traditional Rioja winemakers against modern wines is that they are too tannic and aren't ready to drink right away. Traditional Rioja winemakers believe that wines should be released only when they're ready to drink. As a result, the wines of Rioja are classed according to how long they've been aged in barrel and in bottle. The simplest, thus youngest, such designation is Crianza. A Crianza wine is aged for the shortest time (one year in barrel, one year in bottle). A Reserva wine, made of better-quality grapes in better years, is aged for a minimum of one year in barrel and two years in bottle, while a Gran Reserva will only be made in the best years and is aged at least two or more years in barrel and at least three in bottle.

"How odd to classify a wine based on time," Peter exclaimed. "I wonder if Rioja winemakers get competitive about it—try to keep their wines in barrel longer than anyone else." I assured Peter this was unlikely: after all, time is money. A wine sitting in a barrel brings no money in. (And of course it would taste pretty tired after so long in barrel.)

I had three Riojas of varying ages and styles for Peter to try: two from Bodegas Contino (Contino is a Rioja winery that manages to straddle both the traditional and modern winemaking worlds), the 1996 Contino Gran Reserva and the 1999 Contino Reserva, and a Rioja from Telmo Rodríguez. For Peter, no fan of tannin, the Contino Gran Reserva was a revelation. "There aren't any tannins in this wine, and the finish is long and velvety," he reported in awe. The Reserva was "a little less velvety."

"They should have left it in the barrel longer," Peter opined. "How do they decide when to hold on to the wines and when to release them? And what if they wait too long? This reminds me of the way Hollywood will sometimes hold a film back—usually because they know it's no good—like the Sean Penn remake of *All the King's Men*. They kept waiting to release it. Then they finally released it but it still wasn't good. Do winemakers ever do anything like that?"

A few notable Rioja producers: Telmo Rodríguez, Bodegas Muga, López de Heredia, Marqués de Riscal, Bodegas Contino.

RIBERA DEL DUERO

Ribera del Duero is the second-most important winemaking region after Rioja, and, like Rioja, its most important grape is Tempranillo. (Although Rioja wines are more often a blend of Tempranillo and other grapes, including Garnacha, while Ribera del Duero wines are more likely to be 100 percent Tempranillo.) Ribera is also the trendiest wine region in Spain right now, thanks to an influx of money from Madrid millionaires (the city is less than an hour away), and they've built some large, ugly wineries—as new millionaire producers so often do.

Ribera del Duero is also the home of the most famous wine in Spain—Vega Sicilia—although the region never really had much cachet until a few decades ago. Some date the advent of the new Ribera to the time that Peter Sisseck made his first vintage of Pingus in 1995.

If one wine could be said to be responsible for modern Spanish winemaking, it would be Pingus, the most expensive wine made in Spain. Aged in French rather than American oak, for less than half the traditional length of time in barrel, Pingus is also a nontraditional blend of Cabernet and Tempranillo. While this may not seem so revolutionary now, it was back then.

"I'm fascinated by this Peter Sisseck character," said Peter. "Will we be tasting his wines?"

We would, but not the $350 Pingus. Instead, I had a bottle of the $40 Hacienda Monasterio, another Ribera wine, for which Sisseck serves as consultant. This would at least give Peter an idea of Sisseck's style, for much less money than Pingus. Peter, a fan of the modernist style, found the wine rich and ripe. It reminded him of the Telmo Rodríguez wine.

"These two guys Telmo and Sisseck remind me of what Pedro Almodóvar once said: 'Don't tell me what the rules are; I want my films to be the world,' " commented Peter. Were Telmo and Sisseck popular in Spain? he wanted to know. Almodóvar wasn't very popular at home, according to Peter—at least not the way he is in the rest of the world. Was the same true for Sisseck and Telmo?

I couldn't vouch for Sisseck's national standing or Telmo's popularity one way or another, although it was certainly possible that plenty of other Spanish winemakers were jealous of them both. As others might also be envious of Alvaro Palacios, a third, highly successful young Spanish producer.

Palacios, like Rodríguez, attended enology school in Bordeaux, and he too made wine at his family's winery in Rioja before breaking away. But Palacios chose to break from tradition and go off to

Priorat, a wine region in the far eastern reaches of Spain near Barcelona. At the time (some twenty years ago) Priorat had pretty much been forgotten; certainly no great wine had ever been made there—until Palacios produced the wine L'Ermita, whose first vintage was 1993. Palacios and a handful of other producers such as Daphne Glorian (Clos Erasmus) helped make Priorat one of the most important winemaking appellations in Spain.

L'Ermita is another rich and intense, remarkably concentrated, extracted, and expensive wine (upward of $300, depending on the vintage), made predominantly of Grenache (known as Garnacha in Spain), and as Pingus did for the Ribera del Duero region, it attracted lots of new winemakers and new money to Priorat.

"Don't tell me, let me guess—we won't be tasting L'Ermita either," said Peter bitterly. In fact, we wouldn't, but I did have Palacios's second wine, Les Terrasses, which has much of the same richness and intensity at well under half the price.

"These wines remind me of a Sergio Leone western," Peter said afterward, naming the famous director who made movies in Spain that imitated American westerns (Clint Eastwood was Sergio Leone's big star). "They aren't what I thought the wines of Spain would taste like. Although I don't even know what that would be. But they remind me of wines we've had from other places. And that's what Leone's movies were—spaghetti westerns that were an imitation of American movies, but they were even more excessive. They were practically operatic.

"And yet those movies had nothing to do with Spain. And when Leone tried to make a Spanish movie—that is, a movie made for a Spanish, not American, audience—he failed. I wonder if these wines are like that—if they succeed everywhere else but fail in Spain."

Without realizing it, Peter had touched upon one of the biggest debates raging in the wine world today—so many new wines being made in old places bear no resemblance to what they once tasted like (e.g., Rioja) or to the region where they were made but are like many wines made in other parts of the world. This has been called the "internationalization" of wine and was the subject of the documentary *Mondovino*.

A few top Ribera del Duero wines: Pingus, Vega Sicilia, Pesquera. Some top Priorat wines: Clos Erasmus, Clos Mogador, L'Ermita.

SPANISH WHITE WINES

"You've only mentioned red wine so far," noted Peter. "Don't they make white wine in Spain as well?"

Actually, a fair amount of white wine is made in Spain, but until recently it wasn't much good—mostly because the wines were tired and oxidized by the time they were (finally) released, sometimes as many as four or five years after the vintage.

But about ten or fifteen years ago, everything changed. Now Spanish white wines are as youthful and lively as the white wines of other modern countries, and they're also some of the best values in the world. Good Spanish whites can be found for $10 or less.

Telmo Rodríguez makes a bright and lively white wine he calls Basa, in the region of Rueda, a region next to Ribera del Duero. Some of the best Spanish whites are made there as well as in Galicia to the west (Galicia is on the northwest coast and borders Portugal). The main grape of Rueda is Verdejo (although Viura can also be blended in), while the grape of Galicia is Albariño. "That sounds like a dance step," observed Peter. It does produce a pretty lively wine—full of acidity and flavor. It's a bit like a Riesling aromatically (floral and spice notes) and in the mouth (stones and minerals come to mind), although it's a rare Albariño that becomes more interesting with age. Peter noted the resemblance of the 2004 Martin Codax Albariño to Riesling almost immediately, commenting on its similarly "peachy nose."

Peter was less admiring of the two Rueda whites: the 2004 Bodegas Nora and Telmo's 2004 Basa. Although Peter liked them well enough to suggest that they too might be a substitute for Anne Martin's expensive Pinot Grigio, as they were clean and bright, he was dissatisfied that neither had much of a nose—especially compared to the Albariño. ("Noses are starting to mean a lot to me. They're what I like about Riesling," Peter said.)

Peter recounted a recent Riesling-related disaster when he and his wife, Robyn, had gone to dinner with another couple, a neurosurgeon and his wife. Peter had tried to order a glass of Riesling, but the waiter refused to serve him one. The waiter insisted that Pinot Grigio went with the fish that he was having.

"So I asked the waiter, 'Do you mean the fish has no personality either?'" Peter said. "I don't think the neurosurgeon appreciated that. And I ended up having a glass of Chardonnay, but it was too fatty. And it was expensive too."

Some great bargains in Spanish white wine: Marqués de Riscal white (Rioja), Basa (Rueda), and Martin Codax (Albariño).

PETER'S SHERRY PREJUDICE

One of the most famous Spanish wines is rarely recognized as Spanish and isn't even particularly popular outside of Spain. And yet in Spain, Sherry is still important and people still drink it as an aperitif or a digestif (depending on its degree of sweetness), but everywhere else Sherry is seemingly lost to the past. Or worse. As Peter said, "I think of Sherry as something an old lady drinks in order to pass out." In the hope of changing Peter's perspective, I had assembled some lovely Sherries for him to taste—complex wines at prices no old lady would pay. Perhaps a bit of background on Sherry would help Peter to better understand what made it so great.

Made in Jerez in southernmost Spain, Sherry (the name is an English corruption of the name *Jerez*) is actually just as complicated to make as Champagne and even more time-consuming. Like Champagne, Sherry is made through blending that begins with a fairly neutral high-acid wine. (The main grape of Sherry, Palomino, is nothing special, prized mostly for its acidity.) But it is not the grapes, it's the *solera* blending that makes Sherry great. This takes place after an ordinary fermentation (stopped at a certain point and a neutral alcohol added to fortify the wine to between 15 and 18 percent alcohol). The wine is then put into a cask, where yeasts, called *flor*, are growing on the surface. As the yeasts develop, the wine is gradually removed degree by degree (up to 33 percent of the wine can be removed at any one time) and replenished with young wine, so that no barrel is ever empty.

The range of sherry styles is considerable—from very dry (*fino*) to quite sweet (*oloroso*), a rich, dark, nutty Sherry whose name means "fragrant") and cream sherries, which were actually invented for the English export market. None of this appeared to interest Peter. "If I'm going to drink any sweet wine, it's going to be port," he declared.

The wines I'd chosen to try to convince Peter otherwise included a bone-dry, pale *fino* Sherry from the respected producer Lustau and a rich, nutty (and expensive) Osborne Bailen Rare Oloroso Sherry ($90), which I thought Peter would love despite himself.

Alas, he was not converted by either, though he grudgingly admitted he could imagine the *fino* as an aperitif "instead of a gin and tonic," but he couldn't imagine ever wanting the *oloroso*.

"It would just remind me of my grandmother," he said, adding, "even though my grandmother actually drank Canadian Club—by the slug.

"Sherry just isn't sexy," he added. "I can't even think of a movie where people drink Sherry except *Arsenic and Old Lace*."

Port, on the other hand, belonged in the movies, said Peter. Or as he put it: "Port means intelligent conversation. Sherry just helps you pass out."

A few Sherry producers worth a search (never mind what Peter thinks): Emilio Lustau, González Byass, Osborne, Pedro Domecq.

PORTUGAL

That Portugal is almost exclusively identified with port, the most famous fortified wine in the world, has been both a blessing and a curse to the country's winemakers. A blessing because port is such an iconic wine and has created an awareness of the country, but also a curse because so many other wines are made in Portugal that no one really knows about—and some are quite good. Peter, an avowed port lover (though he couldn't name a single producer), seemed pretty representative of most wine drinkers when it came to his knowledge: all he knew was that port came from Portugal.

In fact, a lot of wines are made all over Portugal—white as well as red. One of Portugal's best-known white wines, Vinho Verde, is made just outside the city of Oporto (where all the port houses or "lodges" are headquartered). Vinho Verde (whose name means "green wine," which signifies youth rather than color) is a lively, low-alcohol white wine that's one of the most appealing cheap wines in the world. I gave Peter a glass of 2005 Famega Vinho Verde, and he was immediately enthusiastic.

"I've never had a white wine that's this immediately delightful," he remarked of the light, spritzy wine. When I told him it only cost $5 a bottle, he grew even more enthusiastic. "Maybe this would be a good Santa Margherita Pinot Grigio substitute?" And he could save nearly $20 a bottle!

Some good dry red wines are made near Oporto as well, many by the port producers themselves. Port houses such as Ramos Pintos and Quinta de Roriz both make good rich and earthy red wines. And while many port producers have only been making dry table wines for a few years, the wines have been remarkably good. The market for port, after all, is limited; there aren't many people (outside of English wine drinkers and characters in Merchant-Ivory films) who finish off dinner with port. Port producers had to figure out what to do about their excess grapes (and insufficient income) and thus decided to make nonfortified wine—something they could sell sooner than port. A good example of one such wine is the 2004 Quinta de Roriz, made from Roriz, one of the chief grapes of port. (Roriz is known as Tempranillo in Spain. It's one of the authorized grapes that can be blended into port, though only six are used regularly, including Touriga Nacional.)

Peter was impressed with the Roriz flavor, though he found it wasn't what he called "refined." But he was impatient to move on. "Now can we get to the port?" he asked, eyeing the five bottles I'd lined up on my kitchen counter.

"I never knew there was more than one type of port," Peter said, marveling at the selection. "People talk about port as if it were just one thing. And yet there are so many kinds." In fact, the five I'd opened were only a small sampling of the various port styles, not to mention the many producers of port (which are not called wineries but "houses").

PORT STYLES

There are essentially five types of port. The best (and most famous and most expensive) is vintage port. Vintage port is a wine made of a particular year's grapes, a harvest that is so successful it is "declared" by port producers, who agree as a group that it is outstanding. (An individual port house may "declare" a vintage in any given year regardless of the decision of the consortium, but this doesn't happen often. Vintage port is the flagship product of any port house, and it doesn't make sense to produce anything but a top-quality wine.)

Second to vintage ports are Colheita ports, which are wines made from a single harvest in a good though not great year; they may be kept for several years or consumed in their (relative) youth. The same is true of the third type, late-bottled vintage ports, which are ports made in a particular, though lesser, vintage and bottled after a few years' aging time. They are ready to drink upon release. And fourth are the simple blended ruby ports that have names instead of vintage years: these include ports such as Graham's Six Grapes, Sandeman Founder's Reserve, and Dow's Boardroom Port.

All of the first four types of port are "ruby ports," so-called because they age in the bottle, whereas the fifth type, tawny port, ages in barrel. A tawny port can spend as long as thirty years in barrel, although twenty years is considered by connoisseurs to be the ideal length of time.

"Why is it called tawny?" Peter asked, looking at the port. "To me it just looks a little brown." (Peter was right; tawny port does lose its color as it ages and becomes a bit brown, but *tawny* is a much nicer-sounding word than *brown* when applied to a wine.)

"But how does port work?" Peter wanted to know. "How are they all made?"

All port is made in pretty much the same way. During the middle of fermentation a neutral brandy is added and the fermentation resumed, thereby increasing the alcohol level to 17 or 18 percent (several percentage points higher than table wine). After that comes the crucial decision to age the fermented wine in barrel (as with a tawny) or bottle (a ruby).

"None of these ports have Portuguese names," Peter observed, looking over the bottles. "Or are these English names actually translations?"

Nearly all the famous port houses were, in fact, founded by Englishmen, some as far back as the seventeenth century. The English controlled the trade and made the rules, one of which stipulated that port could only be shipped down the river from the vineyards to a port house that had its headquarters, or "lodge," in the city of Oporto. Since the Portuguese were mostly too poor to own a lodge, they were pretty much left out. They had to sell their wines or grapes to English firms. And while times have changed and this rule no longer applies, almost all the great names—Taylor Fladgate, Dow's, Graham's, Warre's—are still English, although a few non-English producers show up too, including Ferreira and Niepoort (whose tawnies are particularly good).

The first port I gave Peter was Dow's Finest Reserve, a simple ruby that cost about $10. Fairly fruity and sweet, it's the sort of port most restaurants offer by the glass and was probably the kind Peter drank most often. But a simple ruby bears as much resemblance to vintage port as a Beaujolais nouveau does to a grand cru Burgundy.

"I'm never drinking cheap port again," Peter declared when I told him this, although he admitted the Dow's was "agreeably fruity." And it was soft and easy to drink.

The second Port, a step up in complexity, was the 1998 Cockburn's Late Bottled Vintage Port, which is a midpoint of sorts between an inexpensive ruby and a vintage port that's ready to drink upon release. A good late-bottled vintage port costs about $20 a bottle (Cockburn's was a bit more). Peter declared it much superior to the ruby. "There was more than just simple fruit, but also layers of other flavors, and it wasn't quite as cloyingly sweet. It could easily become my house port," Peter declared.

Peter seemed more like a ruby port guy than a tawny port man to me (most people are one or the other), so I was curious to see what he thought of the tawny, which is much less fruity than a ruby port, almost austere by comparison. I gave him a Dow's Ten Year Old Tawny ($30). A ten-year-old tawny is a good place to start with a tawny port novice, who might otherwise be put off by the oxidized flavors (i.e., more wood and earth notes than fruit) that come with a very old tawny.

"This doesn't taste anything like the others," Peter reported. "It tastes a little like wood. But it has a wonderful aroma, kind of caramel, like a Cognac." The only thing Peter really didn't like was the word *tawny*, which he didn't find accurate. To Peter, a tawny port was slightly brown or "just a little less red."

Finally, I gave him the 1997 Taylor Fladgate Vintage Port ($85 a bottle), one of the best wines of a great vintage. Although it was easily two decades too young to drink (a young vintage port has immense tannins), I wanted Peter to have at least one great vintage port.

Peter was primarily struck by the price. "This costs eighty-five dollars a bottle?" he asked incredulously. "I want to make it last as long as possible then. How long can port last anyway?" A guy Peter knew had the same bottle of port open three Christmases in a row. "Does port last forever?"

The endless shelf life of port is a popular misconception, right up with the everlasting bottle of sherry. Port is a wine, and no wine, except Madeira, can last forever. (Madeira is an already oxidized wine, therefore further exposure to oxygen can't harm it.) Port, because it's fortified, can last longer than, say, Cabernet, but not indefinitely. A bottle of port properly stored (somewhere cool and dark) and tightly stoppered could probably last a week or so. In fact, I had an idea: Why didn't Peter taste all of the five ports every day for a week, while keeping a chart to see how well each of them aged? Peter agreed readily; he liked the idea of drinking all that port.

The following week, Peter returned, chart in hand. "I rated the ports between one and ten, with ten being the top, the closest to what it tasted like on the first day," he said, adding that by the seventh day he'd started to feel like "a total alcoholic" drinking so much port, even if there had only been four bottles in the end. (Peter had eliminated the simple ruby port right away. "I didn't even like it the first day," he said.) Unsurprisingly, the vintage port did best. In fact, Peter determined that it got even better with each passing day. By the end of the week, it had only dropped from a ten to a nine.

The tawny did pretty well too. Peter gave it a nine, and by the seventh day it was still going strong. I wasn't surprised. A good tawny port can be an amazingly long-lived wine. Peter gave it a seven by the last day. The Colheita and the late-bottled ports, however, dropped off precipitously—going from nines to ones by the last day. "That late-bottled vintage was lucky to get a one by the end of the week," said Peter. "There wasn't anything left to it except alcohol."

Peter offered to repeat the experiment if I gave him four new bottles. Didn't I need further proof? Or perhaps he could do it all again with just one bottle of vintage port?

A few great port producers: Taylor Fladgate, Graham's, Dow's, Warre's, Croft.

GERMANY

"I got incredibly nervous when I first visited Germany," said Peter. "I felt like everyone was out to get me. For example, I ordered some bread in a bakery in the Black Forest, and the woman there yelled at me. I don't know what she said, but it didn't sound good."

Peter was basing his impression of an entire country, never mind its wines, on some mean woman in a bakery? Didn't he realize that was something that could (even more easily) have happened in France? "I'm just telling you how I feel," he replied.

Since Peter professed to care so much about Riesling, I suggested he keep an open mind about Germany, since some of the best Rieslings in the world are made there. The wines we would taste would make him forget all about the bakery clerk.

But Peter isn't the only wine drinker put off by Germany (though he may be the only person who would indict a country on the basis of a bad-tempered woman in a Black Forest bakery). For most people, the bad feeling about German wine begins with the wine labels, which are virtually impossible for a non-German to read.

A big part of the problem is the typography: most German wine labels are written in a sort of Gothic style and run several lines long, featuring all kinds of information, even government-issued registration number. (The Germans are nothing if not precise.)

Some streamlined German wine labels are around, mostly from a newer generation of German winemakers who choose a non-Gothic typeface and put information like registration numbers on the back.

The other challenge for would-be German wine drinkers is the country's Prädikat system, the means by which all German wines of

112

a certain quality are ranked. Unlike other wines of the world, the best German wines are rated according to the ripeness of fruit—the higher the sugar content, the higher the quality of the wine. In a country with lots of bad weather (hail and frost) and challenging conditions (e.g., steep, exposed vineyard slopes), it's easy to understand how this system came to be: ripe grapes (at least until global warming) were not easily achieved.

There are five ripeness levels in the Prädikat system—with increasingly hard-to-pronounce names. The first level is *Kabinett,* which are the lightest and simplest wines. After that are the *Spätlese* wines (this is the first level of truly ripe grapes; these are sweet wines with a good acidity). Third are *Auslese* wines, made from bunches of grapes left on the vines after the Spätlese grapes have been picked. Then there are the *Beernauslese* wines, which are made only in great vintages of grapes left even longer on the vine. Finally there are the rare *Trockenbeernauslese* wines, made from grapes that are shriveled like raisins from botrytis, the same noble rot that creates the dessert wine Sauternes. (There's a sixth type too— *Eiswein,* wine made from botrytised grapes that actually freeze on the vine.)

Peter's first German Riesling was a Kabinett from the Mosel, the region in southern Germany on the Rhine River, which is said to produce the lightest and flowcriest (and some say purest) of all German Rieslings. I'd chosen the 2004 Weingut Kerpen Wehlener Sonnenuhr Riesling Kabinett because Kerpen is a progressive producer, one of several in the Mosel making modern wines. "You say the producer is Kerpen, but what does the rest of the label stuff mean?" Peter asked.

That's another problem with German wines: their labels can have a huge string of names that won't mean much to anyone who doesn't know German wine towns or vineyards. As with Burgundy, the name of a famous German vineyard is appended to the name of a nearby town or village, but whereas with Burgundy when the vineyard is great (e.g., Montrachet) the name stands alone, the German town always rates a mention as well. Hence, the *Wehlener* of the label means that the wine is made near the town of Wehlen (*er* indicates "from"), while Sonnenuhr is the name of the vineyard. "This wine has a nice flowery nose that says Riesling to me, but it's a lot sweeter than I thought it would be," said Peter. "I thought Kabinett meant that it would be dry."

This was a common misperception, I assured him. But Kabinett doesn't necessarily mean "dry." What it really means is "light." The only time you can be assured of getting a completely dry German wine is when the word *trocken* (dry) appears on the label. There's also *halbtrocken,* which means "half-dry," but in reality is more like "half-sweet." And they can coexist with different classes in the system. Spätlese trockens and Auslese trockens are full, rich wines that are still fairly dry. Peter sank his head in his hands in (mock or real?) despair. "I can't possibly learn any more German words," he said. "I'll never remember what they all mean."

But the next wine, a 2004 Gunderloch Nackenheim Rothenberg Spätlese Riesling ($24), perked Peter up a bit. The label was reassuringly modern—a plain typescript with only the barest amount of information on the front. (German producers focused on the export market are particularly keen on plain labels.) And yet the simple label alarmed Peter too.

"What happened in Nackenheim?" he asked, turning the bottle over in his hand. "Where's all the information? Did this winemaker run out of money, or don't they have anything good to say about their wine?"

I assured Peter that Gunderloch was one of the top wineries in the Rheinhessen region, but because they export most of their wines, they have much simpler labels.

"There's more going on with this wine than the first one," Peter reported, inhaling the intense apricot and peach aromas that mark a great Riesling. This was true: Spätlese wines have more body and more aromatic intensity than most Kabinetts. And while there was sweetness, there was also good acidity. But Peter was looking at the wine's alcohol level. "Look at that," he marveled. "It's around eight percent. You could drink a whole bottle and not end up on your ear. Of course, you might end up with a few cavities instead."

The third wine had "thousands of numbers on it," Peter

observed—only a slight exaggeration. "What do they all mean? Is it some sort of code? Or is this guy just crazy?" (The numbers were the same government-issued numbers that Gunderloch had hidden on its back label.) The producer in question, I said to Peter, was a youngish, and decidedly sane, fellow named Ernest Loosen, one of the most successful winemakers in Germany. Loosen makes wine in several places, including the United States, with the winery Château Ste. Michelle in Washington State.

Meanwhile, Peter had fallen madly in love with Loosen's wine, the 2004 Dr. Loosen Erdener Treppchen Riesling Auslese Mosel ($46). Redolent of white peach and nectarine, it was gorgeously ripe and rich ("It has a velvety quality," said Peter) with a tremendously long finish. The only thing Peter didn't like about the Loosen wine was its label. "For a young Turk, Loosen has a pretty old-fashioned look," he commented. "Look at all those numbers and the names. Even though I know one of the names is the town and one is the vineyard, I can't remember which order they're in."

KEY GERMAN WINE REGIONS

Mosel-Saar Ruwer—The lightest, most delicate Rieslings are made in the Mosel region.

Nahe—This is a small but important region; some of Germany's most respected producers are located here.

Rheingau—This region is home to the longest-lived, most classic German Rieslings.

Rheinhessen—Although the Rheinhessen was once almost exclusively associated with cheap commercial wines, it's now experiencing a renaissance.

Rheinpfalz (Pfalz)—The most full-bodied Rieslings are produced in this region.

A few great German producers: Schlossgut Diel (Nahe), Dönnhof (Nahe), Kunstler (Rheingau), Müller-Catoir (Pfalz), Robert Weil (Rheingau).

PETER COMES TO TERMS WITH GERMAN WINES

"German wine labels are confusing, but they're a little romantic too," Peter decided, "like the wines themselves, which are intense and kind of remind me of the Wim Wenders movie *Wings of Desire,* which is possibly the most romantic movie ever made about a city, in this case Berlin. Yet the fact that it's a romantic movie means it's not very German. German directors are really better known for their cynicism, not their romantic nature." Peter believed that *Wings of Desire* was truly the last great German movie (*Blue Angel,* starring Marlene Dietrich, was the first). "*Wings of Desire* is a city haunted by ghosts, by its past," said Peter. "And German wines seem a little like that as well."

AUSTRIA

"I don't know why, but I have a much more positive feeling about Austria than I did Germany," said Peter. "Even though I really loved some of those German wines. In fact, the only bad association I have with Austria is Arnold Schwarzenegger, and he's our problem now, not theirs." But what about real Austrian movies, rather than those made by Hollywood stars? There was only one Austrian director whom Peter really respected: Michael Haneke. "But he's not making movies in Austria; he's making movies in France," Peter pointed out.

While not much of global significance might be happening with Austrian filmmaking, the opposite is true with Austrian wine. In fact, we might even be in a golden age of Austrian winemaking—albeit one that had a shocking start.

The new era of Austrian wine actually dates back to the mid-1980s when a handful of Austrian producers were accused of putting antifreeze, or diethylene glycol, in their wines. The repercussions were so great that no one in the world (except maybe some gas station owners) would buy Austrian wine. So the government stepped in and imposed tighter controls and a stringent review process; as a consequence, the quality of Austrian wines improved rapidly.

Austria's most important grape in terms of quantity as well as quality is Grüner Veltliner, a white grape notable for its high acidity and characteristic "white pepper" aroma. It's not grown in many other places in the world, and only in Austria does it achieve true nobility. Perhaps that's why it seems to provoke so much national pride. For example, the first time I met my neighbor Doris, an Austrian, she served me a glass of Grüner Veltliner. "How great is this wine?" she asked me, and it was clear that the question was only rhetorical. It was, in fact, nothing special—there's a wide range of quality of Grüner Veltliners—but I told her it was simply sublime.

"The name Grüner Veltliner doesn't sound like a grape. It sounds more like a cheap foreign car," commented Peter. "Or maybe a name for something that isn't very beautiful."

And the 2002 Steininger Grand Cru Grüner Veltliner that I gave Peter didn't help change his mind. "It's kind of yeasty," Peter reported. "Like a German lager, in fact. It tastes like an old wine."

The wine did have a few years' age, but a great Grüner Veltliner can age for a long time. Some even think it can age as long and as well as Riesling.

"Does that mean there might be some of those Austrian antifreeze wines left around?" Peter asked. "I'd love to find out how well antifreeze ages."

Fortunately, the next wine, a delicately flavored 2004 Schloss Gobelsburg Grüner Veltliner, was a lot more to Peter's taste, as was the 2004 Riesling from Nigl. Both producers are based in Kremstal, which, along with Wachau, is one of the most important regions for Riesling and Grüner Veltliner.

Riesling is the second-most important white grape in Austria, and to some, it's the first in terms of prestige. Riesling is grown quite successfully by many of the top growers of Grüner Veltliner, and I thought Peter would like the style of the wines, which tend to be bigger, drier, and more alcoholic than German Rieslings. The only drawback for Peter was that Austrian Rieslings are ranked by the same German Prädikat system that he found so troublesome.

"This is totally refreshing," Peter declared, savoring the Nigl Riesling. I was surprised that he wasn't put off by its acidity, but Peter, newly enlightened as to acidity, declared it a perfect food wine. "I want to eat something with this wine. The German Rieslings made me want dessert. This wine makes me hungry."

A few top Austrian producers of Riesling and Grüner Veltliner: Nigl, Bründlmayer, F. X. Pichler, Prager, Schloss Gobelsburg.

SOME AUSTRIAN REDS

While Austria (like Germany) is famous for its white wines, Austrian winemakers (like some Germans) like to talk about their red wines, of which they make a surprising number, mostly from grapes with multivowel names. There's Blauberger, a simple juicy red, and Blaufrankisch (also called Lemberger), which can be rather tart and acidic, and then there's Zweigelt, a soft, spicy red that's a cross between Blaufrankisch and St. Laurent (a red German grape said to resemble Pinot Noir).

"That's just ridiculous," Peter declared. "Why would they put two grapes like that together? Why wouldn't they blend one of them with something like Cabernet? I can't believe Jeff Zacharia would carry a wine with a name like Lemberger at Zachys." (Jeff Zacharia had apparently risen from being a mere Bordeaux retailer to a man who could avenge Peter's feelings about "ridiculous" wines like Zweigelt.)

But more and more Austrian red wines are being exported to the States, so I thought Peter should try one or two. I chose the 2003 Zweigelt from Anita and Hans Nittnaus, well-regarded growers in Burgenland, an Austrian region renowned for its reds. Their Zweigelt is generally considered one of the best.

Peter, to say the least, was unimpressed. "That's foul!" he fairly shouted. "I think I speak for the nation when I say, 'Blech!'"

In fact, Peter did have a point. The aromas were rank, almost fetid. They were certainly well beyond "rustic" and into the realm of the truly bad. Peter, of course, had the last word: "Austrian whites sure have it all over Austrian reds."

HUNGARY

As much as Peter's feelings about Germany had been colored by that brusque bakery clerk, his feelings about Hungary were exactly the reverse. A recent trip to Budapest had been such a success; Peter had decided Hungary was one of the best countries in the world. "Hungarian people are so friendly, and the women are all beautiful," he exclaimed. Alas, Peter could say nothing about the wine. On his trip he'd only drunk beer.

In fact, not many people have even tasted Hungarian wine, outside Hungary at least. And until recently, there hasn't been much reason to consider this much of a loss. In fact, the last time Hungary really mattered to anyone, at least enologically, was well before the Communist rule. Hungary's most famous wine, Tokaji (made in the region of Tokaj), was once the world's most famous dessert wine, as far back as the seventeenth century, when it was the drink of emperors and kings. Communists changed that: vineyards were neglected, the quality of the wines declined.

Communism ended, and by the mid-1990s, outside investors, particularly French and English, arrived, determined to restore Tokaj vineyards to glory (and to make some money too). Most started in Tokaj, although some began elsewhere as well. English wine writer Hugh Johnson created the Royal Tokaji Company, while the Spanish winery Vega Sicilia founded the winery Oremus, and a large French corporation, AXA, in conjunction with Bordeaux winemaker Jean-Michel Cazes, created a winery called Disznoko, with the intent of producing world-class Tokaji.

"What's so great about this wine that so many people wanted to make it? Especially a Frenchman?" Peter asked skeptically. "Didn't he have enough work to do in France?"

I supposed part of the venture was the challenge of the wine. As with every great dessert wine, Tokaji is made in a time-consuming, costly way. The (handpicked) grapes are allowed to develop the same noble rot as Sauternes and are put in small containers called *puttonyos*. These are later added to a normally fermented base wine and numbered according to how many are added to the mix: from three to six, with six being the richest, ripest, most decadently glorious dessert wine. (There is a seven-*puttonyos* wine called Eszencia, which is almost like syrup.)

A great Tokaji, like a great Sauternes, can last a long time, developing wonderful flavors of raisin, walnut, and almond. I had a glass of 1995 Disznoko Tokaji, designated a five-*puttonyo* wine, for Peter to taste, which he declared "awesome," adding, "It has a wonderfully toasty flavor that somehow seems Old-World to me. I think I'd like a cookie made from this."

"A cookie with it?" I replied.

"No, I want a cookie filled with these flavors."

NEW WORLD WINE

❧

ARGENTINA

When I heard that Susana Balbo, the most famous female wine-maker in Argentina (in fact, she's pretty much the only famous female winemaker in Argentina), was going to be in New York for a few days, I was determined that she and Peter meet. I'd been a fan of Susana's wines for almost nine years, ever since her first trip to New York, when she'd poured a few bottles in a tiny room off the lobby of a tiny hotel.

Nine years ago Argentine wine was new in this country, and Susana was likewise new to the business of selling wine abroad. (She later admitted she'd slept in her clothes in that tiny hotel.) But now Argentine wine has an established place in the American market, and Susana was in a much better hotel. "The room is so big," she'd marveled.

I'd called Susana's importer, Nick Ramkowsky, of Vine Connections, and asked if Peter and I could spend some time with Susana and taste a few wines. But when I arrived, there was no sign of Peter. Ten minutes more and he was still missing. Some twenty minutes later, Peter arrived, dressed in a white suit. "We'll be tasting a lot of red wine," I warned him, eyeing his suit. Peter affected nonchalance. "I wore white for Susana," he said.

Was Peter being flirtatious? "I thought that white was what an Argentine would wear," he added, giving Susana, a middle-aged woman with short, sensible hair and glasses, a meaningful look. She blushed.

"Why don't we taste some wines?" Nick and I suggested almost simultaneously.

The four of us sat down in the restaurant of Susana's boutique hotel. Nick had brought along quite a few samples of Susana's wines; she made wine under three labels, starting with Crios, her most accessible and reasonably priced line of wines. "The word *crios* means 'children' in Spanish," Susana told Peter. "You use it when talking to very small children." The label depicted the hands of her three children. "Well, then I'm not going to spit my first sip of Crios," Peter replied gallantly. In fact, the Crios wines are some of my favorite inexpensive Argentine wines (they're all under $15 a bottle). The Crios Bonarda, made from a red grape of the same name, was soft and juicy, almost like Beaujolais.

Bonarda was the most planted grape in Argentina until recently, when it was overtaken by Malbec. "This wine is very mischievous," said Peter, a wine-tasting word I'd never heard him employ. He certainly seemed to be working awfully hard to impress Susana. Or did he just like her (very good) wine?

"I was interviewing George Clooney the other day," Peter remarked to Susana, "and I asked him, 'What kind of wine do you like?' and Clooney answered, 'Red or white.'" Susana laughed. Peter laughed. Did Susana know who George Clooney was? (Were there even movie theaters in Mendoza?) But Susana laughed again, even more heartily. Nick and I stared at the two of them. The next wine was the Crios Rosé. It's one of my favorite rosés: dry but savory, and a great deal at less than $15 a bottle. Nick poured a little of it into Peter's glass. Peter, still fixed on Susana, drank that too. You weren't actually supposed to drink that little bit of wine, I said to Peter. That was just a rinse. "When you drink the wine, it's called a French rinse," Nick said to Peter.

"That's beautiful," Peter replied.

The second group of wines were those that Susana made under the Ben Marco name. Her husband, Pedro Marchevsky, is the leading viticulturalist in Argentina, and the label Ben Marco means "son of Marco" because "Marchevsky was too much," said Susana to Peter.

"I went out to dinner with Viggo Mortensen the other night," Peter said suddenly, referring to the actor who played the *Lord of the Rings* hero. "Mortensen spent several years of his childhood in

Argentina," he added in case Susana hadn't read that in Argentine *People*. (How many more celebrity names was Peter going to drop?)

"Viggo wanted to order Argentine wine, but they only had Spanish wine, and Viggo"—how many times was Peter going to say "Viggo"?—"said to the waiter, 'What kind of place is that?' I wish that I had your wine." Susana nodded, looking intently at Peter.

"Viggo was raised in Argentina, from age eight to fifteen. He told me they were his best wine-drinking years!" Peter laughed. Susana laughed too. I laughed and wondered when we could get back to discussing the wine.

"I used to drink a little soda and wine when I was little," Susana recalled. "The older I got, the more wine there was in the glass, and the less soda. The glass got darker and darker," she declared with satisfaction.

"No wonder you're obsessed with color!" Peter responded, then continued, "I was telling Viggo about the difficulties of learning about wine." I wondered how much Viggo enjoyed hearing about that. "I told Viggo I was learning the vocabulary of wine, and he sent me a poem that said, essentially, don't work it out, don't reduce it to words."

Susana nodded as if she understood exactly what the wordless Viggo had meant, while I wondered how an actor who was paid lots of money to use words written by other people got away with writing such stupid poetry. Good old Viggo seemed perfectly content to reduce things to words when it involved, say, a $10 million paycheck. But Susana appeared entranced by Viggo's idea, so I said nothing.

"You know what I didn't understand," Peter continued, "was that after making such a big deal out of Argentine wine, Viggo sent me a bottle of Francis Ford Coppola's wine, Rubicon, a few days later. Why would he send me a California wine? Why not something from Argentina?"

Susana nodded sympathetically as if she too were regularly confounded by the gift-giving ideas of famous Hollywood actors. "I will send you some Argentine wines," she said to Peter. "Especially from the 2005 vintage, which was great for Argentine wine."

"Why is that?" Peter replied, looking at Susana. "Why was the vintage so good?" For all intents and purposes, it seemed that Nick and I had become invisible.

"Because we did not have big problems with hail in 2005. Hail is a very big problem in Argentina," Susana said. I thought Peter was going to leap out of his chair in joy at the mention of his favorite meteorological condition.

"I don't believe it! I've been trying to resist asking about hail!" he declared.

"Hail is a huge problem in Argentina. There's always hail; it's just a question of how much. When it's bad, it looks like Al Capone came through the vineyard with a machine gun," Susana said with a dramatic gesture I was sure was for Peter's benefit.

I interjected, "When I visited Mendoza for the first time a couple of years ago, I was amazed to see all the nets over the vineyards. I thought they were to keep birds away from the grapes, but they were for hail!" Peter and I hadn't talked much about Mendoza, before meeting Susana, though the province is the most important grape-growing region in Argentina, located just over the Andes mountains from Chile and about an hour's plane ride from Buenos Aires (or a ten-hour car ride).

"We had the strongest earthquake in twenty years in Mendoza just last week," offered Susana.

"Hail! Earthquakes! When can I go?" asked Peter excitedly.

"You can come stay with me anytime. Up to six months if you like." I wondered what Susana's husband, Pedro, might have to say about that. Or, for that matter, Peter's wife, Robyn.

But most Argentine winemakers I've met are quite friendly and welcoming (though none, for the record, have ever invited me to live with them). Perhaps, like Susana, that's just the way that they are, or perhaps it's because they're doing so well.

A few top Argentine producers: Bodega Achával Ferrer, Bodega Catena Zapata, Bodega Terrazas de los Andes, Bodega Cobos, and Dominio del Plata (Susana Balbo's wine company.)

AN ARGENTINE WINE OVERVIEW

Argentina is one of the most dynamic wine-producing countries in the world today. And just about every winemaker I talk with these days has visited Argentina or is developing vineyards there. But the story of wine in Argentina is really the story of wine in Mendoza, an arid province at the foothills of the Andes, about six hundred miles west of Buenos Aires. It's where Argentina's wine industry began five hundred years ago, and it's still the most important in the country in terms of volume—75 percent of the country's total production—and quality. Just about all the quality wine made in Argentina comes from Mendoza.

Although all the usual grapes are grown in Argentina (Cabernet, Chardonnay, and Merlot), the country's reputation is almost entirely based on one red grape: Malbec, a native to Bordeaux. Although fairly undistinguished in France and mostly used just for blending there, in Argentina Malbec produces a truly distinctive wine: fleshy and intensely flavored with sweet tannins and a spicy bouquet. Argentine Malbec is one of the world's great wine bargains, and even some of the best can be found for less than $30 a bottle (and many for much less). Top Malbec bargains are found under the labels of Susana Balbo, Alamos, and Altos las Hormigas.

AUSTRALIA

"I think nature is very important to Australians," Peter opined at the outset of our discussion of Australian wine. "It plays a big role in their filmmaking, and I think they imbue nature with a spirituality that's lacking in most American movies." I was surprised; I'd always thought of Australian films as *"Crocodile" Dundee.*

"But Australia is both," Peter insisted. "It's *'Crocodile' Dundee,* which is all about entertainment, and it's also about movies like *Rabbit-Proof Fence, Breaker Morant,* and *Walkabout,* which is all about a mystical connection to weather and nature."

This sounded a lot like the world of Australian wine. Australia is the source of some of the most successful commercial wines in the world (Yellow Tail is the most obvious example), and it's also a place where small producers make some extraordinarily intense, high-quality wines. But the overall success of Australian wine could be said to come down to two things: marketing and weather.

Australia has a near ideal grape-growing climate—it's almost always hot and dry—and that means the grapes can completely ripen. And if they don't get quite ripe, i.e., sweet enough, they can be "fixed" by any number of the Australian-designed technological tools such as alcohol-removal machines. "That doesn't fit with my idea of Australia," commented Peter. "It sounds more like something they'd do in Bordeaux."

This isn't to say that all inexpensive Australian wines are simply manufactured creations; in fact, I like a number of well-priced Australian wines very much (none of them have animal labels—though Peter and I did taste some of those). They come from wineries that make wines in a range of prices, both high and low—such as Wolf

Blass or Yalumba Winery or Jim Barry, whose under $20 Cabernet Sauvignon "The Cover Drive" may be the best inexpensive Cabernet in the world.

Conversely, the number of Australian producers making boutique Shirazes from hundred-year-old vineyards continues to grow—as do their prices, which can exceed $100 a bottle. (Or, in the case of Astralis from Clarendon Hills, it could be a wine that cost twice that amount.) These are the wines that have earned big scores from critics—most notably Robert Parker—though many may only have been in production for ten years.

Most of these boutique wines come from the Barossa Valley, in South Australia, which produces some of the greatest Shirazes in the country. Barossa is one of the many famous wine regions in South Australia (which accounts for about half the country's wine production). Other key districts include the Clare and Eden valleys, McLaren Vale, and Coonawarra.

Wine is made in other regions of Australia too, such as the Hunter Valley, north of Sydney. This is the home of some of Australia's oldest vines, and some of the country's best Semillon is still produced there. And in far-western Australia, the Margaret River district is particularly famous for its Cabernet Sauvignon.

A FEW AUSTRALIAN WINES FOR PETER

Although Peter had a vague idea of what kind of wine was made in Australia (red), it came as a complete surprise to him that some of the best Rieslings in the world are made there too, specifically in the Eden and Clare valleys.

"Isn't Australia too hot for Riesling?" Peter wondered. The Clare Valley (about an hour north of Adelaide) is a pretty warm region and yet seems to be suited to the production of great Riesling. The first man to make a world-famous Clare Riesling was Jeffrey Grosset, whose wines are some of the country's very best.

"It's very austere," Peter commented of the Grosset Riesling I gave him, meaning the wine had a lot of acidity and not a lot of obvious fruit. In fact, Grosset makes one of the more austere Australian Rieslings; his is one of the few to improve with age (Pewsey Vale is another). Grosset's wife, Stephanie, also makes excellent Riesling. Her winery, Mt. Horrocks, is located near Grosset. "Will we be tasting Stephanie's wines?" Peter asked. Unfortunately, the Mt. Horrocks wines are harder to locate; I had to tell him I couldn't find any of her wines. Peter shook his head disapprovingly and said, "Not only does he make a really tough wine, but this Grosset guy can't even get his own wife good distribution."

But quite a few Clare Rieslings are exported to the States; two other good producers are Knappstein and Jim Barry—the latter makes excellent red wines too. (The Jim Barry Armagh is one of the most intense old-vine Australian Shirazes and, as mentioned, its Cover Drive Cabernet is a great-value wine.)

This sort of diversity sets Australian producers apart from the rest of the world—their ability to make a wide range of wines well, and (mostly) at fair prices. The producer D'Arenberg is a perfect example; D'Arenberg makes dozens of good wines—from Semillon to Chardonnay to Grenache and Shiraz and Cabernet. All D'Arenberg wines have catchy names too, such as The Old Footbolt and Peppermint Paddock. (Lots of other producers' wines have silly names too—such as Reilly's Barking Mad Cabernet, Hentley Farm's The Beast Shiraz, and Tait's The Ball Buster Red—this has been another great service of Australian winemakers to the world.)

Gold medals are another important contribution of the Australians. It's hard to find an Australian wine that doesn't have a few medals on the neck of its bottle. Australian winemakers love wine competitions, and whether their wine wins a gold, a silver, or a bronze medal in a competition or fair, they'll immediately paste the medallion to the bottle. Some have so many of these stick-on medals it's hard to see the label at all.

"I had no idea Australians were so competitive," commented Peter. "They always seem so laid-back to me. But maybe that's all a big facade?

"What about wines without medals?" Peter asked. "For example, why doesn't this wine have a medal?" He looked at the 2003 Mitolo

GAM Shiraz that I'd brought him. GAM (the initials stand for the first names of Mitolo's three children) Shiraz is one of the most sought-after, superconcentrated Australian Shirazes. Parker rated the wine "possibly" 100 points.

Producers like Mitolo don't much care about medals, I said to Peter. Especially when they get 100-point scores. Peter nodded and tasted the wine—an explosion of dark fruits and spice. "Wow," he said. "This wine is amazing—there's a lot of sweetness, but there's also a lot of tannin. And yet the tannin doesn't bother me because there's so much of everything else. If they don't enter this wine in a competition, they're fools. I'd give it every gold medal there was."

Mitolo is one of many wineries founded relatively recently in South Australia by winemakers focusing on making ultrapremium wines, mostly Shiraz and Shiraz blends. One of the best of the (recent) blends is Plexus, a superconcentrated, smoky Rhône-style blend (Grenache, Shiraz, and Mourvèdre) made by former Penfolds winemaker John Duval. It's an Australian take on Châteauneuf-du-Pape—which is to say, it's even more rich and intense than the Rhône original.

"This wine smells wonderful," Peter observed. "And it tastes even better, like a piece of perfectly ripe, red fruit." That's the Grenache, I told him. It adds sweetness to the wine as well as perfume. "Then Grenache seems like a very good thing," he replied. "I think I'd use Grenache in everything."

AUSTRALIA'S FIRST GREAT WINE

For over fifty years there was only one great Australian wine name: Penfolds Grange. Created in 1951 by famed Penfolds winemaker Max Schubert, it was originally called Penfolds Grange Hermitage as an homage to the greatest wine of the northern Rhône, but the French protested and the name had to be changed. The wine is still considered the standard by which all other wines in Australia are measured.

"It doesn't sound like I'm worthy of a wine like that," Peter said nervously. "I mean, you've only given me the second labels of famous wines before. Is there some sort of catch?" No catch, I assured Peter. I just wanted him to taste a great wine and, unlike the other Australian wines he'd tasted, a wine that had some history.

"This isn't a wine label, it's a short story," Peter exclaimed when I produced the Grange. (Penfolds Grange could have the most prose-dense label in the world.) Peter began reading aloud: " 'During an extensive tour of Europe in 1950, Max Schubert studied winemaking practices that have now become an integral part of Penfolds' winemaking technique. He also observed the practice of maturing wine in new oak barrels, a method previously unused in Australia.'

"This isn't a label, this is a biography!" Peter exclaimed. "I can almost feel Max Schubert breathing down my neck just holding the bottle. Look! It even tells you the year Max was born and the year he died. I've never read so much about a wine before drinking it. Can I take the bottle home to read the rest?" He could. But first we had to taste the wine.

The wine was, in a word, spectacular—though terribly young and quite tannic. (Max Schubert would not like that we drank it so young.) Grange is made from a blend of vineyards in the Barossa Valley, and it has the characteristically ripe, intense fruit of the region, but also more subtle notes—or, as Peter said, "This wine is intense but at the same time delicate. I had no idea that Australians could do both those things."

Important Australian Wine Regions

Barossa Valley—This southern Australian region is home to some of the most intense old-vine Shiraz and the country's most famous Shiraz producers, including Penfolds, Torbreck, and Henschke.

Clare Valley—This southern Australian region produces excellent old-vine Shiraz and great dry Rieslings from such producers as Jeffrey Grosset and Jim Barry.

Coonawarra—A cool, flat region in South Australia where red soils are the key to some good Cabernet produced by such wineries as Parker Estate.

Hunter Valley—About three hours from Sydney, this region in New South Wales is one of the oldest wine-producing areas in Australia. A lot of commercial wine (e.g., Lindemans) is produced here, but some good Shiraz and old-vine Semillon is grown here as well. (Hunter Valley Shiraz was once famous for a characteristic "sweaty saddle" aroma.)

Margaret River—The most notable wine region in Western Australia, Margaret River is chiefly famous for elegant Bordeaux style Cabernets.

Tasmania—This island is thought to be a promising place to grow Pinot Noir. Several particularly good Pinot-dominant sparkling wines are made here, including Jansz, a venture started by the French Champagne house Louis Roederer.

Yarra Valley—A newly fashionable region outside Melbourne touted for its suitability for Pinot Noir, Yarra Valley shows promise, although the grape has been grown here for only a short time.

PETER AND THE ANIMALS (YELLOW TAIL AND COMPANY)

Much has been written about the "animal brands" that have dominated the Australian wine scene for the past few years (notably the wine megabrand Yellow Tail and its equally "cute" competitors Little Penguin, Little Boomie, and Black Swan). But the kangaroo of Yellow Tail is the animal that looms over them all—and has done so since 2000; it's the number-one-selling imported brand in the United States. (It's reported that in November 2005, a million cases of Yellow Tail were sold in a single month.)

"But how good are these wines?" Peter wanted to know. He'd

never had any of them before—which I found hard to believe. But apparently Peter's retail wine guru, Charlie Rodriguez, wasn't an animal-brand fan. So I pulled together a couple of wines from each brand (none cost more than $9 a bottle), and we sat down for a tasting.

"These wines look like something that should be served at Disney World," Peter commented, looking over the bright blue, pink, and yellow labels.

"We're tasting the wines, not the packaging," I reminded him.

So we tried the Chardonnay and the Shiraz from each brand (those were the original two wines of Yellow Tail), and Peter, the former fatty Chardonnay man, actually found them too sweet.

"Like candy!" Peter pronounced of one wine after the other. Even the oaky Chardonnay failed to move him; the Yellow Tail Shiraz probably fared best of all. "It's juicy, I guess, but I don't really see the point," he said. I'd heard there were some new Yellow Tail wines, Pinot Noir and Riesling, which had arrived fairly recently. Should I find a bottle? Peter didn't seem particularly enthused. "As much as I love Riesling, I can't think a Yellow Tail Riesling is a good thing," he said darkly.

PETER MEETS MCWILLIAM

Although Peter had tasted some of the greatest wines made in Australia—Grosset Riesling and Penfolds Grange—there was one that he couldn't get out of his head: McWilliam's Cabernet. Which was peculiar, to say the least, considering the McWilliam's was a nice $12 Cabernet but hardly the stuff of which vinous dreams are made. But Peter had his particular point of view: "It's so smooth." So when I got a call from Scott McWilliam, in town on a visit, I asked if I could introduce Peter to him.

"I'm amazed that Lettie invited me to lunch today," Peter said to Scott McWilliam as they shook hands. "Every time I've ever liked a wine, she never lets me have it again." Young Scott McWilliam smiled affably enough but looked a bit nervous.

The three of us sat down at a table in the front room of DB

Bistro in midtown Manhattan, and Peter began chatting as if he and McWilliam had known each other for years. Or, more precisely, as if McWilliam could benefit from all that Peter had learned about wine. "Australia is so much easier than Burgundy to understand," he told McWilliam. "You just have to look at the label to know that Burgundy is a living hell. In Australia, they always give you a lot of information on the back of the label. That's a very good thing," he added (somewhat ingratiatingly, I thought).

Scott McWilliam nodded agreement. "We do like to give people a little bit of information on the vintage, the production, and maybe what to eat with food," he said, and poured Peter a glass of his Hanwood Estate Riesling (the McWilliam's wines have two different labels: McWilliam's and Hanwood).

"This is a Clare Valley Riesling," Peter observed.

"Do you know the Clare Valley?" McWilliam replied.

"The Clare Valley is well-known for its Riesling."

"The soil structure is particularly suited to Riesling; there's a real minerality to the wines," McWilliam said.

I felt as if I were watching a tennis match. Point Peter. Point McWilliam. "But even with all that minerality, there's no harshness to it," said Peter. "There's a real approachability to Clare Valley Rieslings."

McWilliam agreed. Although he couldn't have been much older than thirty, McWilliam was impressively smooth.

"I love that word *approachability*," Peter said approvingly. "It's not like those Alsace Rieslings that really smack you around. This is more like a New York State Riesling."

McWilliam had to admit he had never tasted any New York Rieslings, so he couldn't say.

"I have some in my house. Next time you're in town, let me know. I think you'd like them," said Peter expansively.

McWilliam opened his 2001 Brand's Laira Coonawarra Cabernet. "I think we should have this wine next. Or do you think we should have the Syrah?" He turned to Peter politely.

"I think Shiraz is heavier; I'd have that after the Cabernet," said Peter.

"But Cabernets can be even heavier. The skins are thicker and therefore more tannic."

Peter nodded. "That's where the bitterness comes from."

McWilliam shook his head. "As a winemaker you're looking for astringent tannins, not bitter tannins. We want your mouth to turn to velvet after you drink our Cabernet."

"Turn to velvet?" Peter sounded puzzled.

McWilliam nodded. "Sometimes a wine is so tannic it turns your mouth inside out. We don't want that to happen."

"Neither do I," said Peter, who sounded alarmed.

"What's your favorite Australian movie?" McWilliam asked Peter, who offered up *Breaker Morant* and *The Last Wave* by Peter Weir. McWilliam nodded. "We sponsor an Australian film festival," he said. "Are you a fan of Naomi Watts?" Now engrossed in the mutually absorbing topic of Naomi Watts, they forgot to pour the Cabernet. I kept drinking the Riesling.

"I love Naomi Watts," Peter said. "I was at the New York Film Critics Circle lunch and she said, 'I have to give you an Australian hug.' So we went outside and she jumped on me and wrapped her legs around me. It was fabulous. Ian McKellen was watching and said, 'If that's what you wanted, I would have given you a hug myself.'"

I watched McWilliam's eyes widen at the idea. He'd clearly forgotten all about Cabernet or Riesling or Shiraz.

A few top Australian names: Burge Family, Clarendon Hills, Grosset, Henschke, Penfolds, Rockford Estate.

NEW ZEALAND

"Peter Jackson says that the red wines of New Zealand are no good," Peter reported, not long after his dinner with the New Zealand–born director of *Lord of the Rings*. That sounded like a pretty sweeping statement to me, I told him. "Well, all I can tell you is that Peter Jackson won't drink them," Peter replied. "When I had dinner with Peter Jackson in his suite at the Plaza Athenée Hotel, he and his wife were eating Indian food and drinking white wine. There was a Sauvignon Blanc and a Riesling. I only drank the Riesling. I thought it was really good—I used the word *closed* to describe the Sauvignon Blanc and they were really impressed. But I couldn't go on after that. They asked me some questions about wines and sauces that I couldn't answer. I said the nose, the aroma, it's eighty percent, and I'm not getting it from this Sauvignon."

Did Peter remember which Sauvignon he'd had? Had he perhaps written it down in his notebook? He had not. But he did remember talking about Cloudy Bay to the Jacksons. That was one of John Irving's favorite wines; Peter had shared it with John Irving at a film festival in Nantucket at a screening of the movie *The Door in the Floor*.

"Cloudy Bay is actually the original New Zealand Sauvignon," I told Peter. "It was the prototype for just about every New Zealand Sauvignon that came afterwards. And amazingly enough, it was the only wine that was needed to put New Zealand on the world map when it debuted about fifteen years ago."

"Would you call Cloudy Bay the Pétrus of New Zealand?" Peter asked.

Whether or not Cloudy Bay Sauvignon Blanc could be called the

Kiwi Pétrus, it had certainly led to the creation of a lot of other great New Zealand Sauvignon Blancs, if not an entire style of Sauvignon Blancs all over the world: fresh, green, ripe fruit flavors and acidity so vibrant it could only be described as "zingy." It actually changed the way people thought about Sauvignon Blanc and the way wine-makers approached the grape too. For example, in California, they used to make Sauvignon Blanc as if it were a second-class Chardon-nay, putting it in a lot of oak and trying to make it richer, more structured—in other words, making it what it was not. But when they saw the success of Cloudy Bay, winemakers around the world worked to replicate the style. From California to South Africa, even in the Loire Valley, the home of Sauvignon Blanc, I've seen wine lists that feature "New Zealand–style" Sancerres.

"This wine is pale as parchment, although there is a fatness to the swirl," Peter commented on the 2005 Cloudy Bay Sauvignon Blanc.

"You mean the wine has a good viscosity," I corrected him.

"That too," Peter replied amiably. I wondered if it was a good sign that Peter often used the wrong word and didn't particularly care. Was I failing in my mission, or was Peter simply growing confident in his ability to choose his own tasting words?

I gave Peter a second New Zealand Sauvignon to try: the 2004 Villa Maria, which was a year older, and the difference was apparent in terms of freshness and spark. "It tastes kind of flat and herbal," Peter commented. And he was right. When New Zealand Sauvi-gnons get older, they lose acidity and can take on a kind of canned-green-bean note.

In fact, green bean was a flavor that New Zealand producers used to think was typical of their wines. When I was a judge at the Air New Zealand Wine Awards a few years ago, another experienced judge (and New Zealand winemaker) told me that it was a character-istic they actually once sought to cultivate. Fortunately, that style has changed to something much more fresh and citruslike.

"What about New Zealand red wines?" Peter wondered. "Is Peter Jackson right that it's better to drink the red wines from Aus-tralia than New Zealand?"

Well, Peter Jackson was right and wrong. In terms of red wines such as Cabernet and Shiraz, it's better to look to Australia (although the Cabernet-based wines of Hawke Bay in the North Island are getting better—particularly those from the Gimblett Gravels area), but in terms of Pinot Noir, there's no place in the New World that shows more potential for Pinot Noir than New Zealand.

Certainly no country is planting it at a faster rate than New Zealand, which has more Pinot Noir under vine than the entire population of the country could drink now or in decades to come. Pinot Noir has been the most fashionable grape in that country—even more so than Sauvignon Blanc. In fact, there has been a mini-internal backlash against Sauvignon Blanc in New Zealand, as if it's no longer good enough to warrant full concentration. Or that it's too easy to make—unlike the difficult Pinot Noir.

"But why are they all insisting on Pinot Noir? Why aren't they happy to make something like Sauvignon Blanc really, really well?" Peter wondered. This was, of course, the question that could be put to any number of winemakers all over the world who aspire to do more than just what they know they can do well—wines that are difficult and represent a challenge. Pinot Noir is certainly that grape. Even in Germany there are winemakers who make great Riesling but also want to make a great Pinot Noir.

"Well, I'm curious about how good New Zealand Pinots could possibly be," Peter commented, "especially since Peter Jackson takes such a dark view of them."

Peter could taste and decide for himself. I had two wines on hand, both considered among the best New Zealand Pinots: the 2004 Felton Road Pinot Noir and the 2002 Carrick Vineyard. Both were from the region of Central Otago, currently the most fashionable place in New Zealand to grow Pinot Noir. "Fashionable?" Peter remarked skeptically. "Central Otago sounds like a place where cars are made."

In fact, Central Otago is a beautiful region, the southernmost wine region on New Zealand's South Island. Thanks to a combination of high mountains and frequent high winds, it can be a hard place to reach; a few years ago I spent all day in the airport at Christchurch trying to get a flight there.

"Christchurch!" Peter exclaimed. "There's a movie called *Until They Sail* set in Christchurch. It was made in the fifties and starred Paul Newman and Sandra Dee. I remember Christchurch was hard to get to in the movie—but it was incredibly beautiful." Peter continued to surprise me with some unlikely film associations. Who else could invoke Sandra Dee in a conversation about New Zealand Pinot Noir?

"The Felton Road was awfully charming," Peter conceded. "It really smells like Pinot Noir," meaning it had a characteristically sweet, ripe-fruit nose, while the Carrick Vineyard was more substantial and earthy, a more savory style. I admired it, but Peter was more reserved in his praise.

"I like these wines," he allowed, "but I think I like Australian reds better. New Zealand wines just seem so . . . tentative by comparison."

"But you're comparing Pinot Noirs to Syrahs—they're not the same thing," I protested. I'd actually thought the Carrick Vineyard was a pretty big wine.

"I don't know," Peter said, "I just think the Australian wines have an abundance of character; they're more overt, and I guess I prefer that. Although I do like New Zealand Sauvignon Blanc." Was Peter Jackson, I wondered, somehow to blame?

Some great New Zealand producers: Cloudy Bay, Felton Road, Kumeu River, Ata Rangi, Martinborough Vineyard.

Three top bargains in Sauvignon Blanc: Babich, Brancott Estate, Spy Valley.

SOUTH AFRICA

Are there any great South African filmmakers or films? I asked
Peter as we sat down to discuss South Africa. I couldn't name
one. Nor, apparently, could Peter. Except for Gavin Hood's *Tsotsi*,
which had recently won an Oscar for Best Foreign Film. And Peter
did like the work of model-turned-actress Charlize Theron. She is
the only South African who has made an impact on American film,
according to Peter. But Peter couldn't name any other recent filmmakers who had made a mark in the larger cinema world. Alas, I had
to tell him that much the same was true for South African wine.

Not that there aren't some well-made, good South African wines,
but there aren't any world-class examples as in other New World
countries such as Australia and New Zealand. New Zealand has
Sauvignon Blanc as its flagship (whether they like it or not), and Australia has cornered Shiraz of a certain big, muscular kind. But South
Africa's two key varietals to date—Pinotage and Chenin Blanc—
aren't grapes people outside South Africa seem to care much about.

Pinotage is a strange grape to be sure—a cross between Pinot Noir
and the rustic Cinsault grape of southern France. Chenin Blanc is, of
course, the grape of the Loire. It's also known as Steen in South
Africa. (Why did South Africans have such an affinity for ugly
grape names?) Of course, other grapes are grown in South Africa
besides Pinotage and Chenin Blanc, aka Steen (which, incidentally,
South African winemakers are pulling up as fast as they can in favor
of more internationally popular grapes such as Chardonnay and
Syrah). But nothing has earned South Africa superstar status or, for
that matter, even universal praise (although its Syrahs are promising
and its Sauvignon Blancs can be good).

"Well, that's really making me look forward to this chapter of the book," said Peter sarcastically.

That's not to say there isn't enormous unrealized potential in South African wines, and more and more ambitious, well-funded wineries are turning out more and more good wines—such as the Sauvignon Blanc from Mulderbosch or the Pinot Noirs from producers Hamilton Russell and Neil Ellis. But there is still a long way to go.

Pinotage is the particular problem. As it's the only truly South African grape (first planted in that country almost a century ago), it's been an awkward flagship for South Africa for a long time, producing wines of a certain rustic, even wild or feral, quality. In short, not much to build a national reputation upon.

Peter looked apprehensive at the name. "I don't like the sound of that grape—it sounds like something went wrong."

Try to keep an open mind, I counseled him, though I knew what he meant. Peter was, meanwhile, still mouthing the word *feral.*

"I doubt Charlize Theron would be drinking this stuff," Peter remarked when I opened a bottle of 2003 Kumkani Pinotage. Aromatically, it certainly had a unique profile—earthy, almost bacony—while in the mouth the texture was rustic and the flavors reminded me of an animal pelt. Peter spit.

"Animal pelt!" Peter fairly shouted, and took another sip. "Animal pelt! It does smell like that! But what kind of description is that?" He took one more taste and asked, "Can we bury this bottle now in the backyard?"

Instead, I gave Peter a second Pinotage to try, the 2002 Simonsig Redhill. This was an improvement over the first wine; that is to say, it didn't taste like animal pelt but, instead, a sort of polished example of a rustic grape. "It's not hideous," Peter reported cautiously. "But why are they doing anything with this grape at all? It's so weird. Why don't they just rip it all up and plant some Cabernet?" And I had to agree.

Peter and I aren't the only ones who wish there were less Pinotage: a number of South African vintners are focusing on other red grapes such as Syrah and Cabernet. The winery Fairview turns out a number of good Rhône-style Syrahs in the region of Paarl, and the Rupert & Rothschild estate (also located in Paarl) crafts a Cabernet-Merlot blend that's a good example of the sort of ambitious, international-style wines that forward-looking South African winemakers are producing more and more. The 2001 Baron Edmond was a particularly polished example, although the most Peter could say at the time was that "it takes the flavor of Pinotage out of my mouth."

The white wines of South Africa are a different story from the reds. That is, a lot more good white wines are made, from Mulderbosch, as noted (which packages its wines in a distinctive racing-stripe bottle), and Simonsig, which makes an excellent-value Sauvignon Blanc for $10 a bottle. But South Africa still seems to have a way to go in terms of making truly distinctive, world class wines.

Or, as Peter put it, "It's hard to understand a country that would willingly make a wine like Pinotage."

A few top South African producers: Mulderbosch (Sauvignon Blanc), Hamilton Russell (Pinot Noir), Thelema (Chardonnay), Rupert & Rothschild (Cabernet blends), Fairview (Syrah).

CHILE

Although Chile is the twelfth-largest wine-producing country in the world, Peter, like most people, had no particular vision of the country or its wines. Peter couldn't even remember whether he'd ever tasted a Chilean wine. Or, as he said, "I think I've had a Chilean Chardonnay sometime in my life—maybe at a movie screening—but I'm not sure."

Peter wasn't entirely to blame for this failure of memory. Chilean producers make a bewildering number of wines from a wide array of grapes. And many producers make more than one tier of wines—from simple $6 Chardonnays to $60 Cabernets. Chilean producers themselves seem confused as to which wines they should focus on—the cheap wines that they began exporting back in the eighties, or today's more ambitious wines?

Certainly there's a lot more competition in the cheap-wine market since Chile dominated it some twenty years ago. Australia, Italy, and Spain now all contribute lots of bargain wines to the world, and enough expensive wines are made everywhere else; a producer of a fancy Chilean Cabernet faces fierce competition in the $100 wine market.

"I didn't even know that Chile made such expensive wine," Peter commented. "Who would be buying a hundred-dollar Chilean wine anyway? Besides some Chilean guy who made a fortune in sea bass?"

In fact, nearly all of Chile's wine is aimed at the export market (about 80 percent), and little is purchased by native Chileans, with or without fish-derived fortunes. This includes the cheap wines as well as the most expensive.

One of the most successful wineries in Chile, Montes, exports almost all (90 percent) of its production. The winery is also notable for making excellent wines at both ends of the price spectrum (unsurprisingly, not a commonplace feat). Their Montes Alpha Syrah has terrific Syrah character and is always reliable, while its fancy, superconcentrated Syrah Montes Folly was one of the first successful high-priced "Super Chilean" wines. I opened a bottle of Montes Folly for Peter.

"Why did they call this a 'folly'?" Peter asked. "That doesn't sound very promising." He turned over the bottle (whose front label is a wild design by British cartoonist Ralph Steadman) to the information-dense back label and started to read "This is like some filmmaker's statement of what he was trying to do," said Peter. "Except that it basically says, 'I don't care if you like this wine or not,' which I think is a pretty interesting thing for this winemaker, Aurelio Montes, to say. He must be a pretty confident guy to put that on the label."

Aurelio Montes is probably the most important winemaker in Chile right now; he has been a consultant to a number of important wineries in the country in addition to his partnership with Montes winery. "Is he like the Harvey Weinstein of Chile?" Peter asked, tasting the wine. "Because his Montes Folly wine really slaps you around. It's just really big and intense. Which isn't necessarily a bad thing, but it's not something I'd expect from a Chilean wine."

Such big, intense wines are increasingly the focus of Chilean producers (often in partnership with French, Italian, or even American wineries), who are turning out Cabernet-dominant, Bordeaux-style blends with fanciful one-word names, often beginning with the letter *A*, including Altair (a wine made by San Pedro, Chile's largest winery, and Château Dassault of Bordeaux), Albis (a partnership between Chilean producer Haras de Pirque and Italian superstar Piero Antinori), and Almaviva (Concha y Toro and Château Mouton Rothschild). All are priced to compete with some of the best wines in the world. Almaviva currently leads, price-wise, at about $90 a bottle.

Most of these wines are made in the Maipo Valley appellation,

Chile's premier red-wine region, which surrounds the city of Santiago and runs roughly between the Andes mountains and the coastal mountain range. In fact, one of the most legendary Cabernet vineyards in Chile, Tocornal, is just about within the city limits of Santiago. (It's the source of Almaviva as well as Don Melchor, the flagship single-vineyard Cabernet Sauvignon from Concha y Toro, arguably Chile's first truly great wine.)

Of course, other wines are made in Chile, including Carmenère (a red French grape that Chile produces almost exclusively, sometimes impressively so and sometimes indifferently), Chardonnay, and Merlot. But most notable right now are Chilean Sauvignon Blancs, which are some of the best deals in the world—with excellent examples coming from newly developed coastal regions such as San Antonio and Leyda. The wines are a lot like those from New Zealand—fresh and zingy—though often at half the price of the wines from that country. Some of my favorites include the rich and minerally Floresta Sauvignon from Santa Rita Winery and the Sauvignon Blanc from EQ, a relatively new producer in the maritime (only two miles from the ocean) San Antonio region. Casa Lapostolle winery, one of the earliest Chilean-French joint efforts, also makes a great $10 Sauvignon Blanc, which I poured for Peter.

"I have a feeling that even Peter Jackson would like this wine," Peter said.

A few top Chilean producers: Santa Rita, Concha y Toro, Montes, Casa Lapostolle.

A few promising new producers: Altair, Tabali, EQ.

NEW YORK STATE

"I have a really good feeling about the Finger Lakes," Peter said, recalling the wines I'd brought back from my trip to New York's Finger Lakes region a few years earlier. The wines of Standing Stone were particularly memorable for Peter, especially the Gewürztraminer. "I had no idea that Gewürztraminer could be so good. Or that it could come from someplace like New York. Although at the time I didn't even know that wine was made in New York."

THE FINGER LAKES

In fact, the Finger Lakes region of New York is particularly well suited to such grapes as Riesling and Gewürztraminer—even if the region's varietal visionary, Dr. Konstantin Frank, was denounced as a madman when he made this observation some fifty years ago. At that time, only hardy native varietals such as Catawba and Baco Noir were grown; noble grapes such as Riesling were considered too delicate to withstand the cold. But Dr. Frank, a native of Germany, believed the climate was much like that of his home country and therefore suitable to the same grapes. The local grape-growing forces not only disagreed with him, but at one point discussed having the exceedingly vocal Frank carted off to the loony bin. (Perhaps the first time that growing Riesling has been thought to be a sign of insanity.)

Now, of course, terrific Rieslings are made all over the Finger Lakes, especially in the Seneca Lake region, from such wineries as

Standing Stone, Lamoreaux Landing, Red Newt, and Hermann Wiemer (a disciple of Dr. Frank's). Dr. Frank's winery is actually on a different Finger Lake, Keuka.

"Dr. Frank sounds a lot like Werner Herzog to me," Peter said admiringly after hearing the story of his near incarceration. "Herzog is such a crazy director that in his film *Fitzcarraldo* he decided that the actual actors should drag the boat over the mountains of Peru and they did. Herzog did the same thing in his 1972 film, *Aguirre: Wrath of God*. There isn't anyone who doesn't think Herzog is crazy—but he is a great filmmaker.

"Is Hermann Wiemer crazy too?" Peter asked hopefully as we tasted Dr. Frank's 2004 Riesling and Wiemer's 2004 Dry Riesling alongside each other. Not as far as I knew, although he was intimidating when I met him. Meanwhile, Peter enthused over his Riesling. "It reminds me of some of those really dry Alsace wines we had—although I like the Dr. Frank a little more. It's a little richer. Maybe a little sweeter. But they're both really good; why don't more people know about these wines? I'd never heard of them till you told me about them. Is this Hermann Wiemer really that obscure?"

Peter held up the bottle of the Wiemer Riesling for a closer look at the label. "According to Hermann, the whole world knows him. He says his 'high-quality wines are recognized throughout the world.' It also says he came from Bernkastel, Germany, from a family with a three-hundred-year tradition of vinifera wines. That sounds pretty impressive to me.

"I really like the wines of Hermann Wiemer," Peter said. "And I'd like to think that he's as crazy as Dr. Frank or even Werner Herzog. I think when someone does something really, really good, they're probably just a little bit crazy. But I don't have any data on psychopathic winemakers, so I can't really say. But I'd like to find out."

A few good wine producers from the Finger Lakes region: Hermann Wiemer, Standing Stone, Dr. Frank, Red Newt.

THE REST OF NEW YORK

The two other wine-producing regions in New York are the Hudson Valley and the North and South Forks of Long Island. The wines of the former are rarely seen much farther south than the Catskills, but I've actually spotted some Long Island wines on lists in California restaurants (or at least one).

The Long Island wine industry is newer than that of the Finger Lakes, but it's attracted a lot more money in a much shorter time—recent investors include movie industry moguls such as Michael Lynne, head of New Line Cinema, who bought Bedell Cellars, and royalty such as Prince Marco Borghese, who bought Hargrave Vineyard and renamed it a very un–Long Island like Castello di Borghese.

But with all the money invested and all the individual good wines (a Riesling here, a Merlot there), the Long Island wine industry, in global terms, is still very much in a state of becoming.

A few notable Long Island producers: Macari (Chardonnay), Wolffer Estate (Merlot and Rosé), Osprey's Dominion (Riesling), Schneider Vineyards (Cabernet Franc), and Channing Daughters (Pinot Bianco, Tocai).

Oregon and
Washington State

Peter's first question about Washington and Oregon wines was one I've been asked many times: Where do they stand in comparison to Napa wines? Never mind any comparison isn't really valid, as the two states grow very different grapes from Napa. Oregon specializes in Pinot Noir and Pinot Gris, which don't really matter in Napa, and in Washington, a much broader range of wines are important: Merlot and Cabernet to Riesling and Semillon and Sauvigon Blanc. While it's true Napa does produce a number of different wines, the name is almost completely synonymous with Cabernet. But I knew what Peter had in mind when he asked the question. Napa is not just another place to grow grapes; it's synonymous with all that is great in American wine.

Peter had never been to either Oregon or Washington State, though he expressed a mild interest in Seattle, mostly on account of independent film director Alan Rudolph, whose work Peter admired. And of course, Peter added, Tom Hanks was sleepless there too. Perhaps one reason the region failed to resonate with Peter was that he couldn't think of many movies that were set in the Pacific Northwest, with Paul Newman's *Sometimes a Great Notion* a notable exception.

"All the movies that they pretend take place in the Northwest are actually filmed on a back set in L.A.—or in Vancouver," Peter contended. "So I don't really have a sense of Washington State."

Nor do many people have a sense of Washington State winemaking regions. And as far as both Washington State and Oregon go, the general picture is probably one of ceaseless rain. Furthermore, most people probably still think Washington wines are made in the suburbs of Seattle—or grown somewhere near the Potomac, as in Washington, D.C. Yet Oregon and Washington are producing some benchmark American wines, particularly Oregon Pinot Noir and Washington State Merlot.

OREGON: TALE OF TWO PINOTS (GRIS AND NOIR)

One of Oregon's great values is its Pinot Gris (which must always be called Pinot Gris, not Pinot Grigio, in Oregon, according to state law). Oregon Pinot Gris is a fairly rich white with good natural acidity and is usually quite affordable—around $15 or so. "I had no idea. And it would never occur to me to order a white wine from Oregon," Peter said, "but I do like the idea of a bargain."

One of my favorite Oregon Pinot Gris for both consistency and value ($14) is the Elk Cove Pinot Gris, which I gave to Peter, who declared it to be "fatty like a Chardonnay, but it has a spiciness and a really good acidity. A terrific food wine."

Then, of course, there's Oregon Pinot Noir. Although the wines are now acclaimed, some thirty years ago things were quite different. Oregon wasn't thought to be a good place to grow grapes at all, let alone one as temperamental as Pinot Noir. For a long time (and many seasons of rain), it looked as if the skeptics were right. But a handful of winemakers persisted and the weather improved (global warming?) so much that the past several years have been particularly good vintages for Oregon Pinot Noir.

There are four major grape-growing regions in Oregon, but only one of major consequence: the Willamette Valley, less than an hour's drive from the city of Portland. It's a fairly cool region, and of course, it gets a fair amount of rain, for which Oregon is famous. But many great wines are made in marginal climates, and the Willamette Valley could certainly be described as marginal, at least in terms of rainfall.

A handful of Oregon winemaking pioneers arrived in the early seventies, mostly on trips north from California. (David Lett is famously considered the "father of Oregon Pinot Noir" and accorded the honorific "Papa Pinot" by his admirers.) Another early believer with arguably even more influence over the state's winemaking fortunes was a Frenchman, Robert Drouhin, a producer from Burgundy. Drouhin had come to Oregon's Willamette Valley in the 1980s after tasting an Oregon Pinot that bested a number of Burgundies in a wine competition in France. Drouhin purchased land in Willamette and gave the winemaking job to his daughter Véronique, who now divides her time between France and Oregon. The Drouhins make several Pinot Noirs, including a small production bottling, Laurène, named for Véronique's daughter.

Drouhin Pinots owe more to elegance than power, although powerful Pinots are increasingly common in Oregon, thanks both to changes in climate (drier, hotter years that result in higher-alcohol wines) and changes in winemaking technique (more new oak) and style (more concentration). I had one of each kind for Peter, beginning with the Drouhins' 2002 Laurène, but Peter seemed more interested in the bottle's back label. "'The red hills of Dundee,' I love how that sounds," Peter said. "It's very poetic. But what does it mean, 'a traditionally Burgundian wine'? That sounds like it's going to cost an arm and a leg. Particularly the part about 'French soul and Oregon soil.'"

What did Peter think was wrong with the Drouhins' wanting to point out a two-continent winemaking experience? After all, plenty of Americans made as much out of their one decade of winemaking experience. Peter didn't see it that way. "I feel like there are a lot of hidden agendas in this label," he said. "A lot of code words. Like 'French soul.' That's probably their way of warning you that this wine will cost a lot."

The Laurène Pinot Noir costs about $65 a bottle—not cheap—but by comparison to a number of Oregon Pinots priced over $100 a bottle, a relative deal. Oregon Pinots have become more expensive over the past several years in part because the quality of the wines has dramatically improved. This has resulted in higher scores from the critics, who have in turn created a wine-buying public willing to pay more for Oregon Pinot Noir.

The second Pinot that Peter and I tasted was another Elk Cove wine, the 2004 Mount Richmond Vineyard bottling. A few wineries make Pinot Noirs from the Mount Richmond vineyard, and nearly all of them are big, tannic wines. This bottling was no exception.

Peter read the label skeptically. "'Spectacular'? 'Renowned'? I want to know who's doing the renowning." The Elk Cove Pinot was a much bigger, chewier wine than the Laurène. "This Pinot Noir would stand up to a steak," Peter remarked, and I had to agree. "The Laurène, on the other hand, you could have with a fish," he continued. "But not this one. Maybe some Pinot Noirs aren't really that versatile. And I have a feeling this wine isn't cheap."

For a man who professed great love for French Pinot Noir, aka Burgundy, never mind their cost, Peter seemed unwilling to cut Oregon producers the same deal. "I think I'll stick with Pinot Gris when it comes to Oregon," he declared.

The discussion of money reminded Peter of a recent chat he'd had with Sigourney Weaver at an awards dinner at Tavern on the Green. ("The Tavern on the Green waiter wouldn't show me the name of the wine, but it sure was awful," Peter said.) Sigourney Weaver didn't even drink it, although she and her husband were interested in wine. "Sigourney's husband, Jim, asked me if I could tell the difference between a fifty-dollar and a two-hundred-and-fifty-dollar wine," Peter reported, "but I told him the question was too hard. Even though there are a lot of people who want to know the answer to that sort of question, it wasn't one that interested me."

Had Peter really said that? It sounded a little, well, arrogant to me. But according to Peter, Jim had understood. Furthermore, Sigourney Weaver told Peter that she wanted to learn more about wine. She even said she'd like to attend one of Peter's wine lessons. She'd had a bad experience in California wine country. "Sigourney went to Napa once with Candice Bergen and Louis Malle, but she didn't have a great time visiting the wineries," Peter recalled. "She said that no one would explain any of the wines to her. And she's a really smart woman. I think she could learn a lot if she was tasting wine with me."

The idea of Sigourney Weaver sitting at the table while Peter declaimed on the virtues of a particular Riesling or castigated some South African Pinotage was too hard to imagine. I did suggest that Peter ask Sigourney if she and her husband might like to have dinner sometime, to which I would bring some truly good Napa wine.

"I'll give her a call," Peter said.

A few top Oregon Pinot Noir producers: Domaine Serene, Brick House, Domaine Drouhin, Patricia Green, Beaux Frères.

Two great buys in Oregon Pinot Gris: King Estate, Elk Cove.

WASHINGTON STATE

If Sigourney Weaver couldn't find a winemaker to talk to her about wines in Napa, she'd certainly find plenty of producers willing to chat in Washington State, where most of the wineries and their tasting rooms are run by the owners themselves. Although it's the second-largest wine-producing state in the country, it's still pretty folksy and there aren't many large Washington wineries except Château Ste. Michelle.

"But aren't Washington wines just for tourists?" Peter asked. He'd never had wine from Washington before. Not even a wine from Château Ste. Michelle? I asked. "Perhaps," he allowed, "but if so, I didn't know it was from Washington State."

That's one of the problems of Washington State: it lacks a cohesive identity. Even the site of its flagship winery, Château Ste. Michelle, is obscure. (In fact, plenty of people I know think Château Ste. Michelle is in California.) And unlike Oregon, which has developed a reputation for its Pinot Noir, Washington doesn't have a reputation for a particular grape. Washington grape growers can do many things well: Cabernet Sauvignon (many good, a few great); Merlot (many better than Napa); Riesling (the best American versions, aside from a few from New York); some good Syrahs and excellent Semillon—and on and on. Maybe they are too versatile? Peter wondered.

"Do you think that Washington should specialize, like Oregon?" Peter wanted to know. "And why don't they grow Pinot Noir too?"

Because it wouldn't do particularly well. The state's grape-growing regions are almost all located in the far eastern corner of the state—about five hours from Seattle—and it can get hot there, too hot for Pinot Noir.

Although most of Washington's vineyards are in the eastern part of the state, its most important wineries are located around Seattle, which means a ten-hour round-trip car ride just to check on the grapes. Some of Washington's most famous winemakers do this quite regularly—including Chris Camarda (Andrew Will Winery), who lives on an island off the coast of Seattle, Alex Golitzen (Quilceda Creek), who lives north of the city, and Ben Smith (Cadence), who's a Seattle suburbanite as well.

Not that there aren't quite a few wineries and winemakers located in eastern Washington State too, in such regions as Red Mountain, Columbia Valley, and Walla Walla (a town as well as a wine region). One of the oldest wineries in Walla Walla is L'Ecole No. 41, established in the early eighties, when winemaking in Washington was still new. L'Ecole makes several different types of wines, from Chardonnay to Merlot to Cabernet and Syrah. They also make one of the best Semillons in the country. (Semillon is one of the two key grapes of a white Bordeaux.) L'Ecole No. 41 is one of the few producers of Semillon in the state, although Chinook Winery also makes a terrific Semillon.

"If it's so good, why don't more winemakers make Semillon?" Peter asked sensibly as I handed him a glass of the 2004 L'Ecole No. 41 Barrel Fermented Semillon.

It was time to remind Peter of the practical business of winemaking, and that no one is likely to stake his reputation on an obscure grape such as Semillon. Not when there's so much money in Chardonnay. There's not much prestige with Semillon either—not as there is, for example, in Cabernet.

"Well, I think it's completely delightful," Peter reported. And it was—a rich, almost waxy white with a fair amount of balancing acidity.

Peter also liked the 2004 Eroica Riesling, declaring that it reminded him of a German wine. It was a perceptive observation, as Eroica is actually a joint project between German winemaker Ernst Loosen and Château Ste. Michelle. It was created to showcase the potential of Washington State Riesling, and though at $21 or so a bottle it wasn't cheap, it was definitely one of the state's benchmark wines.

"Has anyone else in Washington made a Riesling this good?" Peter wanted to know. I had to tell him that nobody in Washington seemed any more set on making a great Riesling than they did a great Semillon.

Instead, Cabernet Sauvignon, Merlot, and Syrah are the grapes that Washington producers seem to be pinning their hopes and their fortunes on. Overall, they're probably focusing on Cabernet the most, even though they make some of the country's best Merlots. The last time I traveled to Washington to taste Merlot, I was told over and over by producers that they believed their "real future" was with Cabernet. Or as one winemaker put it, "We want to prove we can make wines as good as Napa's."

"That doesn't sound very folksy to me," Peter commented. "That sounds kind of combative. I thought you said Washington wine-makers are folksy."

To me the attitude revealed just how ambitious Washington wine-makers are. A new generation of winemakers in Washington are determined to make wines that will compete with the best in the world. Not just Napa. Take Ben Smith of Cadence, a relatively new winery whose red blends have already won high praise. I gave Peter a glass of the 2003 Cadence Ciel du Cheval Vineyard red blend.

"All it says on the label is red wine. That sounds pretty unsophis-ticated to me, like 'Good Eats' on a restaurant sign," commented Peter. He changed his mind after tasting the wine.

"Red wine" doesn't mean that the wine is mediocre, I told Peter. It just means that the wine is made from more than one grape. This wine in question was a Bordeaux-style blend of Cabernet Sauvi-gnon, Cabernet Franc, Petite Verdot, and Merlot. Peter studied the back label and noted the percentage of every grape. "It seems like all these grapes add up to more than one hundred," he said critically.

The fact is, blended wines are becoming more and more common, not just in Washington but all over the world. Even among talented winemakers such as Chris Camarda of Andrew Will. Camarda, who once made some of Washington's best Merlots and Cabernets, is concentrating on blends instead.

Peter didn't approve. "I don't like this whole blend business. It just doesn't seem pure."

I had a couple of older Andrew Will wines dating back to when Chris Camarda was still "pure," so I poured them for Peter. The first was the 2000 Andrew Will Sheridan Vineyard Cabernet, a polished wine, with ripe, sweet fruit and well-integrated tannins.

"What's wrong with this Camarda guy?" Peter asked. "This wine is terrific. Why does he want to make it part of some blend?"

The second wine, 2001 Andrew Will Pepper Bridge Merlot, further convinced Peter that blends were a mistake. "How can you not want to make Merlot when you make a Merlot this fantastic?" he raved.

While Peter might have been raving, he had a point. Some wines are good enough to be a pure expression of a single varietal. The Pepper Bridge wine was a perfect example; it had every virtue of a true Merlot: the fruit was ripe and lush but not excessive; it was restrained yet seductive. In short, it showed what great Merlot could be. As Peter put it, "This wine doesn't make any false promises."

Peter asked, "Why are so many winemakers focused on blends? They seem like stylized movies to me, when a director adds things on when they didn't get the picture right in the first place. It's like a filmmaker saying 'I tried to take a pure line but I had to worry about what the audience wants' sort of thing. I want a purist filmmaker; I want to feel that even if it doesn't have a happy ending, I experienced the real movie as the filmmaker intended it to be."

I promised Peter I'd call Camarda and let him know how Peter felt, though I wasn't sure how Camarda would react to an accusation that he was stylistically impure.

Some great Washington State producers: Quilceda Creek, Andrew Will, Cadence, Pepperbridge, Leonetti Cellars.

A few great-value Washington State producers: Château Ste. Michelle, Columbia Crest, Hogue Cellars.

CALIFORNIA

If there was one place I expected Peter to feel a deep connection to, it was California. Not just because it's where so many movies are made and almost every director Peter admires calls home (except Marty Scorsese and Woody Allen). But I also thought Peter would relate to California best because its wines are labeled by the name of the grape—the way Peter (still) liked best.

Of course, grapes aren't all that's important in California; geography counts too. There are one thousand officially designated growing regions in the state, otherwise known as AVAs (American Viticultural Areas), although not many are well-known. A few, such as Oakville and Howell Mountain, are famous, but others, such as American Canyon, have questionable origins—created not because they produce distinctive "American Canyon" wine but because a large winery is located there. (When was the last time Peter had ever heard anyone looking for an "American Canyon Merlot"?)

Peter liked these facts, so I gave him more: the United States is the fourth-largest wine-producing country, and almost all the wine comes from California, which produces double the amount of Argentina, the world's fifth-largest wine-producing country.

That production is spread over a thousand wineries, and even though most people equate the words *California wine* with *Napa*, less than a third of the state's wineries are located there. (Around two hundred wineries are in Sonoma, and the rest are scattered all over the state—some as far south as the Mexican border.) Peter diligently wrote these facts in his notebook. Would he spring them on Spielberg sometime, I wondered, the way he had given Scorsese a volatilized-ester show?

Wine has been made in California for hundreds of years, but the modern era of California winemaking is widely considered to have started in 1976, the year the now famous Paris Tasting took place. The tasting had been organized by an English wine merchant, Steven Spurrier, then living in Paris. Spurrier pitted the top wines of California against some of the best Burgundies and Bordeaux in France and invited nine judges, all French, to taste the wines blind and deliver a verdict. (Spurrier later said he'd assumed the French wines would win.) Instead, two California wines, Château Montelena Chardonnay and Stags' Leap Winery Cabernet, took the top honors, and thanks to a reporter from *Time* who broke the story, the entire world took notice and the so-called golden era of California wine began.

The triumph in Paris begat a few decades' worth of experimentation as California winemakers set about figuring out what to do with their wines. In the beginning, a lot of them turned out wines that were too oaky, then they went the other way and made wines that were too high in acidity. About 1985, winemakers began to really get it right, making wines that were better balanced. They started to focus less on what happened in the winery and more on the vineyard. It all came together in the nineties, when the real boom in California wine began.

By the mid-1990s, the price of the most sought-after California wines had reached staggering levels as the "cult" Napa Cabs emerged—wines such as Screaming Eagle, Harlan Estate, Colgin Cellars, and Dalla Valle, with prices rivaling first-growth Bordeaux. Suddenly everyone with a few hundred million dollars seemed to want to be a vintner in Napa.

And the prospects looked promising: after all, every California vintage was great—1994, 1995, 1996, and the most hyped of all, 1997. Then everything changed. The 1998 vintage proved less than stellar, the next one was difficult, the next even worse. Prices dropped and people began to doubt what they'd taken for granted: Was every Napa Cabernet really worth $100 a bottle?

Other developments were taking place in other parts of California at the same time. Vineyards were being developed in promising new locations such as the coast of Sonoma and the Anderson Valley in Mendocino, as well as the Santa Rita Hills outside of Santa Barbara. And for the first time, California winemakers seemed to have figured out where to plant and to make Pinot Noir. (In fact, the rise of Pinot Noir may be the single greatest varietal triumph in California in the past twenty years.)

"Whenever I think of California, I think of Hitchcock," Peter offered in reply. "Many of the locations of Hitchcock movies — *The Birds, Shadow of a Doubt* — were in California. Hitchcock actually lived in Santa Rosa for a long time while he was making those movies. In fact, he set his most fiendish movies in Santa Rosa."

This was surprising news to me: Santa Rosa is a small town in the southern end of Sonoma whose only famous resident I'd ever heard of was Charles Schulz, creator of *Peanuts*. Had Peter ever visited Santa Rosa or Sonoma? Peter confessed he'd never been anywhere in California north of Los Angeles. "But," he added, "I'd like to go."

A ROAD TRIP IS PLANNED

It's an accepted truth that to truly understand a wine you must visit the place where it is made. And that the most iconic American wine region is Napa. What if I took Peter there? Not only would he gain a deeper understanding of wine, but maybe he'd even get over his fear of Cabernet Sauvignon.

"That's great," said Peter when I proposed the Napa excursion. "But I think we'll need a month at least." How about four days? I countered. "Done," Peter said.

Just because Peter and I decided to go to Napa isn't to say that other winemaking regions in California are not equally important. Before Peter and I embarked on our Napa adventure, he needed to learn something about the rest of the state too.

SONOMA

Sonoma County is bordered by the Pacific Ocean on the west and the Napa Valley on the east; it's probably the most diverse grape-growing region in the state. Several types of grapes grow here very, very well. (Other California regions may claim equal diversity, but Sonoma's top wines are consistently first-class.) Sonoma is a great region for Chardonnay as well as Pinot Noir (particularly in the Russian River Valley and the Sonoma Coast) and Zinfandel (some of the best Zinfandels in California come from Sonoma's Dry Creek Valley region). Good Cabernet is made in Sonoma too.

Peter seemed troubled, rather than pleased, that Sonoma winemakers did so much so well: "Is Sonoma's diversity really a good thing? Wouldn't it be better for Sonoma winemakers to be more like Napa producers, who are famous for one wine, Cabernet? Isn't there more money in specialization?"

It was an interesting notion, one I'd never considered before: diversity as a marketing drawback. I told Peter that I figured Sonoma winemakers were probably pretty happy to have all the options they had.

To give Peter a perspective on the breadth of Sonoma, I lined up a few of my favorite wines, starting with a Chardonnay from David Ramey, who makes Chardonnay from vineyards all over Sonoma. Ramey is considered one of California's top Chardonnay producers, although he also makes an acclaimed Napa Cabernet. Peter seemed to view this last fact as some sort of geographic betrayal.

"Why does he do that?" Peter asked. "If Ramey cares so much about Sonoma, why is he in Napa? Is he just hedging his bets? Or is his Napa wine just about money?"

Ramey is hardly the only California winemaker to make wine in different parts of the state—or for that matter, the world. In fact, it's quite commonplace. Some of the best California winemakers, such as Adam Lee of Siduri Wines and Wells Guthrie of Copain Cellars, don't even own vineyards at all but buy grapes from vineyards all over the state. If they get access to great grapes from the right place, good winemakers will want to see what they can produce regardless of where they're actually based.

Some winemakers, such as Paul Hobbs, who's based in Sonoma, make wine as far away as Argentina. Working in two hemispheres means two harvests a year. ("Twice as much money!" exclaimed Peter. "That's what it's all about!") Certainly Hobbs wasn't doing missionary work, but it was likely as much about the challenge of working in a different climate and place as it was the money. Peter just looked skeptical.

But a taste of Ramey's Chardonnay made him forget his money-grubbing charge. "I love this wine. It has layers and layers of flavor," he said.

I'd chosen Ramey's 2002 Russian River Chardonnay because it was not only a good example of Ramey's style—rich, unctuous fruit, backed by beautiful acidity and a mineral edge—but also of how good California Chardonnays can be when they're possessed not only of ripe fruit but finesse. "I want to know this guy Ramey," Peter declared. "You say he lives in Sonoma—do you think he knows anything about Hitchcock?"

Our next wine, the 2002 Merry Edwards Olivet Lane Pinot Noir, was also made in the Russian River region. Merry Edwards, like Ramey, was a winemaker for several different wineries before going out on her own. Her wines are quite elegant, though also quite rich. "This is one of the richest Pinots I've ever had," Peter declared. "Would I have to be on some sort of list to get this wine?"

In fact, Peter would have to be on a list, and not just to buy Merry Edwards's wines but just about any wines from a sought-after pro-ducer. Such wines can only be bought via the winery's mailing lists or by paying a premium in a handful of top restaurants.

"How do I get on her mailing list?" asked Peter. I suggested that he write Merry a letter describing how much he liked her wine. (While many producers, including Edwards, have waiting lists of people who want a spot on their mailing lists, a personal plea can't hurt. At least the producer will know how much you love his or her wine.) But when you write the letter, I said to Peter, do me a favor and don't mention Hitchcock.

Our next Sonoma wine was from the Dry Creek Valley, a warm region just north of the Russian River. Dry Creek wines are completely different from those of the Russian River—not just in style but in varietals too. Zinfandel is the most important grape grown in Dry Creek, and some of the vines there are over a hundred years old.

Accordingly, several top Zinfandel producers are located in Dry Creek, including the "three R's," as they're known: Ridge Vineyards, Rosenblum, and Rafanelli. One of my favorite Zin producers, Seghesio Vineyards, is also based in Dry Creek, where the Seghesio family has been growing Zinfandel for over a hundred years. The Seghesios make a remarkable range of wines—from single-vineyard bottlings to a basic Sonoma Zin that costs around $20 a bottle and is always a great value.

Zinfandel is the only grape in California whose vine age is regularly touted: some producers will cite the actual number of years (one hundred is the perennial favorite number) on their labels, while others simply proclaim that their wine is made from "old vines." (No one really mentions old-vine Cabernet, as it's often replanted and rarely attains such an old age.)

"There's such an exuberance to this wine it's hard to believe it comes from anything that's one hundred years old," Peter said approvingly of the 2003 Seghesio Sonoma Zinfandel I gave him.

Exuberance is the perfect word to describe the aromas and the flavors of a great Zinfandel, which run the gamut from black cherry to strawberry to black raspberry. There are also notes of pepper and spice—all of which are even more pronounced when the wine is made from old vines. And yet, for all its intensity, richness, and obvious appeal, Zinfandel is not considered a noble grape capable of producing a serious wine.

"Is Zinfandel nonnoble because it's so easy to like?" Peter wondered. "If that's the case, then I think noble grapes must be considered antipleasure."

I reminded Peter that his favorite grape, Chardonnay, was noble.

"But I still feel bad for the nonnoble grapes," Peter replied. Yet Peter admitted he couldn't find a lot of "complexity" in the Zinfandel, although he liked it a lot.

And yet he didn't admire the Zinfandel. "It doesn't have enough layers for me. Which I guess is what nobility means. And yet it's still perfectly pleasant. Could there be another category perhaps for grapes that give pleasure?"

I liked this idea of a new varietal subgroup: grapes that give pleasure. I considered other grapes that might fit. Zinfandel would certainly be at the top of the list. Maybe followed by Malbec, the star red grape of Argentina, and grapes such as Semillon, which give softness to Sauvignon Blanc in white Bordeaux, and of course Viognier, the lush, tropical white grape of the Rhône and a growing favorite among California producers.

Top Sonoma producers: Mark Aubert (Chardonnay), Merry Edwards (Pinot Noir), Martinelli (Zinfandel), Williams Selyem (Pinot Noir), Rochioli Vineyards (Pinot Noir, Sauvignon Blanc), Seghesio Vineyards (Zinfandel).

MORE THAT IS NOT NAPA

SANTA BARBARA

If Sonoma is first in terms of geographical diversity and varietal versatility, then Santa Barbara would probably (still) be at the top as California's most promising region. It's been up-and-coming for years. Indeed, more than two decades ago Santa Barbara's wine pioneers were boasting about their renegade status and how "un-Napa" they were. The region was (and mostly still is) fairly "unfancy"; that is, there aren't many wineries with gift shops or restaurants. But Santa Barbara is hardly undiscovered—thanks in no small measure to the movie *Sideways,* which has brought masses more tourists to the region, people who had probably never heard of any wine region but Napa before.

"Like me," Peter said.

There are two primary appellations in Santa Barbara: the newest is Santa Rita Hills, a cool region near the coast that is turning out some of the most interesting Syrahs and Pinot Noirs in the state, from producers such as Sea Smoke and Melville.

The Santa Maria Valley has been established many years longer than Santa Rita and is home to the region's most famous vineyard, Bien Nacido, which was actually planted several decades ago. At well over eight hundred acres, Bien Nacido may be the largest single vineyard in the entire United States. And yet it's a hard place to find. When I first visited Bien Nacido several years back, I expected to find road signs, perhaps even a billboard, pointing the way. What I found instead was a dirt road leading to an unmarked white shed and acres of the Bien Nacido vineyard beyond.

Two of Bien Nacido's most famous tenants, Au Bon Climat and Qupé, actually have wineries on the grounds of Bien Nacido (which, incidentally, has no winery of its own). Today dozens of wineries produce Bien Nacido–designated wines, but Qupé was the first to make Bien Nacido famous, with its Bien Nacido Vineyard Syrah.

Bob Lindquist, owner and winemaker of Qupé, was one of the first champions of California Syrah, although now Syrah is grown almost everywhere in the state and is considered nearly as important as Cabernet. It's hard to imagine that Lindquist and his fellow Syrah makers, once called "the Rhône Rangers," were considered quite radical twenty years ago.

I gave Peter the 2000 Qupé Bien Nacido Syrah, and he declared himself immediately impressed by the wine's aromas of herb, spice, and smoke—trademark Syrah notes—as well as its taste.

"It's not as aggressive as I thought a Syrah would be," Peter said, meaning tannic and hard. Part of this could have been the wine's age—tannins usually soften with time—and also the wine's terroir, that is, the place and the circumstances where it was made. The Bien Nacido vineyard lies in a valley whose climate is almost maritime—which means it has the moderating influence of ocean breezes and a longer, slower ripening period (wines from cool climates aren't as high-alcohol as wines made in warmer climes).

Other Rhône varietals besides Syrah grow well around Santa

Barbara—Grenache (Beckman Vineyards makes a particularly good one) and white Rhône varietals such as Roussanne, Marsanne, and Viognier. I'm a big fan of Santa Barbara Viognier, when it's made right. (Viognier can be a difficult grape to grow, and its many virtues—intense flavors, aromas, and richness—can easily turn to excess.) But a great Viognier, marked by notes of honeysuckle and flowers, is one of the wine world's aromatic wonders.

One of my favorite California Viogniers is made by the Santa Barbara–based producer Morgan Clendenen, who grew up in the same small North Carolina town as my father. But Morgan apparently liked her hometown even more than my dad did since she took the town's name (Morganton) as her own while my father's name is (still) just Ed.

Morgan is completely dedicated to Viognier and produces three wines under her Cold Heaven label. She also makes a wine called Deux C with Yves Cuilleron, a young Frenchman who is one of the top makers of Condrieu, the Viognier–based wine of the northern Rhône. The Viognier that they produce together is a perfect synthesis of California opulence and Gallic restraint. Peter, as I might have predicted, was a fan.

"I've never had a wine this rich before that isn't Chardonnay. It tastes like some exotic tropical fruit," Peter enthused. "I think my new favorite white grape is Viognier."

Some top Santa Barbara producers: Qupé Vineyards (Syrah), Au Bon Climat (Chardonnay), Brewer-Clifton (Pinot Noir), Jaffurs Wine Cellars (Syrah), Ojai (Pinot Noir), Sea Smoke (Pinot Noir).

Two More California Wine Regions

Mendocino

Another winemaking region in California is Mendocino, which has become particularly important in the past several years. A wide range of grapes are grown in Mendocino, but Syrah and Pinot Noir do particularly well—especially in the cool Anderson Valley. (One of the best

California sparkling wines, Roederer Estate, is made in Anderson Valley.) There's a bit of a cult around Anderson Valley Pinot Noir right now, and two of California's most talented young winemakers—Wells Guthrie (Copain Wine Cellars) and Eric Sussman (Radio-Côteau)—are making wines from Anderson Valley fruit.

There are also some good Syrahs and some full-flavored Zins made in the northern (much warmer) end of Mendocino in the Redwood Valley, but they aren't as sought-after as Mendocino Pinot. At least not yet.

Some notable Mendocino names: Edmeades (Zinfandel), Goldeneye (Pinot Noir), Lolonis (Zinfandel), Handley (Pinot Noir), Roederer Estate (sparkling wine), Radio-Côteau (Pinot Noir), Copain (Syrah, Pinot Noir).

Amador County

Amador County is the climatic opposite of Anderson Valley. Located in the foothills of the Sierras about an hour east of Sacramento, Amador County is easily one of the hottest wine regions in California. Once famous as Gold Rush country, it's now best known for men in cowboy hats, horses, and brawny, briary, high-alcohol wines, mostly Zinfandel and Petite Sirah (an oxymoronically monikered grape that produces big, tannic reds that are far from petite and no relation to Syrah).

Some notable Amador County names: Easton Wines, Montevina Wine, Terra Rouge.

PETER FACES HIS FEARS, OR FOUR DAYS IN THE NAPA VALLEY

While four days may not sound like a long time to spend in one of the greatest wine regions in the world, I'd never spent more than half an hour in a car with Peter before our Napa tour. Four days was as long as I could imagine traveling together and still remaining friends while also ensuring Peter received a proper education in Cabernet.

When I mentioned our upcoming trip to my friends, almost every one of them seemed to believe it would end in a fight. How could we spend four days tasting a wine that Peter doesn't like? they wanted to know. Some even predicted that Peter would refuse to drink Cabernet at all. Peter's wife, Robyn, told me, "Peter will make you crazy," though she offered no specifics as to his technique. Personally, I figured I could cope with almost anything—as long as Peter learned to love, or at least to drink, Cabernet.

Had people told Peter they expected us to fight? I asked him. He seemed surprised. "Not at all," he replied. "Everyone expects me to have a fabulous time.

"I just want to leave Oakland," Peter said, looking disconsolately out the car window after we'd collected our rental Ford in the airport parking lot. "It's gray and disgusting." I wasn't sure if Peter meant the day or the city, but I promised it would get better once our trip was under way. And when we turned off Interstate 80 onto Route 12 toward Napa, it did. The weather not only improved, but the view became, as Peter put it, a scene straight out of *Brigadoon.* The sun shone and the vineyards came into view. Soon some Disneyesque bluebirds would surely fly by, though if it were Brigadoon, grouse would have been the appropriate bird.

I asked Peter if he thought we would see Coppola. Peter had told the famous film director the dates of our Napa tour. "I don't know, he just sent me an e-mail and said that he might be around," Peter replied. "I gave him my cell phone number, but he hasn't called. I think he may be off shooting a movie in Romania somewhere."

Peter and I were on Highway 29, heading north to the town of St. Helena. The highway is the main north-south valley route, and it's usually crowded with cars, but since Peter and I were traveling in the middle of the week in the winter, traffic was light.

"Where are all the tourists?" Peter wondered. "I expected to see hundreds of cars on the road." On a summer weekend, I assured him, it could take an hour just to get from one town to the next.

Think New York City to the Hamptons in August. Peter said nothing; he was engrossed in taking photographs of the road.

Peter's photography reminded me of the way my sister and I would document our vacations from the backseat of the family car; nearly all our pictures seemed to include part of a car door. And, often as not, a few shots of the door handle too. Would Peter, I wondered, end up remembering Napa by the interior of our rental car?

Peter, however, insisted he wasn't photographing our Ford. "I'm taking pictures of Napa," he said, without taking the camera away from his eye as we passed Napa's famous (and admittedly dorky) welcome sign: a barrel carved with a bunch of grapes emblazoned with a quote from Robert Louis Stevenson: "Napa: . . . and the wine is bottled poetry." (Stevenson had stayed in the Napa Valley on his honeymoon in the late nineteenth century.) Had Peter seen the sign? He had not; he was too busy taking pictures of the highway on the other side.

"We'll be back," Peter declared. "I'll take a picture of the sign then."

Peter and I were booked into the Wine Country Inn, about a mile outside of St. Helena, surely the most charming town in Napa and consequently the most touristed. The inn is owned by the family of vintner Jeff Smith, who owns Hourglass Vineyard. Jeff Smith, forty-two, is a relative anomaly among Napa vintners today: he is a native, or near-native, son, having grown up in the valley. Smith has witnessed its change firsthand from a farming community with some vineyards to a Brigadoon for billionaires. Smith's father had moved his family from San Francisco to Napa when Jeff was only five, buying the inn on the advice of a friend. It was a bit risky: there weren't many other lodgings in Napa—or for that matter tourists—back then.

Today, of course, Napa is crowded with hotels and resorts, and the Wine Country Inn has long since been eclipsed in size (though not charm) by fancier places such as Meadowood and Auberge du Soleil. Smith's brother and sister now run the inn, and their mother lives nearby. Smith runs the vineyard, once planted to Zinfandel, now planted to Cabernet. When the vineyard was Zinfandel, his father didn't make wine; he just sold grapes. It was Jeff's idea to make wine, albeit many years later, in 1990, when his father died. Jeff asked his mother if he could take over the vineyard.

Smith—"Call me Jeff," he said to Peter—walked Peter and me out for a look at his vineyard. He'd named it Hourglass, Jeff explained, because the Napa Valley is roughly the shape of an hourglass, wide at each end and narrow in the middle. (The valley is about thirty miles long but only a few miles wide at its narrowest point.) "Our vineyard is right in the middle of the hourglass; therefore the name," Jeff explained. "We really knew it was a good name when we got a call from Gallo asking if they could buy it from us. We thought about it for a while because we really needed the money, but we figured that if Gallo wanted it so much, it had to be good."

Peter followed Jeff's gaze as the three of us stood facing east toward Howell Mountain. The sun was just beginning to set, washing the vineyard and the hills with gold, brown, and even lavender light.

"This is amazing," Peter said. "I don't know what I expected the Napa Valley to look like, but it looks even better than I could have imagined it."

Jeff nodded. "I wake up every day and say, 'How the hell did I get so lucky?'"

Not that any of it had happened easily. Jeff's mother hadn't given up control of the vineyard entirely willingly; she had to be convinced over a period of years by the combined forces of a famous enologist from UC-Davis (the top winemaking school in the country) and Jeff's boyhood friend Bob Foley (now a famous and sought-after wine consultant). Together, the two men told her the vineyard had the potential to make great Cabernet. So she finally relented and allowed Jeff to develop the vineyard as he pleased.

The result was a wine that has received some high praise and high scores from the critics—in short, a Napa fairy tale come true. Even though the first Hourglass vintage was 1998 (a rare bad vintage in Napa, one of the worst of the decade), it didn't affect the quality of the wine. More important, the winery, now in its ninth year, was finally turning a profit. And it had all happened by word of mouth.

"But how can you sell a wine like yours by word of mouth? Doesn't a fancy Napa wine have to be marketed?" Peter persisted.

"We don't have a marketing budget," Jeff confessed.

"No marketing plan?" Peter replied, shocked. "How can that be? There's hardly a movie made in Hollywood these days without a marketing budget almost as big as its production cost. If it takes fifty-five million dollars to make a movie, it costs thirty-five million dollars to market it. I figured in a place like Napa, since it's the Hollywood of wine, it was pretty much the same thing."

Jeff only laughed and held up his hands.

Then we walked back to the inn, where Jeff poured Peter and me glasses of Hourglass Cabernet, from two vintages, 1999 and the recently released 2002. Peter continued to talk about the high costs of marketing movies. "*King Kong* cost 207 million to make and 60 million to market!" Peter exclaimed. "Isn't that insane?" He couldn't seem get over that Jeff got away without marketing his wine at all.

"We're small enough that we can," explained Jeff, sounding more surprised than smug. "We've gotten some good response from some important people." He means he's gotten some very good scores from the wine critic Robert Parker, I said to Peter in an aside. That may be the only marketing plan a small Napa winery needs—it's certainly an important factor in determining its success or failure. "I'd like to meet this fellow Parker," said Peter. "As critics, I think we'd have a lot to discuss."

I watched as Peter picked up his first glass of Hourglass Cabernet, looking remarkably comfortable, as if it were a glass of fatty Chardonnay. He even managed to swirl it a bit on the table before tasting it.

"It's delicious," Peter declared. Then he tried the 2002 wine, as did Jeff, who pronounced it "shut down." Peter looked into his glass. This was a new expression to him. How did a wine "shut down"? Was it something that had happened in Jeff's car on the way to the inn? Or was it a storage problem? Jeff shook his head. He didn't understand how it had happened either. The 2002 Hourglass had been a lot more accessible than the 1999 just a few hours ago. It didn't make sense. But wine is a living thing and therefore unpredictable. Sometimes a wine can just close down for no reason at all.

"What happens when a wine shuts down?" Peter wanted to know.

Everything becomes muted and the wine will taste tight and compressed, I told him.

Peter looked alarmed. "How can you stop that from happening?"

Unfortunately, you can't. It's just what happens to some wines in a certain stage of their evolutionary development—it usually occurs in a wine's early middle age. (Five to seven years of age seems like the typical time that this happens to many wines.)

"But what if you bought a wine for some special occasion and when you opened the bottle, it was shut down? Could you ask for your money back?" Peter persisted. I noticed that as we were talking Peter had been drinking, not tasting, the wine and appeared quite content. Could his Cabernet conversion actually happen that easily? With the very first taste of the trip?

The next morning I discovered Peter in the entryway of the hotel, taking pictures of a couch. They're going to mistake you for a claims adjuster, I said to him as he took one picture after another of the furniture. Why are you taking so many pictures? Why don't you save your film for the wineries and the winemakers? "It's a digital camera," Peter replied. "And besides, I want to document every moment of our time."

There would be a lot more for Peter to photograph: I had scheduled three busy days, arranging for Peter to meet some of the Napa people I admired the most—not just for their wines but because they represent the best of Napa to me. (Since Peter and I only had a few days, there were plenty of other winemakers I like that we didn't visit. When I mentioned this to Peter, he suggested that we do a sequel: Napa Part Two.)

HARLAN ESTATE: A 100-POINT LUNCH

Our first meeting that morning was with Bill Harlan and his team at Harlan Estate, winemaker Bob Levy and general manager Don Weaver. Harlan is possibly the most acclaimed winery in Napa today, thanks primarily to the single-minded vision of Bill Harlan, a slight, bearded man (who looks like a prosperous, two-eared Vincent van Gogh), and his winemaking team. Harlan is not only a visionary in the world of wine who decided some twenty years ago to create what he calls "a first growth Cabernet," he's also a powerful real estate developer who has built properties all over California, including Meadowood, Napa's first luxury resort.

But Harlan, whom I've known for several years, isn't interested in just money and real estate (though he has plenty of both). He's also something of a philosopher, determined to leave a lasting legacy for his children with his winery. Harlan is a fairly serious man, so I was hoping Peter wouldn't say something like what he had to Jeff Smith the day before ("I don't really consider what you do to be work").

Peter and I were late because Peter insisted on stopping several times to take pictures. Once we reached Harlan Estate, Peter must have taken two dozen pictures of the view. Then, of course, the view from Harlan—high above the valley floor—is one of the best that money can buy.

Like most of the "cult" Napa wineries, Harlan Estate is located in the hills not far from Mount Veeder rather than on the valley floor. Harlan was one of the first Napa vintners to recognize that better wines were produced on the hillsides. Earlier pioneers such as Robert Mondavi had planted on the floor of the valley in part because it was more fertile and easier to cultivate. It was also a better position for tourism; it's much easier for a bus to turn off Highway 29 than it is to navigate the steep and winding Oakville Grade. But grapes like Cabernet do better in soils where they have to struggle— as they do in the poor soils of the steep hillsides. Today almost every great Napa Cabernet comes from hillside vineyards.

"We wanted to be on the hillside but not too far out," Harlan explained to Peter. "There were just forests here at the time, and twenty years ago, building on hillsides was a high-risk proposition. But this isn't a business of instant gratification, it's a business of generations. Real validation takes layers and layers of time. If you look at businesses that have lasted hundreds of years, they're based on land and they're family-owned."

"It's like the studio system," offered Peter. "When they started movie studios, they were all family-owned: Warner Bros., Paramount, Fox—the studios we know today were started by families." Harlan looked at Peter with surprise. He didn't know that. Perhaps Peter could hold his own with Napa's winemaking elite after all. Until, that is, he began tasting wine.

Bob Levy, a man in his late forties who said little but had a scholarly air, gave Peter a brief overview of the Harlan winemaking methods (small fermentation tanks, tables where the grapes were sorted by hand). But perhaps most exciting for Peter was when Levy gave him his first look at some real French oak barrels.

Peter was completely taken up by the subject of oak, and Levy seemed more than happy to oblige on a topic that so clearly fascinated them both.

"The trees that these barrels are made from are between 125 to 150 years old," Levy said to Peter, gesturing to one of the hundreds of barrels in the impeccable winery. "They come from government-managed French forests dating from the time of Napoléon. The coopers we use will actually go into the forest and select the trees they're interested in; then they bid on them in an auction."

Peter nodded appreciatively. "I'd love to go to one of those auctions."

Levy nodded. "It's fascinating."

They both nodded and it was time for lunch.

Lunch came accompanied by two vintages of Harlan Estate wine: the newly released 2002 vintage (an excellent vintage) and the legendary 1996 (a great year for both Napa and Harlan). Whether he realized it or not, Peter was about to taste two wines that most wine drinkers can only dream about or at least have to pay a lot of money to drink. Anyone who doesn't hold a place on the long-sold-out Harlan Estate mailing list (where the wine is currently priced at $275 a bottle) will have to pay thousands of dollars for the same wine in a restaurant. Peter was blissfully unaware of his privileged state.

The Harlan wines are as exquisite an expression of Cabernet as I've ever experienced—classic aromas of black currant, smoke, and lead pencil in a ripe, concentrated, and lush New World–style wine. Robert Parker gave the 1996 vintage of Harlan 98 points and a resounding 100 points to the 2002, proclaiming, "It literally has everything one could ever want in a great Cabernet Sauvignon–based wine." How could these wines not convince Peter of the greatness of Cabernet?

But Peter didn't appear to be tasting either wine. Instead, he was, well, drinking them. First one and then the other as if they were just wines poured at some Tuesday-night film screening. I overheard him telling Harlan about a recent dinner with George Clooney. "George said to me that the second and third stages of your career define who you are, and once you attained a certain level of achievement, you have a responsibility to the world," Peter said. Bill Harlan nodded at this bit of Clooney wisdom.

I wondered if Harlan was thinking he'd give George Clooney a call, maybe chat over their respective ideas about larger responsibilities in the world, or was he perhaps thinking he'd offer Clooney a spot on the Harlan mailing list, since according to Peter, Clooney liked wine, however, as Peter had noted before, he didn't go much beyond "white" or "red."

Suddenly Peter burst out, "Everyone is so silent—why hasn't anyone said, 'This wine is fabulous!'" and with that he promptly drained his glass of the 1996 wine. (The 2002 was already gone.) Bill Harlan, whose glasses were both almost as full as mine, looked amused, though I noted Bob Levy had drained his glass of 1996 too.

"Why didn't you drink more of those Harlan wines? They were amazing!" Peter exclaimed as we drove away, headed east across the valley to Dalla Valle Vineyards, our next stop. I didn't want to get picked up by the Napa police, I replied. Jeff Smith had described how the local authorities were cracking down. They'd even invented a new category of offense just below DWI called "wet and reckless," which meant that while you weren't officially drunk, you were "borderline." This happens with as little as half a glass of wine, according to Jeff. I didn't want to be thrown into a squad car with the label "wet and reckless" attached to my name. Peter said he wouldn't mind. In fact, he kind of liked the idea. But drinking all the wines didn't make any sense, I reminded Peter. He wouldn't remember any of the wines if he didn't spit. Peter didn't answer; he was asleep.

DALLA VALLE VINEYARDS: WET AND RECKLESS

Naoko Dalla Valle may be the most elegant and gracious woman in Napa; she exudes a contentment and serenity I think she would even if she weren't the proprietor of one of Napa's most famous wineries, with an incredible view. Naoko's winery and house are every bit as dramatically sited as Harlan Estate—high in the hills, facing west. (Dalla Valle also has a following nearly as fanatical as Harlan's and a mailing list with a similarly long wait.)

Naoko and her late husband, Gustav, arrived in Napa nearly three decades ago, intending to open a hotel and spa. Their real estate agent was Jean Phillips, the founder and (until recently) owner of the acclaimed winery Screaming Eagle. Peter and I were also trying to meet Jean Phillips, but she was proving every bit as elusive as Francis Ford Coppola.

Jean Phillips had suggested Naoko and Gustav look at a house in the hills while they pursued their idea of creating an inn. The house Phillips suggested came with five acres of Zinfandel and a sweeping view of the valley. Gustav liked the idea of growing grapes, so they kept buying land and finally, almost inadvertently, ended up with ten acres and some of the choicest parcels for Cabernet in all of Napa. The winery's flagship bottling, Maya (named after Naoko's daughter), actually comes from a vineyard that Dalla Valle purchased for the price of an RV—something the vineyard's owner apparently prized more than his grapes. "That was the steal of the century. But no one really knows about that deal," Naoko said, laughing. Peter just stared. I could tell he was charmed; either that or he was simply awed by Naoko's bargaining skills.

"The first ten years we made no money," Naoko continued. "And we didn't start making money until 1995, the year my husband died. That was also the vintage that our wine Maya got ninety-

two points from Robert Parker." Peter tried to look simultaneously sad and impressed. Ninety-two points! Robert Parker! Now,
at least, he knew what that meant. "Those days you were lucky if
you could charge twenty-five dollars a bottle," Naoko continued as
we sat down to taste the four vintages of Maya that Naoko had chosen: 1996, 1997, 1998, and 2002.

The wines were elegant yet intense. Peter praised them effu-
sively.

Naoko deflected his praise with predictable grace. "You'll have to
come back and have dinner another time."

"I'd like that very much. Or maybe I can just live here?" Peter
replied, staring out at the valley.

Naoko, ever gracious, just nodded as if she were accustomed to
people demanding to move in to her house. "Sometime, I'm sure."

MEADOWOOD AND A SARTORIAL REVELATION

Dalla Valle, in Oakville, is just a few miles down the Silverado Trail
from Meadowood resort. (The Silverado Trail runs north and south,
virtually parallel to Highway 29, but it is a much more scenic, less
congested drive.) Since we had a few minutes before our next
appointment, I thought Peter should have a look at Bill Harlan's
other Napa enterprise, Meadowood, a place that is more or less synonymous with Napa-style luxury. A large, wooded compound of
cottages built into the hills of Howell Mountain and centered
around a pool, Meadowood also has a golf course and a
championship-quality croquet field. Created more than twenty-
five years ago, Meadowood was the first of the great luxury Napa
resorts.

As we wandered around Meadowood's perfectly manicured
grounds, Peter mused, "So far, no one I've met is unhappy with
their lives. I'm not used to that. It's not like New York. In a way,
this is the most surprising thing about Napa to me."

Peter was also surprised by Napa attire. "Napa people have a certain casual nonchalance that I didn't expect. I think it all starts with

a vest. Everyone we've met with so far has worn a vest. If I'm going to get a true sense of what it means to be from Napa, I'll need a vest."

Peter was tasting some of the best Napa Cabernets from the region's top winemakers, and all he could think about were the clothes that they wore? If a vest was all Peter needed to care about Cabernet, I would happily buy one for him. When I said this to him, he replied, "I don't want you to buy me my vest. I'm happy to buy it myself. In fact, I'd spend up to four hundred dollars to look like a man from Napa."

For a vest? I was sure that even Bill Harlan didn't spend that much on his.

THE SPLENDOR OF SPOTTSWOODE

By the time we reached our next stop, Spottswoode winery, in St. Helena, Peter seemed to have forgotten about vests, even though Beth Novak Milliken of Spottswoode was wearing one too. But Peter's attention was diverted, at least temporarily, by the beauty of Spottswoode—and the Novak women, Beth and her mother, Mary.

Spottswoode is an anomaly among Napa Valley wineries: a beautiful Victorian-era estate actually set within the town limits of St. Helena. The centerpiece of the winery is a 1882 manor home surrounded by gardens and vineyards where Mary, an elegant woman in her seventies, still lives; Beth and her family live nearby. Peter asked me to take his photograph with Mary on her front porch.

As they posed together, I overheard Peter tell Mary, "Jack Nicholson once told me, 'I need a bottle of Scotch and a meatball wedge to sit for any photographer.'" Mary appeared to be charmed by the tale; Peter closed in for the kill. "Do you think I could move into your house for a while?"

"Don't forget you're going to be spending six months with Susana Balbo in Argentina," I reminded Peter, who seemed to be turning his wine education into a quest for a second home.

"I could live six months here and six months in Argentina," he replied. "I would be like those winemakers who split their time between two hemispheres."

The Novak family moved to Napa in 1972 when "land prices were really low," according to Mary. They bought their house, along with forty-five acres of land, as a hobby and retirement for Mary's husband, John, a physician. But John Novak died of a heart attack a few years after they arrived, and Mary and her daughters took over the running of the winery. Today, along with winemaker Rosemary Cakebread, they turn out some of Napa's most polished Cabernets as well as a terrific Sauvignon Blanc.

"Isn't that odd? That they can make both red and white wines in the same place?" Peter wondered. "I didn't even know they made white wine in Napa." In fact, it's not uncommon for a top Napa producer to make an excellent Sauvignon Blanc and a great Cabernet—after all, they do the same in Bordeaux. In regions like Pessac-Léognan, famous châteaux such as Haut-Brion and La Mission Haut-Brion make Sauvignon Blanc blends that are almost as acclaimed as their reds, I reminded Peter. He nodded, but clearly Peter had forgotten all about Bordeaux now that he'd found a new love in Napa Cabernet.

Other Napa wineries besides Spottswoode make great Sauvignon Blanc and Cabernet too: four of my favorites (in no particular order) are Rudd Estate, Cakebread Cellars, Duckhorn Vineyards, and Araujo Estate.

Beth and Rosemary arranged for Peter and me to taste their Sauvignon Blanc as well as half a dozen Spottswoode Cabernets, dating back to 1987. This was as much a privilege for me as it was for Peter, as Napa Cabernets nearly twenty years old aren't that easy to find. They don't often show up on restaurant wine lists (except in steak houses, where they tend to be pricey). Peter was amazed they existed at all.

"I didn't even know Napa Cabs could age," he said.

A great Napa Cabernet in a top vintage can age well, gaining in complexity and depth. But only a handful of wines have been made for long enough to have a real track record of several decades or more. Beringer Vineyards, along with a few others such as Phelps and Château Montelena, have produced ageworthy wines for thirty years. But the older Spottswoode Cabernets were impressive, particularly the 1994 bottling, which was still firm and full of life. The younger wines were rich and intense, particularly the 2002, which Robert Parker had described as the winery's "best effort yet."

"I thought every one of those wines was an experience," said Peter to Beth when she asked his opinion of what we had tasted.

Peter, though still lacking the technical terms to describe what he found in his glass, had unwittingly grasped one of the crucial facts of tasting a wine, especially a wine with history attached. It wasn't just a matter of finding the right adjectives, the right fruit names, cherries and blackberries, and spice and wood, but of locating the wine's place in the larger context in the world. That is, the 1994 Spottswoode Cabernet was as much a look back at a different era in Napa as it was a wine. It was a marker of a time when not only the winemaking was different (e.g., the technology was less sophisticated, the grapes were harvested when much less ripe), but the Valley was too—a slower, less commercial, less trafficked place. All of that, it seemed, could be found in the wine.

As we said our good-byes, Peter paused to ask Beth what she thought about Coppola and his wines. Did she know him? Beth ventured that he seemed nice but he wasn't around much. "We were hoping to see him while we were in Napa, but he's filming in Romania. He hasn't called us," Peter said, adding wistfully, "I hope he will."

But we can visit Coppola's winery, I reminded Peter. My friend Larry Stone had recently been named Rubicon Estate's general manager (the winery had changed its name from Niebaum-Coppola to Rubicon Estate), and Larry had offered to give us a tour.

"It's not the same thing as Francis," said Peter dolefully. He'd told Beth the story of his lunch with Coppola, when Coppola had told Peter he couldn't drink wine or he "would become sleepy or affectionate or both." Beth seemed charmed by this anecdote, which meant that Peter's Hollywood stories impressed people more than I realized, or that the women at Spottswoode were just very polite.

THE SEARCH FOR COPPOLA AND A BIG SURPRISE
ALONG THE WAY

By the next day, Coppola still hadn't called (was he in Romania or not?) nor, for that matter, had Jean Phillips of Screaming Eagle. Peter and I did have our appointment with Larry Stone, who had assumed directorship of Rubicon Estate the week before. Larry is a small and always sharply attired man (who usually sports a bow tie). He is one of the most famous sommeliers in the United States; in fact, Larry had worked with Coppola for years as the wine director of Rubicon restaurant in San Francisco. He was also the first man we'd met in Napa who wasn't wearing a vest.

"Maybe it's because he just started the job and he hasn't had time to get his wardrobe together," speculated Peter.

Rubicon Estate is one of the oldest wineries in Napa Valley; it was built in 1879 by a Finnish sea captain, Gustave Niebaum, and later became the home of the Inglenook Winery, which was legendary in the 1940s. By the time Coppola bought it some fifty years later, the winery was well into a decline. Coppola spent about $10 million upgrading the old stone château and expanding the vineyards. The result is grand in a Hollywood movie-set sort of way, a sort of historical ideal of a winery.

Until recently, a large amount of the winery's floor space was devoted to its gift shop—considered one of the best in Napa. (Coppola has a staff dedicated to tracking down some spoon or sauce or clock that he's discovered while traveling.) While this all sounds whimsical, the men and women working in the gift shop the day Peter and I arrived seemed quite sober. Attired all in black, they looked more like the staff of a particularly posh funeral home. They circled around Peter and me as we roamed around the cavernous space, peering into cases filled with expensive corkscrews, clothing, and Coppola movies. And pasta sauce. One black-clad woman asked Peter if he was interested in trying a pasta sauce. (Unbeknownst to us at the time, all the attendants and pasta sauces would soon be gone—transferred to the old Souverain winery in Sonoma that Coppola had recently bought.) There wasn't anything Peter wanted to buy in the gift shop. "There wasn't anything that said 'Francis' to me." Not even a vest.

Peter's mood lifted when Larry led us to a room upstairs for a tasting of the Cask Cabernet, one of the winery's best-known wines, second only to the winery's flagship wine, Rubicon. (Coppola actually makes quite a few other wines, including a line of relatively inexpensive, commercial Coppola wines that he is now producing out of his winery in Sonoma.) But Rubicon is his bid for the Napa big time. The 2002 Rubicon that Peter and I tasted, a blend of Cabernet Sauvignon, Cabernet Franc, and Merlot, was a surprisingly soft and supple wine. It was delicious and well made.

"But was it great?" Peter wanted to know. Peter was such a big fan of Coppola's movies, he wanted his wine to be great too. Yet the Rubicon just didn't impress him the way the Harlan Estate had. "It just doesn't seem as profound."

Although Coppola was apparently in Romania, Peter and I still hoped to meet with Jean Phillips, of Screaming Eagle (which she sold a few months after our visit—for, some have speculated, as much as $30 million). Jean had sent me a fax a few weeks before saying she wasn't sure if she'd be in town. But, she added, if she wasn't, she could leave us a bottle of wine. A bottle of Screaming Eagle? Did Peter have any idea what that meant? Had he ever heard of Screaming Eagle? He had not.

Screaming Eagle is one of the original Napa cult Cabernets, if not the ultimate cult wine—an ultrarich, concentrated Cabernet made in a tiny amount, sometimes as little as a few hundred cases. It's sold almost entirely to mailing-list customers and usually later resold for thousands of dollars. (For example, only two hundred cases were made of the first vintage of Screaming Eagle, and a bottle of that wine is now worth close to $4,000.)

I'd tried to meet Jean Phillips over the years, but she'd proven as elusive as her wine. She was traveling or busy with one thing or another—harvest, pruning, replanting—although her faxes were an artful study in polite rejection. On one occasion several years ago, I'd actually thought we might meet, but Phillips left behind a character-istically polite note and a bottle of Screaming Eagle instead.

"But what was the wine like?" Peter persisted. "And what makes people pay so much for it? Was it really amazing?" It was a beauti-fully made wine, I recalled, with incredible balance and finesse. What struck me the most was its aroma—one of the most unusual I'd ever found in a Napa Cabernet: billowing, exotic notes of sandal-wood and spice. But why people wanted it so much they'd pay $4,000 for a single bottle was hard to say. That sort of madness was-n't about wine anyway.

"Do you think Jean Phillips will leave a bottle in some secret loca-tion for us if she doesn't actually show up herself?" Peter asked. He liked that idea; it sounded like something out of a mystery novel. I couldn't say. In some ways, Phillips reminded me of Harper Lee, the woman who wrote one remarkable book, *To Kill a Mockingbird*, and then disappeared. She didn't do magazine interviews or television talk shows or, for that matter, write the sequel, *To Kill a Mocking-bird Two*. Her mystery, like that of Jean Phillips, remained intact.

At the end of our second day, when Peter and I returned to the Wine Country Inn, I got a call from Peter in the room next door. "There's a package here with your name on it," he said. "It looks like a bottle. The return address says Jean Phillips."

I ran to Peter's room and opened the package, pausing to read the note inside. *I'm sorry not to be able to meet with you and Peter,* Jean Phillips wrote. *But I had hoped that a bottle of my first vintage, 1992, might give Peter an idea of the wine and perhaps a better understand-ing of Napa Cabernet.* Phillips noted that the wine had been awarded 99-plus points by Robert Parker. *I took this to mean you go, girl, you can do better,* she wrote, and added that she thought Peter and I "deserved" it for all of our hard work in Napa.

"That's a lovely note," Peter said. It's an amazing present, I replied. Then the same terrified thought struck Peter and me at precisely the same time: How would we get our bottle back to New York? Or, more important, which of us was going to be responsible for it? "I'm not carrying it," Peter said immediately. "I'll carry the box, but I don't want the responsibility of a four-thousand-dollar bottle of wine."

While the separation of box from bottle didn't make any sense, it was decided that I should take the bottle and Peter the box. We fitted both carefully into the trunk of our rental car for the last day's drive around Napa. We had a few visits remaining, including lunch at Beringer Vineyards with winemaker Ed Sbragia, or, as Peter called him, "Big Ed."

PETER AND BERINGER'S BIG MAN

Founded in the 1870s by two German brothers, Beringer is one of the oldest wineries in Napa, located just outside St. Helena. ("Is everything located just outside St. Helena?" asked Peter, and in fact, sometimes it seems that it is.) But Beringer is the most famous St. Helena winery, a Napa Valley landmark with possibly Napa's most popular winery tour. (It certainly attracts fun-loving types; whenever I've been in the Beringer tasting room, I've been surrounded by raucous, laughing crowds. Was it simple joie de vivre, I wondered, or Beringer White Zinfandel?)

Beringer's most famous wine is, in fact, white Zinfandel, which accounts for much of the company's 3 million–plus case production. They also make many prestigious wines, including several single-vineyard Cabernets and Merlots, all highly sought after and much acclaimed, thanks in no small part to Ed Sbragia, who has directed Beringer's winemaking for nearly three decades. Sbragia is synonymous with the Beringer name.

Ed Sbragia made the wine that Peter had fallen in love with during one of our lessons—one of the biggest, richest, oakiest Chardonnays he'd ever had: the Beringer Ed Sbragia Private Reserve. Ever since tasting that wine, it was Peter's greatest wish to meet the man who had made it. "It's like meeting a director of a film I admire," Peter explained.

Ed Sbragia, a large, bearded man with a flushed face and an open, friendly demeanor, makes large-scale wines in his own image—rich and powerful, with a heavy dose of oak. When Peter and I pulled into the Beringer parking lot (already crowded with cars at 11 a.m.), he told me he was nervous at the prospect of finally meeting Sbragia in person.

"What if I don't like him?" Peter fretted. "It will ruin the wine for me; I won't be able to think about his wine in the same way. And I really like that Chardonnay." As Peter was saying this, I spotted Ed Sbragia ahead. Too late, I told Peter, Ed is less than ten feet away.

"I just checked myself out of the hospital so we could have lunch," Ed Sbragia said by way of a greeting. It was certainly a memorable opening line. But Ed wasn't kidding; in fact, he was still wearing a hospital bracelet (along with a green Beringer Vineyards vest).

"You're scaring me, Ed," Peter replied.

"It was nothing," said Ed, waving his hand. "Just a little shortness of breath. I even drove myself over from Sonoma. I wouldn't have missed this lunch for anything." (Exactly what Peter's winemaking god should say.)

Thirty minutes into lunch, I realized that Ed and Peter would become friends when Peter admitted his fear of Cabernet, and Ed, in turn, confessed, "*Jurassic Park* scared the crap of me." (Ed had been about thirty years old at the time he saw the movie.) Soon enough, Ed began opening wines, including a bottle of the 2001 Private Reserve Chardonnay that Peter had declared "the *Citizen Kane*" of wine. At that, Ed mentioned how his son Adam, at age twenty-two, had thought he wanted to be a movie star (but later decided to join his father in the family winemaking project in Sonoma, where Ed also makes his own wine).

"Ed's amazing," Peter said to me later. "But he's just one of the remarkable people we've met, and his wines were just some of the extraordinary wines we tasted; it's all been so much more than I ever thought it would be. But, I can't believe after all this time in Napa I don't have a vest."

A Sartorial Emergency Stop

We were driving down the Silverado Trail when Peter was lamenting his lack of a vest. Quite a few wineries are along Silverado, but they are less tourist-oriented than the wineries on Highway 29. In other words, there aren't many places to buy vests.

And we were late for our appointment with an old friend of mine, Carl Doumani, who once owned Stags' Leap Winery, before he sold it to Beringer and built a small winery next door that he called Quixote. Carl is a well-known figure in the valley for a number of reasons, most famously for his long-running feud with Warren Winiarski of Stags' Leap Wine Cellars over the name Stags' Leap. It was finally resolved sometime in the late seventies, and according to Carl, the two are now friends, or at least friendly acquaintances. Carl has lived in the Napa Valley almost forty years. Carl, I knew, would be wearing a vest.

I drove past the entrance to Carl's winery toward Silverado Vineyards. Founded by the daughter of Walt Disney in 1981, Silverado is not a superstar winery but produces some solid wines (Silverado Cabernet is a particularly popular steak-house wine), and I knew I could buy Peter a vest there.

Peter and I tasted several of the Silverado wines (we both liked the special Cabernet called Solo), and Peter noted the view. Even the least-distinguished winery in Napa, he noticed, has something to look at. (While Peter was gazing at the scenery, I bought him a vest— for much less than $400, incidentally.)

"I really wanted a Harlan vest, but I guess this will do," Peter said, fingering—rather ungraciously, I thought—the blue fleece Silverado garment I'd just bought him.

We drove back to Carl's for a cappuccino and a talk about Petite Sirah (a grape that Carl makes well at his winery, Quixote, and that he helped to make famous when he owned Stags' Leap next door). Then it was time to hit the road. This time we drove out of Napa, south toward the Oakland airport and our flight back to New York.

Peter was in a contemplative mood. There were still things about Napa he didn't understand. Such as their focus on Cabernet. And the importance of hillside vineyards. Not to mention their curious attraction to vests. But there was more that Peter hoped to discuss.

He was incredibly impressed by all that the winemakers were able to do. "They worry about weather all the time," Peter noted. "And it's not like any of them sets out to make a bad wine, just like nobody sets out to make a bad movie—except maybe Oliver Stone. Yet unlike movie directors, there are so many variables beyond a winemaker's control. But no one I've met in Napa seems like Oliver Stone at all. Everyone has been incredibly gracious and kind. I don't think anyone who isn't an interesting, decent person can make a great wine. Unlike the movies, when a real SOB can make a great movie. But these people are doing what they want to do with their lives, unlike in New York, where it seems like everyone is just looking for a way to escape."

Yet Peter still did not comprehend one thing about Napa. "Why do they sell so many hats in winery tasting rooms? Why don't they sell more vests instead?"

A few Napa greats (Cabernet Sauvignon producers whom Peter and I particularly loved): Beringer Vineyards, Dalla Valle Vineyards, Harlan Estate, Hourglass, Quixote Winery (not Cabernet, of course, but great Petite Sirah), Spottswoode Winery, Screaming Eagle.

OTHER NAPA GREATS PETER DIDN'T GET TO MEET

Although Peter and I visited some of the best Cabernet producers in the state of California (and arguably the world), we didn't get a chance to visit quite a few others on our too short Cabernet tour. The following also make topflight wines: Araujo Estate, Colgin Cellars, Pride Mountain, Shafer Vineyards, Seavey Vineyard.

THE NIGHT
THE EAGLE LANDED

Once Peter and I got our bottle of Screaming Eagle safely home, we immediately began discussing when and where (and who) should drink it. The company was the biggest question of all. Who would really appreciate what it meant to drink a bottle of 1992 Screaming Eagle? Who really deserved a glass of our wine? When I mentioned our dilemma to my friends in the wine business who knew how much the bottle was worth ($4,000), they told me to sell it and take another trip instead. You could go back to Napa, said one friend. Take a trip to Burgundy, suggested another. Peter was present for this last piece of advice and said, "Burgundy would be nice."

We were absolutely drinking the Eagle, I replied. It was a gift. How could Peter entertain the notion of selling it? And what would we say to Jean Phillips?

"But just think—we could see Burgundy together!" exclaimed Peter, quickly adding, "I'm just kidding, of course."

After several months of wrangling over dates (no New Yorker ever agrees on a date right away; it's as much a matter of pride as scheduling), Peter and I ultimately decided to invite my friend Jeff, whom I called the Collector, and his wife, Pat, who, fortunately, preferred white to red wine. "Pat won't really care about drinking the Eagle. She'll probably only have a tiny taste," Peter said confidently, sounding awfully possessive about a bottle he'd been willing to sell to finance a trip to France.

The Collector was agreeable, though he hardly seemed overwhelmed by our offer. He was, after all, the Collector, which meant he'd already had every great wine, several times over. "It's a nice wine," the Collector said, "but I'll bring something too. A backup wine." A backup bottle for Screaming Eagle? How insulting was that?

On the appointed Night of the Eagle, as Peter and I called it, the Collector arrived, bearing a bottle of 1989 Chapoutier Hermitage, a great Rhône red from a famous producer and a great vintage. I was about to point this out to Peter when the Collector remarked, before putting his bottle down, "I don't usually like this wine, but I brought it along anyway."

We started the evening with a bottle of 2005 Garcés Silva Sauvignon Blanc, one of my favorite Chilean Sauvignon Blancs. I'd just visited Chile a few weeks before and had been impressed with the Garcés Silva wines. Peter and I admired the wine's flavor, its nuance, its mineral finish, while the Collector declared it "not as good as the Terrunyo I had in Puerto Rico," naming another Chilean Sauvignon Blanc. The Collector was nothing if not competitive.

"We saw *The Constant Gardener* the other night," the Collector said to Peter. "Did you like it?"

"I thought it was provocative," Peter replied.

"I thought it was over-the-top," said the Collector. "I hated it."

The evening wasn't getting off to a particularly auspicious start. Perhaps Peter and I should have cashed in the bottle and gone to Burgundy instead.

Yet nothing is more exhilarating, or frankly more terrifying, than opening a bottle of much-prized wine. From the act of pulling the cork (hoping it won't crumble or break in two) to actually tasting the wine (hoping it won't be corked or over-the-hill). Peter and I stood over our Eagle in a collective pose of supplication.

"Let it be good," Peter intoned in what I thought of as his Cabernet Prayer.

Then I poured us each a glass. "Oh my God, it's really, really good," Peter declared as he took a sip. "I thought there was no way it was going to be as good as our anticipation of it," he added, taking a bigger mouthful. "But it is. It simply . . . resonates."

"It smells like a young Burgundy," offered the Collector, who pushed his glass forward for more.

"Do you realize that no one in the country is drinking a Screaming Eagle that's older than ours?" Peter asked suddenly.

"Well, you'll never know unless one of us spends four thousand dollars to find out," the Collector replied.

The Screaming Eagle meal itself was a pretty simple affair, just ham with sweet potatoes and a salad—nothing that would distract from the wine. "I wouldn't have thought ham," the Collector mused when the ham was served. Was that a criticism? I wondered, bristling a bit. (In fact, ham was the perfect slightly salty, fairly neutral background that a wine as complex as the Eagle required.) After all, as the Collector had observed, the Screaming Eagle not only smelled but tasted a bit like a Burgundy more than a Cabernet: it was that subtle—and therefore delicious with something as simple as ham.

When the bottle of Eagle was nearly empty, Peter turned to me. "I didn't think this wine could possibly live up to all of the hype, and yet it's one of the most . . . alive wines I've ever had. Usually when you anticipate something, it's a disappointment. But not this. It was an absolutely perfect wine."

Peter was right. There was no disappointment for either of us that night. Was it because the wine was magnificent or was it the thought of Jean Phillips and her incredible generosity? Or was it maybe even more than Jean or her wine? Perhaps it was that together they were a symbol of all that Peter had learned. Peter stared into his almost empty glass and cleared his throat. I turned expectantly.

"I wonder," Peter mused, "if Ed Sbragia has ever had a bottle of Screaming Eagle before."

PETER AT LARGE
IN THE WINE WORLD,
OR
PETER GOES PUBLIC

❧

PETER AT THE ZACHYS
WINE AUCTION

While most aspiring oenophiles would probably be daunted by the idea of buying wine at auction, Peter didn't seem intimidated at all. In fact, when Jeff Zacharia (whose family owns not only the retail store Zachys, but one of the country's largest auction houses) asked Peter if he wanted to attend an auction, Peter immediately responded in the affirmative.

Did he know what he was getting into? I asked, worried that Peter would be intimidated by the seriousness and the silence—and frankly, I was afraid he'd raise his paddle at just the wrong time. But Peter declared that he was unafraid and eager for the experience. Besides, Jeff had said something about lunch being served at the auction. Wasn't that reason enough for us to go?

All Zachys's New York–based auctions are held at Daniel, a fancy French restaurant on East Sixty-fifth Street. They're usually large, two-day affairs. Though the auction is free (as all auctions are), the lunch costs $50, which includes a buffet and a glass of Champagne.

"I love the idea of a buffet," Peter said when he showed up beside me at the registration table. He looked hungry. "I didn't have breakfast. I thought I would wait to eat at the auction. Do you know when they start serving lunch?"

Soon enough, I replied. In the meantime, Peter needed to focus; we needed to talk about proper auction protocol. Do you know how an auction works? I asked Peter, who brushed my fears aside. "Don't worry," he said, "I know enough not to start waving my arms around."

Anyone who wants to bid at an auction must first register. This means giving the auction house some background information along with your credit card number. In return, you get an auction catalog and a paddle. Peter looked excited at the idea of a paddle, less so at the prospect of a catalog.

Then he caught sight of it. "This is beautiful," he said, fingering the heavy paper, admiring the full-color photos of bottles. "It's like something out of an art gallery. Except it has all kinds of information in it. Look, here are some vintage ratings for these wines. Why do they list this sort of stuff? Doesn't everyone at this auction already know that stuff?" he asked, his voice loud in the hushed dining-turned-auction room.

In fact, the dining room was nearly museum-like in its silence— much quieter than during the restaurant's regular dining hours. The only sound that broke the silence was the voice of the auctioneer, Ursula Hermacinski, a tall, blond woman who's considered the best in the business. When Peter and I took our places, Ursula was exhorting the crowd to consider a mixed case of Bordeaux. It's from the superlative 1989 vintage, she urged them. No time to waste.

"I'm surprised this place isn't jam-packed," Peter said, looking around the room. "And no one here seems to have that lean and hungry look." Wine auctions aren't really the province of the lean and the hungry. Indeed, the reverse is true. (There tend to be a lot of lawyers present.) But most serious bidders don't actually attend auctions in person—they do their bidding by fax or more commonly by phone. "But that takes away from the excitement," Peter complained.

Peter was looking at Ursula, the auctioneer, and listening intently as she spoke. "She's fantastic," Peter raved. "She's really fast but you can understand everything she says. I don't know how you could listen to her and not be impressed." Peter leaned forward and pointed to a page in the catalog. "According to Ursula, this bottle has 'signs of seepage.' What does that mean? Although it sounds terrible, I love the sound of it. It sounds like the title of a mystery novel."

Signs of seepage, I told Peter, simply means that a bottle is showing some evidence of leakage from the cork. Usually, this happens with age, though it could also happen through some kind of physical trauma to the bottle. The wine itself might be good or not. The buyer has to be willing to run the risk.

The condition of every bottle has to be checked and noted just as the wine's provenance (or origin) does. This protects the buyer, though it also protects the auction house too. For example, a wine with a low "ullage" is simply a wine with a low fill (a certain amount of the wine may evaporate over time).

"I love the wording in this catalog—it's almost like reading poetry," Peter said, pointing to one passage, then another. "Look, there's a wine here with 'a touch of a sweetness leading to a strong finish.' There's something else about a wine's 'shoulders.'" Peter flipped the pages as if he were skimming a book. "But what do they mean by 'shoulders'?" Then he was distracted by another set of bottles, which he'd now learned to call "a lot." "Look, here's a lot of 1947 Burgundies. Maybe we should bid on those. After all, 1947 was a great year for movies. The picture of the year was *Gentleman's Agreement.*" It was a great year in Bordeaux too, I said. In fact, 1947 was one of the truly legendary vintages of Bordeaux.

"I want this 1959 Château Latour," Peter said, scrolling down the page to a new lot. "It's reasonable too. You can get a whole case of it for twelve thousand dollars." If Peter, the former $10 Chardonnay man, was now thinking $12,000 was a steal, I was certainly glad I'd kept hold of the paddle. I told him the $12,000 was an estimate. It didn't mean anything in terms of the actual price. As in fact, it did not. This case sold for $24,000. "I guess there really aren't any bargains here," Peter muttered.

Just then Jeff Zacharia appeared beside our table, fairly bouncing with energy and fiscal delight. Clearly, the auction was going well.

"Are you bidding on anything?" he asked Peter, who sat up in his chair.

"Not yet. We lost out on a case of '59 Latour," Peter said mournfully.

Jeff looked puzzled. "Did you want to buy that wine?" he asked in a wondering tone. After all, the last time he had seen Peter and me, we were buying bottles of $18 Bordeaux.

I was afraid Jeff was going to tell Peter he had another case of '59

Latour in the back he'd sell to him at a slightly better price. I pretended not to hear their exchange as Peter assured him he had fully intended a bid.

"Well, that's great," said Jeff a bit dubiously, not clear if Peter was pulling his leg. "Well, even if that case is gone, you should definitely try to bid on something, get into the spirit."

Peter nodded reassuringly. "Oh, we will. We're waiting for exactly the right thing."

When Jeff had gone, I asked Peter if he was really going to place a bid.

"I thought I might get carried away and bid on something totally by impulse. Although no one here looks like they've ever done anything on impulse in their entire lives," Peter said, looking around the room.

He was right; it was a pretty sober-looking crowd, nearly all middle-aged men. But then most auctiongoers are men, and most are professionals—sommeliers or wine directors or sophisticated amateurs with money and serious intentions. No one really goes to auctions to have fun, and people do a lot of research beforehand.

"Well, I think it would be great if they did, because wine auctions should have more emotion," said Peter definitively.

Suddenly Peter found in the catalog what he insisted on calling "his" wine: 1998 Domaine Leflaive Bienvenues-Bâtard-Montrachet. Four cases were offered, each a separate parcel with an estimated sales range of $1,100 to $1,200 per case. This seemed like a very fair price. (The wine was released at around $250 a bottle.)

"Bienvenues-Bâtard-Montrachet is the first wine I ever fell in love with," said Peter dreamily. "Or at least it's the kind of wine I loved. It was a different vintage, of course."

But was Peter really contemplating buying a full case of a white Burgundy that cost ten times the amount he normally spent on a wine? Peter claimed that even though the price made his "palms sweaty," he wanted to place a bid. Looking around at the serious faces, including some sommeliers I knew, I realized Peter was in fact probably the only emotional bidder in the room.

The first lot of Bienvenues sold for $1,416. "That's more than I wanted to pay," said Peter worriedly, putting the paddle down promptly when the number hit $1,200. Peter had decided he would go as high as $1,250. Just then the buyer of the first lot decided to take the second as well. "I didn't know that was allowed," said Peter, shocked. I didn't either. (At some auction houses, including Zachys, the buyer of a first parcel has first right of refusal on all subsequent parcels—which, alas, we only later discovered.)

The bidding on the third lot began. Peter put the paddle up. The auctioneer (not Ursula now but her counterpart, a short, chubby man named Fritz Hatton) hit $1,200 straightaway and stayed there. Peter decided to hold out for the fourth and last parcel. "The price is going down. I think we can get it for even less," he said.

But the buyer of the third parcel wanted the fourth one too. So both were sold to him for the same price: $1,298. An excellent buy. In fact, it was a bit of a deal, the sort of thing that doesn't often happen at auctions much anymore, as the attendees are (generally) too sophisticated and well-informed. "If only we'd known about rule of the option!" Peter and I both said at the same time.

"I can't believe that just happened," Peter said. I'd never seen a man who once couldn't bear to break a ten-dollar bill for a bottle of Chardonnay actually keen over the loss of a $1,300 case of wine.

Just then Jeff Zacharia and his ten-year-old son walked by. "We bid on some wine but the buyer of the third parcel took the fourth," Peter said to Jeff, as if willing him to overturn the sale.

Jeff's son regarded Peter dispassionately. "Didn't you know about the option rule?" he asked with barely concealed scorn.

It was another example of how tricky a wine auction can be for an amateur. As Peter said, "I understood why no one does this spontaneously." But, he added, "if I was ever to attend another wine auction, I will be prepared. And I'm going to make sure I buy my wine from Ursula. I like her style."

I was surprised Peter wanted to attend another auction. Was he sure?

"Absolutely," Peter replied. "In the meantime, I'm taking this catalog home and studying it carefully. It's a fascinating read. There's so much information in it, and not just about individual wines.

There's also all kinds of terminology I've never heard before, and I want to learn all the terms—like *seepage* and *ullage*—and whether or not I should care about a scuffed label, slight stain, or a low neck. I'll be able to buy the wine that I want next time."

Five top auction houses: Hart Davis Hart (Chicago), Zachys, Christie's, Sotheby's, Acker Merrall (all four are based in New York).

Peter in a Restaurant, or a Guide to Pairing Wine with Food

Just as "fatty" Chardonnay was Peter's wine ideal, so too was foie gras the dish by which he measured all others. Peter loved foie gras in a way that was almost operatic. I've never seen anyone enjoy a dish more. "And what's wrong with that?" Peter would say. "What's wrong with eating the food that you love?"

Putting aside issues of political correctness (i.e., whether to support the forcible stuffing of a goose's liver so that it becomes painfully outsize), foie gras was a troublesome food to me because it doesn't pair easily with many wines. The wines served with foie gras are almost always a dessert kind. Most sommeliers I've encountered pair foie gras with Sauternes, though to me this is usually a mistake. Not only because it's often sweeter than the foie gras, but also because a very sweet wine at the start of a meal can bring everything to a sensory halt, particularly when it's served after a dry aperitif and followed by a dry wine with dinner. Personally, I prefer an off-dry, that is to say, slightly rather than entirely sweet, wine.

"I tried to order a Gewürztraminer with my foie gras at Bouley restaurant a few weeks ago," Peter reported, "but the wine guy at Bouley wouldn't let me. He told me they didn't have Gewürztraminer by the glass and he seemed disgusted by the idea. He just gave me a Riesling without asking if it was what I wanted. And the wine was warm. When I asked him if the Riesling came from New

York State, he looked at me like I was crazy. I got so depressed I just drank water the rest of the night."

It was then that I realized Peter's problems were bigger than finding the right wine for foie gras; he really needed to learn how to talk to sommeliers.

A good sommelier doesn't just help someone select a wine, but (theoretically at least) also gives useful wine-and-food-pairing advice, hopefully without imposing too much of his or her own prejudices on diners—unlike the guy from Bouley. I had a couple of sommeliers in mind who I thought might be able to teach Peter a thing or two about wine and food. Before I brought him to meet them, though, I wanted to make sure he knew a few basic wine-and-food-pairing principles. Peter regarded this goal skeptically.

"You mean teaching me rules like white wine goes with fish and red wine goes with everything else?" he said. I assured him that it went a bit further than that.

FOOD-AND-WINE-PAIRING BASICS

A basic rule of food-and-wine pairing is that wines that are high in acidity are the most flexible with food. These wines include some that Peter liked (Riesling and Pinot Noir) and some that he did not (Sauvignon Blanc). And while compatible wines can be found in countries all over the world, in general the wines of Italy, with their high natural acidity, are probably the most flexible with food.

Peter needed to keep in mind a wine's weight and texture relative to the food it was paired with: lighter dishes go better with lighter wines, though the converse of this is not always true. "Oh, great," Peter commented. "Right away you give me an exception."

Color can be useful in determining if a match will work: the lighter the wine, the lighter the food it should be paired to. (I knew the visually oriented Peter would like this rule.) This is called a *complementary* pairing. However, at times a contrasting pairing can work too. For example, a rich dish can be offset by a lighter wine, which can help to cut through the heaviness of butter or cream. The key to it all was balance. Peter professed himself a fan of this word; in fact, he decided it would be his mantra (for better or worse). As Peter said, "I'm all about balance in my wine. I'm less and less interested in depth and complexity." This was, at least, some kind of start.

WINE-AND-FOOD PAIRING GLASS BY GLASS

For Peter's first wine-and-food pairing adventure and interaction with a sommelier, I chose Eleven Madison Park, one of my favorite restaurants in New York, not just for the food—the cuisine is "modern French" and the chef is the young and talented Daniel Humm (who is not even thirty years old)—but also for the wine list, an interesting, intelligent selection put together by the equally young John Ragan.

In addition to a fairly extensive wine list, Ragan also offers a wide array of wines by the glass. Peter professed himself comforted by the phrase. "I like the sound of a *wide array*," he said. "It improves my odds of getting the pairings right."

Peter was even more pleased to discover that the Eleven Madison Park menu featured foie gras, specifically a Seared Hudson Valley Foie Gras with Apple Port Purée appetizer. "It will be especially useful to have pairing options when it comes to foie gras," Peter pointed out. "Particularly since you tell me it's such a tough match, although, except for that guy at Bouley, I've usually liked just about any wine a sommelier has suggested for foie gras."

Perhaps Peter should consider ordering something besides foie gras, particularly since he had it so often anyway. How about the sturgeon?

Peter looked appalled. "Why would I do that? This is a perfect opportunity to find out from someone you say is really reliable what the definitive wine match with foie gras would be. Besides, I hate sturgeon."

At that moment, John Ragan appeared and introduced himself to Peter and me. "Are you just the sommelier or is there a wine director too?" Peter asked when John mentioned his title.

The question sounded a bit combative to me. But if John thought so, he didn't betray it. Instead, he just smiled and replied, "There is no wine director, there's just me."

"But aren't there both sommeliers and wine directors in some restaurants?" Peter persisted. Sometimes, John acknowledged, but wine directors are usually the guys who just sit in an office, ordering wine and looking at the inventory. A sommelier, said John, is the guy out on the floor, making wine suggestions. The sommelier is the wine waiter. That's the definition of a sommelier after all, John added.

"I've never heard that before," Peter replied skeptically. After John left, Peter turned to me. "Wine waiter? Have you ever heard that definition before? I wonder if he just made it up."

Peter's job was to choose a wine to pair with each of our dishes (foie gras and Black Angus steak for Peter, beet salad and poached chicken for me). "But there are so many wines here," Peter protested, looking at the list of wines by the glass. "How am I possibly going to make a decision?"

But he had just said that an array made things easier, I pointed out. And besides, it's a lot simpler to pair every dish with a different glass of wine than it is to come up with one bottle of wine that would work with everything. That was a much bigger challenge, though I didn't tell Peter that choosing a single wine would be his next challenge.

Just then John Ragan reappeared. "You're just in time," Peter said to him in relief. I explained that it was Peter's challenge to come up with an appropriate wine for each of our dishes. "But I also need to learn how to talk to sommeliers," Peter added. "So I can practice that with John here too." John merely nodded and offered the same polite face. Did Peter, he wondered, have some wines in mind?

"I thought about a Gewürztraminer for the foie gras," Peter replied rather grandly, pointing to the list, "but I didn't see one by the glass. Then I thought of Riesling—that's what the guy at Bouley suggested after all. But then I guessed that any idiot could think of a Riesling with foie gras, couldn't they? Then I thought about something totally different, like a Sancerre or maybe a French rosé. Would either one of those work?" Peter scanned the list. "I've never had any of them with foie gras."

John paused for a moment to take this all in. The trouble in either case, he replied, was acidity. Both wines were quite high in acidity and quite dry. "It's a lovely wine," he said of the rosé, "but it's dry and will come across as a little thin with the foie gras. The same thing with the Sancerre." John paused again, diplomatically. "Although you should drink what you want and eat what you want."

"You don't really believe that, do you?" Peter demanded. Not really, John admitted. But it was something he felt that he should say. "Not to me," Peter assured him. "I'd much rather you told me what to do." And the two of them shared a complicit smile. In that case, John said, he would choose two wines for every one of our dishes, and Peter could tell him which wine worked best and why.

"I like that plan," Peter replied, and when John left, Peter looked after him appreciatively. "I like a guy who takes charge. That's my idea of a good sommelier."

Of course, Peter was both right and wrong. Ideally, sommeliers should offer advice on wines that are always first-rate, always food appropriate, and always reasonably priced. But, as Peter had learned that night at Bouley, this wasn't always the case. "But I know I can depend on John," Peter insisted. How could he tell? "Well, for example, I loved the way he handled my question about the rosé. He said it was lovely, but it was clear he didn't think it worked with the foie gras. Besides, that guy at Bouley said the one thing you never want to hear a sommelier say: 'Trust me.' Those two words immediately tell me I'm going to get screwed."

John returned bearing four glasses and four bottles of wine. For the foie gras, John chose a 1996 Clos du Bourg Moelleux Le Haut Lieu Vouvray, a sweet wine from the Loire Valley, and a 1998 Dirler Sélection de Grains Nobles Gewürztraminer (aka SGN), an even sweeter wine from Alsace. "This is an amazing wine," John said to Peter, gesturing to the Gewürztraminer, from which Peter had taken a large gulp. Made from a select amount of botrytised grapes, Sélection de Grains Nobles wines are the richest, most concentrated dessert wines in Alsace and possibly in the world. But as it turned out, the wine was actually a little too sweet—it was even sweeter than the foie gras.

The Vouvray, on the other hand, worked beautifully. It had a fair amount of sweetness but also a terrific corresponding acidity, which helped cut through the fat of the foie gras. And, as Peter observed, the wine was also the "right color," a rich gold that matched the foie gras. That's the color that a ten-year-old wine becomes, especially a grape such as Chenin Blanc—much like Riesling. And Riesling and Chenin have a lot in common.

"Do you think that sommelier at Bouley doesn't know about Chenin Blanc and foie gras?" asked Peter.

For my beet-and-goat-cheese salad, John chose another Vouvray, this time a demi-sec, which means half-dry, though the wine was actually more accurately described as half-sweet. The Vouvray and beets were an excellent combination, and the Vouvray that John had chosen had a creaminess that countered the acidity of the beets. His second choice, a 2001 Dirler Pinot Gris from Alsace, was by contrast a bit too earthy and a bit too dry.

"Vouvray is my new favorite wine," Peter declared, sampling his Vouvray and mine. "I think it should be served with everything. It deserves the technical term *yummy.*"

For my chicken and Peter's beef, John brought out four more glasses and four more bottles of wine. For Peter he'd chosen the 2001 Lucien Barrot Châteauneuf-du-Pape (an excellent vintage and a good producer) and the 1998 Mercurey Clos l'Évêque from Hugues and Yves de Suremain, a red from the Côtes Chalonnaise region of Burgundy. "This is an excellent value," John said of the Mercurey. "I'm a big fan of the Côtes Chalonnaise." John explained his rationale: the beef wasn't a particularly big dish and would therefore work with a wine as light as the Mercurey; on the other hand, he'd reasoned that the spiciness of the beef meant it could work with the earthy, spicy Châteauneuf-du-Pape.

Peter and I both found the Châteauneuf-du-Pape to be the ideal pairing wine: its earthy, spicy qualities were accentuated by the spicy preparation of the Black Angus beef. The Mercurey was not only too light, but this particular wine was showing its age: both visually (a slight orangish rim around the edge of the wine) and in its rather faded fruit flavors. Peter tasted it and declared it "tired." I was impressed by Peter's perceptions as much as I was that he even used the right word. (Although some lesser Burgundies such as Mercurey can live up to ten years or more, the combination of a good-but-not-great producer and a less-than-great year made this wine an unlikely prospect for aging.)

For my poached milk-fed chicken, a light but delicately seasoned dish, John chose a second southern Rhône wine, the 2003 Montueil la Levade Côtes du Rhône, and a Bordeaux, the 2001 Château du Seuil from the Graves region. Both were fairly simple wines but were from excellent vintages, and in this instance, John proved right in his choice of both. The Côtes du Rhône had a lot of bright, juicy fruit and helped to enliven the flavors of the bird, while the Bordeaux was a soft but elegant and polished wine. It was the slightly better match—the subtleness of the wine matching the subtleness of the dish. "I've learned an enormous amount about matching wine with food," Peter declared at the end of our meal. "I'm just not sure I understand the difference between a wine director and a sommelier."

The wine-by-the-glass option was definitely a help to someone such as Peter who was just learning how to pair wine with food. But to my mind, it was a bit of a cheat, an easy way out. (Not to mention expensive: the wines by the glass Peter and I had cost between $12 and $18—multiplied by several glasses, of course.) And with several different glasses of wine, it's harder to make pairing mistakes. It's also a bit unrealistic. Most people don't open several different bottles for dinner at home. Most people only get one chance to get the wine pairing right—in other words, most people only open one bottle of wine. So Peter would also need to learn how to succeed in a real-life scenario. He would have to choose that single bottle sometime (soon).

"But isn't that what the sommelier is supposed to do?" Peter protested when I told him my plan. "When I tell him that I'm having the pork and you're having the sea bass, he's the one who's supposed to figure it out. He's the one who's supposed to come up with the perfect bottle."

Yes, but what about sommeliers such as that guy from Bouley? Did Peter really want to be at the mercy of someone like that? Having a bit of wine knowledge and an understanding of what food and wines went together (and why) would mean freedom for Peter—freedom to figure things out for himself. Therefore, the next time Peter and I went out, he'd have to choose the wine—and only one wine—all by himself.

THE ONE-BOTTLE CHALLENGE

For our next meal, Peter and I had dinner at Cru, a restaurant with one of the best wine lists, and certainly the largest, in New York. The descriptor most frequently invoked to describe Cru's wine list is "telephone-book-sized," though in fact it's the dimension of two telephone directories—one for white and one for red. Both are the work of Robert Bohr, a self-possessed young man in his early thirties, with a knowledge of Burgundy so great that powerful men twice his age come to Bohr for counsel—and to spend lots of money on the wines that Bohr says they should have.

"I just had a look at the Cru wine list online," Peter said in a message on my answering machine later that week. "You actually expect me to be able to order *one* bottle of wine? There must be thousands of wines there. Not just from France but from all over the world." A second message arrived moments later; Peter sounded slightly panicked. "I can only do this if you let me decide what you're eating. I've already decided we're drinking Pinot Noir." (This might have narrowed the field in any other restaurant, but Cru had something like three hundred Pinot Noirs on the list—both New World and Old.)

When our appointed dinner hour arrived, Peter was so late, I thought he'd lost his nerve. He finally arrived, about twenty minutes late.

"The train just stopped," Peter reported. "But that was fine by me—I'd printed out the white-wine section of the wine list and I had time to read it over and over. Except I don't think I'll be ordering white wine." Just then Robert appeared, bearing glasses of Krug Champagne for Peter and me—and the lists, both fat, square, leather-bound books, which he handed to Peter. "Come back in about two hours," Peter said to him.

As Robert later explained to Peter, the Champagne he had brought us was a charitable act. "I just bought you fifteen minutes more reading time," he told Peter, and offered him this piece of advice: "You usually have about six or eight minutes with a wine list before you need to order, so every additional minute counts. When you're not sure what you want, order a glass of Champagne or white wine to begin."

Certainly every minute does count with the Cru wine list— though an hour could easily be spent with it as well. "I was thinking of red Burgundy," Peter said to Robert, setting the white-wine book aside without even opening it and taking up the red.

"But you haven't even looked at the menus yet; how do you know what you're having to eat?"

"I know that Pinot Noir goes with everything," Peter replied.

"You should make her order first," Robert said to Peter, gesturing to me. "Or you could order first and then change your order if hers doesn't work with the wine you had in mind."

Peter nodded enthusiastically. "I like that idea," he said, accepting this rather unorthodox advice.

When I protested, Robert demurred, "I'm just trying to help him out. This guy needs to have a strategy."

Peter nodded. "I like the sound of a strategy. Why don't you order first?" he suggested to me. "That way I can look chivalrous, and if you order something contradictory to mine, something that doesn't work with the wine I want, I'll change my order."

Was this Peter's strategy? Had he even looked at the menu? Which, by the way, contained no foie gras.

Peter pretended indifference. "I know what to drink with foie gras by now."

What about a pasta appetizer? I countered. The pastas at Cru are terrific, as is the food in general. (Cru's chef, Shea Gallante, was a *Food & Wine* Best New Chef in 2005.)

"If I order pasta, then I'll have to drink Chianti," Peter replied. "And I don't know that I want a Chianti."

What about a Rhône wine? Had Peter looked at the Rhône section of the wine list? After all, Peter had liked the wines that we'd tasted in the Rhône lesson, particularly Châteauneuf-du-Pape. They were certainly more affordable than red Burgundy.

"But Burgundy is more versatile," Peter countered. "Laurent Drouhin told me that. He said red Burgundy is more versatile than any other wine." Well, Drouhin does produce red Burgundy, not Châteauneuf-du-Pape, I pointed out. Robert, who had reappeared tableside, simply nodded. Peter looked up at him expectantly. Wasn't Robert impressed that he, Peter, could so casually drop the name of a famous Burgundian such as Laurent? But alas, Robert, who knew all the great Burgundian people and names, merely looked a little bored.

Peter decided to start with the chestnut ravioli followed by Atlantic halibut in a garlic and Genovese basil sauce. I chose grilled quail with Brussels sprouts and a pasta called maccheroni (a wide, flat noodle) with Serrano ham and English peas.

"I think a red Burgundy could work with all of this," Peter announced.

"Do you have a wine budget?" Robert asked Peter, adding that he would usually never ask such a direct question but figured he could with Peter and me. Somewhere around $100, I answered. After all, I was the one paying the bill.

"I hate limits, don't you? That makes it so much less fun," Peter said to Robert in mock despair. "What could we possibly drink that costs less than one hundred dollars?"

Robert paused. "You might want to reconsider and have a Châteauneuf-du-Pape. That would work with what you're having, and the price is good. Châteauneuf-du-Pape is a versatile wine with food. Otherwise, as far as Burgundy goes, with that amount of money you're talking about a village-level wine." (Premier cru Burgundies, I noted, were well north of our budget, and grand cru wines were beyond anything Peter and I could afford.)

"I think I'd like a Burgundy," Peter said.

"I'm not going to argue with that," Robert replied.

"I think I'd like a Nuits St. Georges."

"And why is that?" Robert asked.

"I just like the sound of it. And I remembered that's where a lot of good red Burgundies come from."

"True enough. But are you thinking of a particular wine?"

"I still haven't looked at the red-wine list yet," Peter replied.

I perused my own copy and told Peter to look at some of the village wines from Gevrey-Chambertin and Vosne-Romanée, both from the excellent 2002 vintage. From Gevrey-Chambertin, the 2002 Vieilles Vignes by Bachelet came in just under budget, as did the 2002 Vosne-Romanée of Mugneret-Gibourg. Both were excellent wines from first-rate producers. Peter pretended to look further. When Robert returned, Peter solicited his opinion of the wines. Or did Robert have other suggestions?

Robert complimented Peter on both wine choices (never mind they were mine) and added that it was helpful for him that Peter had a few questions; it made his job as a sommelier easier. Not only did it give him an idea of what wines Peter liked, but also what he was willing to spend.

Robert had a few words on both wines: "The Gevrey is earthy and complex, the Vosne-Romanée is more powerful. The most powerful wines in Burgundy come from Vosne-Romanée." Peter wrote all this down. While Robert approved of both wines, he had another in mind. "I have a great 1994 Clos des Forêts from Domaine l'Arlot, an estate in the Nuits St. Georges. The vintage isn't great and it's a little over your budget, but I've had the wine and it's fantastic."

Peter nodded. "I think I'm going to go with the Vosne-Romanée. I like the idea that it's a powerful wine—I think that will work with what we're having and I don't want to go over budget. And even though you say the wine is fantastic, when you tell me it's from a bad vintage, I'm afraid it might be swill."

Robert nodded. "Well, you've made your bed. It could be splendor or it could be doom."

Peter turned to me. "I like this guy's attitude."

Robert returned shortly with two enormous Burgundy balloons (each held thirty-seven ounces of wine) and produced the bottle

Peter had ordered. Peter just stared at it. I encouraged Peter to make sure the vintage and the producer were, in fact, what he'd ordered.

"Do you remember ordering this?" Robert asked Peter, who looked a bit dazed. Peter nodded, so Robert pulled the cork and presented it to Peter.

"What do I do with this?" Peter asked, running it between his fingers.

"Just what you're doing with it now," Robert answered. "You want to check to make sure it's intact, that it's not old or moldy, since this is a fairly young wine. You'll also want to look for the name of the producer and maybe even the vintage. I use the cork pretty much for identification purposes."

Peter was baffled. "You mean I don't sniff it? I thought people always sniffed corks."

Robert shook his head. "Only people who don't mind looking stupid."

Finally, Peter tasted the wine. "Perfect. It's just what I wanted it to be. It doesn't slap me around like Sharon Stone in *Basic Instinct Two*"—a movie Peter had recently panned. Had Robert seen it? Peter wondered.

Robert shook his head. "If movie theaters were open late, I would go to the movies a lot more often," he said, alluding to the late-night schedule of the restaurant world. As the two of them discussed movies (Robert's all-time favorite was *South Park*, which he'd seen more than forty times), I tasted the wine. It was, indeed, a big, muscular Burgundy, but it was also delicious, with gorgeous ripe fruit and great acidity. After praising Peter's selection again, Robert moved away.

The wine paired beautifully with both our first courses, though I wondered how it would fare with the halibut Peter had ordered. Would it be too big? Impossible, answered Peter confidently. Just then Robert appeared, carrying red wine in more outsize glassware. "Try this and tell me how you think it works," he instructed Peter.

The wine was lush and sweet, a very different style from our

Vosne-Romanée. I though it was a young Burgundy. Maybe a Chambolle-Musigny.

"It's definitely not a Cabernet," Peter offered.

Robert came back to check our reaction. "It's terrific," Peter said, "but I think I still like my Vosne-Romanée after all."

Robert nodded. "I'm glad," he said, and produced the bottle. It was the 1994 from l'Arlot that Robert had suggested.

"It's very pretty," Peter remarked, "but I still liked the wine that I ordered better." Peter had learned another rule about dealing with sommeliers: stand your ground. Even though Robert knew more about Burgundy than probably anyone else Peter would ever meet (except perhaps Laurent Drouhin), wine is, above all, a matter of personal taste.

"Tell me about Burgundy," Peter prompted Robert, who travels to the region six or eight times a year. "I really want to go there. Burgundy is like the movies of D. W. Griffith to me—where everything began, where wines were first formed, where the earliest pioneers walked on hallowed ground."

This was a bit overwrought for the practical-minded Robert, who said that it was a lot easier to understand a wine after visiting the place it was made.

Peter nodded. This had been true of his trip to Napa. "Now," he told Robert confidently, "I know how great Cabernet can be."

But it's not just about visiting the place, but seeing the right people, Robert replied, adding that he visited the same thirty Burgundy producers over and over not only because they made the best wine, but because he trusted them to tell him the truth about their wine. They don't have to lie. "For example," said Robert, "Christophe Roumier won't lie to me and say he didn't have hail in his vineyard. But a great producer can also make a really good wine in a bad year, such as the 1994 you've just tried. And sometimes a wine can improve in the bottle. The 1993 Burgundies are a perfect example of that. Everyone slammed the vintage, and then the wines really improved in the bottle, and now you can't find them at all. So it's always a sense of discovery. When I talk to someone who claims to know a lot of wine, I'm always skeptical. The first rule I learned about wine and I think is still true today is that humility is paramount when it comes to understanding anything."

"I couldn't have said it better myself," Peter replied. "Or ordered a better wine."

Peter Dines
with the Collector

Peter decided his next step was to start collecting wine. His wife, Robyn, had recently bought him a wine refrigerator, which Peter described, with a touch of awe, as "very big—it must hold about fifty bottles of wine." For a man who had until recently kept his bottles in a wooden rack over the stove, this represented a big step forward. Of course, Peter would soon discover, as every budding collector does, that a fifty-bottle refrigerator is, in fact, very small. In the meantime, Peter was determined to "fill it up," as he said. Maybe my friend the Collector could give him some tips?

My friend the Collector is a burly real estate lawyer and company president who spends much of his waking time (in the office and out) planning his next meal. His eating trips to Europe are legendary— lengthy and carefully planned. He will fly to Paris for dinner because a certain restaurant has a few bottles of La Tâche on their wine list for a good price. So when I called the Collector and told him that Peter wanted to have dinner with him, he agreed immediately.

We made plans to meet at Montrachet restaurant in New York on a Monday night, the restaurant's official BYOB night. (The restaurant has since closed.) "What do you want me to bring?" asked the Collector, who takes wine everywhere, whether a restaurant has a BYOB policy or not. He knows his wines will always be welcome. I can't recall a time or place when they were not. The Collector is simply one of the most confident people I know.

"What wines doesn't Peter know anything about?" the Collector asked me the day before our dinner. "Are there are some specific wines that I should bring along to help with his education?" Peter would love to taste Pétrus, I told the Collector. After all, it's film director Alexander Payne's favorite wine. The Collector snorted. "I don't think he's ready for Pétrus." (The Collector believed that people had to earn their way to great wines.)

The Collector did, however, bring some good, if not great, wines. Even if they weren't the best of his cellar (the Collector, needless to say, has an amazing cellar), they were incredible wines, certainly the best wines Peter was likely to taste for a long time.

"Would it be crass to ask how much these wines cost?" Peter whispered once we were seated and looking at the three bottles that the Collector had just pulled out of his bag. I guessed around $1,500 or perhaps more. "I guess it's going to cost a lot more than I thought to fill up my wine refrigerator," said Peter dolefully.

"These Burgundies should be decanted," the Collector said to Montrachet's sommelier, Troy, handing him two of the three bottles of wine.

"What's the business with decanting?" Peter asked the Collector. "It seems like some wines get decanted while others don't. Why do you decant a particular wine?"

"You decant for two reasons," replied the Collector. "You decant either to get air into the wine—the air brings out the wine's fla-vors—or to make sure you aren't pouring the sediment from the bottle of wine."

"What's your reason for decanting these wines?" Peter inquired.

"It's always about air, not sediment, with Burgundy. Sediment is something you'll get with Bordeaux, and with Bordeaux you also need to decant to give it a lot of air."

"You mean, with Bordeaux you decant for both reasons?" asked Peter.

The Collector nodded, but his attention was no longer on Peter, but on the menu. "How many courses could we have? Only four or maybe five?"

The Collector's first wine was a white Burgundy: the 1990 Ramonet Chassagne-Montrachet les Ruchottes, a premier cru. (The Collector's two biggest wine passions were Burgundy and the Rhône.)

216

"I think this will be good with the pan-seared foie gras," said Peter. How could he say that? He knew Burgundy wasn't the right match with foie gras. He'd learned as much in our food-and-wine-pairing session. "But it's what I want," Peter protested, catching my look. "Tell me about this wine," he said, turning from me to the Collector.

"Well, for starters, this isn't a wine that goes with foie gras." The Collector went on to tell Peter a bit about the wine anyway. The winemaker is a guy named Ramonet, one of the greatest wine-makers in Burgundy, and the wine is from a premier cru vineyard that's considered to be close to a grand cru vineyard in quality.

"Then it must be very expensive," said Peter, looking at his glass appreciatively.

"I paid about forty dollars and it's worth around two hundred and fifty dollars." The Collector never minded telling how much (or how little) money he paid for a wine.

"What was the first white Burgundy you ever tasted?" Peter asked the Collector, who said he had no idea, although he did remember the first case of wine he'd ever bought. As well as a magnum of 1966 Latour he'd bought for $50.

"The ad in the newspaper said, 'One to a customer,'" the Collector recalled. "But I drove up to the store one day and bought one and came back the next day and bought another. I guess that's when I really started to collect wine."

"How many bottles do you have?" asked Peter. The Collector didn't know. "I have thirty-four thousand movies," Peter offered in return.

"I didn't know there were thirty-four thousand movies in the world," the Collector answered in a tone that suggested he didn't particularly care either.

While Peter ate his foie gras with the Burgundy (a combination I tasted, and found the foie gras completely obliterated the wine), the Collector and I ate the leek-and-oyster carbonara, which was a perfect match with the wine. The richness of the dish actually made the wine, which was a little high in acidity, seem richer than it was.

I told Peter he had to admit that the foie gras pretty much killed the wine. He insisted he could taste both, if not exactly together. I realized then that Peter simply wasn't rational about foie gras.

"Let me try it," said the Collector, stabbing a piece of Peter's foie gras with his fork. He tasted his wine. "It doesn't work at all."

The Collector's second wine was the 1991 Comte de Vogue Musigny, one of the greatest grand cru red Burgundies in the world.

"Tell me about this second wine," Peter said.

"Well, I think you'll like it—there's a little *merde* in it," the Collector replied, sniffing his glass.

"What do you mean *merde*?" Peter asked innocently. I explained that it meant that the wine smelled like a barnyard, using a polite word for the Collector's term.

"Is that a good thing? You never mentioned anything about a barnyard in our Burgundy lesson," Peter said, looking at me. *Merde* is a word used sometimes to describe red Burgundies of a certain earthy kind. Some people like it and some people don't.

"This wine is a Musigny," the Collector interrupted. "It's a grand cru Burgundy that some people say is the greatest red Burgundy of all. It's probably one of my favorite wines. I've had it from all the great vintages—1947, 1949, 1959. All from magnums." This last point was particularly important among serious collectors, as wine from a magnum ages more slowly and more gracefully than wine from a standard bottle.

"Is this wine a great vintage?" Peter asked. In fact, the 1991 vintage was largely overlooked in Burgundy, following, as it did, the superb 1990 vintage. But the 1991 red Burgundies are excellent wines, and some collectors believe they're even better, or at least more typically Burgundian, than the 1990 wines. "You mean they have more *merde* in them?" Peter asked.

"You might say that," the Collector allowed. I wasn't able to warn the Collector to stay away from using words that he didn't want to hear over and over.

The wine was glorious, with a stupendous nose (from which all notes of barnyard were missing) and glorious fruit whose freshness made it seem a good ten years younger than its actual age. "This wine could easily go another twenty years," the Collector declared with the satisfaction of a man who had more bottles at home.

"Do you have mostly Burgundy in your cellar?" Peter asked the Collector politely, after admiring the wine. I felt like the chaperone of a stiff first date.

"I have a lot of Bordeaux, but I don't drink it," the Collector replied carelessly.

"Really? I'm fascinated by that," replied Peter, mouthing the question *What do you think Jeff Zacharia would say?* to me. Then he turned back to the Collector. "Is that because there are fewer great Burgundies than great Bordeaux?"

"Great Burgundy is more elusive."

"How do you mean? That the highs are higher and the lows are lower?"

The Collector looked at Peter appraisingly. "I guess you could say that." And I knew without looking that Peter was pleased with himself. He'd just figured out Burgundy!

Troy, who had been standing at our table during this exchange, offered his own insight about Burgundy versus Bordeaux. "It's really hard to understand Burgundy unless you immerse yourself in it. Bordeaux is more easily understood. When you get a really great Bordeaux and you say, 'This wine is very Burgundian,' everyone recognizes that as high praise. But it doesn't work the other way around. If you said, 'This wine is very Bordeaux' about a Burgundy, people would think something was wrong."

"I don't think Jeff Zacharia would agree," Peter muttered.

The last wine that the Collector had brought was a great Bordeaux: the 1985 Lafleur Pomerol. The Collector could be a generous man. "This wine is as good as Pétrus in some vintages," I told Peter in an aside. In fact, it's just across the street from that legendary Pomerol estate.

"This wine is amazing," Peter pronounced. "But without undergoing years of therapy, I wouldn't say that I like Burgundy better because it's riskier; I just like it because I like it." A few minutes later, our entrées arrived: the rack of lamb for me and for Peter the Scottish venison. The Collector tucked into his squab pot-au-feu in a black truffle sauce.

As the three of us alternately contemplated and drank from each of the three wines, the Collector abruptly declared the Lafleur Pomerol to be the best. The Musigny is too young and the Ramonet is too high in acidity, he proclaimed. The Lafleur is just right.

I admired the Lafleur too, but my favorite wine of all was the Musigny, if only for the aroma, which was classically Burgundian with notes of earth, spice, and red fruit (and sans barnyard or merde). Peter, however, professed himself incapable of "taking sides" and declared them all "incredible wines." Did he really believe this or was he afraid that the Collector would be offended if he criticized any of the wines? He must have been more impressed by one wine. If Peter was going to be a wine collector, he'd need to have strong opinions, right or wrong. That's part of the game collectors play.

Peter Goes Shopping,
or What to Do in a Wineshop

When I first met Peter many years ago, he shopped for wine exclusively at a local liquor store. Peter had known the store's clerk, Charlie Rodriguez, for many years; in fact, he'd known Charlie back in the days when Charlie sold albums in a record store. How had Charlie gone from touting records to bottles of Merlot? I asked. How had Charlie learned about wine? "He didn't," Peter replied.

Then what exactly had been Charlie's role in choosing a wine?

"I just asked him to give me a good Chardonnay," Peter said, "and Charlie would point me to something that cost around ten or fifteen dollars. Sometimes I'd ask him to give me a Pinot Grigio when my friend Anne Martin was visiting. As I mentioned, Anne Martin only drinks Pinot Grigio, and she likes Santa Margherita, the best, but since it costs over twenty dollars a bottle, occasionally I'd ask Charlie to give me something else instead. Sometimes the wines he gave me were good and sometimes they were pretty bad. That's when I would go back to Santa Margherita."

I'd never met Charlie nor been to the liquor store where he worked, but I was curious to meet the man responsible for shaping Peter's taste in wine for so many years. In the meantime, I wanted Peter to experience a few places that were more challenging—and more rewarding—than Charlie's liquor store. "I'm ready," Peter declared.

There's actually little need to visit a wineshop in person these days, given the proliferation of retail wine websites and that it's now legal in many states to buy directly from wineries. But to me there's nothing like holding an actual bottle, or physically digging through a sales bin in the hope of finding some overlooked, underpriced wine. There's also the value of developing a personal relationship with the retailer, though as Peter's experience with Charlie Rodriguez revealed, it had to be with the right sort of retailer.

Westchester County, New York, where Peter and I live, has a lot of wineshops and a wide range of types to choose from—supermarket-style stores, boutiques that emphasize small producers and feature lesser-known names, and, of course, basic liquor stores like Charlie's that carry only well-known brands.

The biggest wineshop in Westchester, or at least the best known, is Zachys, a kind of cross between a supermarket and a boutique wineshop. But Peter, having been to Zachys twice, felt that he knew it already (or at least he knew where they kept the Bordeaux), so we visited a different supermarket-style store instead.

I'm a big fan of Stew Leonard's in Yonkers, an enormous Costco-style grocery store with a wineshop attached. I've found Stew's selection surprisingly varied—from standard supermarket brands to some well-chosen labels from smaller producers. Stew's has a particularly strong selection of Italian wines.

I'm also a big fan of Rochambeau, a small store not far from Stew Leonard's in the town of Dobbs Ferry. Although the choice of wines is more limited at Rochambeau than at Stew's, the selection is clearly personal, which is, to me, the chief attraction of a boutique store. In the third category, liquor stores, there was Charlie Rodriguez.

THE ROCHAMBEAU RETAIL EXPERIENCE

"This looks a lot like a liquor store from the outside," Peter said dubiously as we approached Rochambeau. He was right. A lot of liquor bottles were in the front window and there wasn't much evidence of anything more promising inside. This seemed odd to me until Peter and I later learned it was deliberately done to reassure longtime residents who still thought of Rochambeau as their local liquor store.

There isn't much free space in Rochambeau—every bit of shelf space and inch of the wooden floor is crammed with bottles. While some people might be put off by such barely restrained chaos, to me it heralded adventure and the possibility of finding a great bottle that had been overlooked.

Was Peter looking for a particular wine? He was. "I'd love to find some of that Andrew Will Merlot that we tasted when you were teaching me about Washington wine," he said as we stood before a shelf full of California Cabernet. "I love the idea that the winemaker Chris Camarda can make such an amazing wine and he doesn't even drink. He reminds me of the director Sam Peckinpah."

Sam Peckinpah? The one who made *The Wild Bunch*? Isn't that a really violent movie? I asked. Peter nodded. "Peckinpah made movies in which people are killed in really violent ways. Peckinpah used to say that he'd be more violent personally if he couldn't make the kinds of movies that he does. But," Peter hastily added, "I don't want to make this guy Chris Camarda sound like a murderer, although I do think there are some creative parallels."

When I mentioned Peter's theory to Camarda when I saw him a few months later in Seattle, Camarda was less than pleased—not because Peter had compared him to a violent filmmaker but because Camarda wasn't a big Peckinpah fan. "I think Peckinpah was an asshole," Camarda said. Was there a director Camarda liked and even identified with? "Paul Schrader," he said immediately. He identified with Schrader's work completely. Really? The screenwriter of *Taxi Driver*? I asked, surprised. That was a pretty violent film. Camarda nodded.

"Paul Schrader makes movies that are the themes of my life," said Camarda. "Like *Bringing Out the Dead*" (a disturbing 1999 film that Schrader scripted and Martin Scorsese directed, in which Nicolas Cage plays an emergency medical technician who is haunted by the people he tries and fails to save). However, Camarda's favorite director wasn't Schrader but Scorsese. Just like Peter.

As Peter and I stood discussing whether Chris Camarda had

anything in common with Peckinpah, a tall man with sandy hair and glasses approached. He asked if we needed help.

"Do you have Andrew Will wines?" Peter asked.

"I have a bunch of Andrew Will wines on order," the man replied. "But I do have wines from Buty, another Washington State producer who's very good." (I'm a fan of Buty wines, particularly Buty Rediviva, a well-priced Cabernet and Syrah blend.) But the only Washington State wine Peter wanted was Andrew Will.

"What about Finger Lakes wines from New York—do you have any of those?" Peter asked, abruptly switching sides of the States. The tall man, the store manager (whose name we learned was Jeff Woody), admitted that although he and owner Dieter Kannapin were "big fans" of Finger Lakes wines, they only stocked a few. There wasn't room for many and they couldn't even properly display the ones that they had.

"We put the Finger Lakes wines between the Beringer White Zinfandel and Gallo wines, and I know that's like saying we don't care about them, but that's the reality of a store as small as ours," Jeff explained a bit abashedly.

To make more room for Sauvignon Blanc? I gestured to what seemed like a prodigious selection of California Sauvignon Blanc on the shelf just to the right. Jeff laughed. "Dieter is kind of obsessed with Sauvignon Blanc right now. We're thinking of changing the name of the store to Dieter's House of Sauvignon Blanc. But Sauvignon Blanc is what's really happening in California right now." Peter, having learned as much during our Napa sojourn, gave Jeff a knowing nod.

"You really have to know what you're looking for in a store like this, don't you?" Peter remarked. I wasn't sure that Peter appreciated the chaos. He was looking at the shelves of wine where California Cabernet abruptly transitioned to Washington State Cabernet, which abruptly transitioned to Oregon Pinot Noir. "We want to be a wine store where you need to talk to someone," Jeff said, as if the jammed-together selection was by design rather than the result of too little space. "And because we taste everything that comes into the store, we can really tell you what it tastes like."

"But what if someone comes in and doesn't want to talk to a salesperson?" Peter persisted. "What if someone just comes in and wants to be left alone? Sometimes I don't want to talk to anyone. Is there some sort of way they could figure the store out?"

Jeff leaned forward in the manner of one about to impart a secret. "When you go into a store, you should look at the wines that are displayed up front—the wines in the nine-to-nineteen-dollar range. Those are the workhorse wines of a wineshop, and those wines will tell you where the retailer's head is at. For example, the guy who has a floor stacked with cases of Yellow Tail and Geyser Peak is a guy who's just pushing product."

The three of us moved to the wines stacked across from the entrance to the store, its workhorse section. There was no Geyser Peak or Yellow Tail in sight. "So this is where it's all happening?" Peter asked, examining the (mostly) Spanish wines.

"They're wines we believe in; wines that you won't necessarily find in every other wine store."

"It's clear to me you're in this business because you have passion," Peter said, examining one of the bottles stacked in the boxes behind Jeff (Tres Picos Garnacha from Spain, which, contrary to what Jeff said, I've found in quite a few stores).

"It's like Ed Sbragia of Beringer, who I met in Napa a few months ago," Peter continued. "He's not in love with his white Zinfandel, but he knows it allows him to do all the things he is really passionate about." (Clearly Peter had learned the lesson of every aspiring oenophile: drop the names of famous people or the great wines you have in your cellar. And preferably do a little of both.) When Jeff didn't respond, Peter tried a follow-up. "Are you familiar with Ed Sbragia's Chardonnay?"

"Of course," Jeff said, and led us to the California section—which simply meant taking a few steps back. He looked for the wine. "We don't have it right now, but I've tasted the '02 and I thought it was great. Really big and rich but not over-the-top, not like the Mer Soleil." Jeff pulled out the bottle. "That Chardonnay is just fat for the sake of fat."

Fat Chardonnay! Peter and I exchanged looks. It was the first time

Peter had heard anyone else employ his cherished wine descriptor. Jeff, unaware that he'd risen considerably in Peter's estimation, continued, "If someone came in and asked me for Mer Soleil, I'd have an immediate idea of their palate. Although I might steer them toward a wine like the Maldonado Los Olivos Chardonnay. It's fat but it's poised." Fat but poised! I saw Peter make a mental note of the phrase. No doubt I'd be hearing a lot of it in the weeks ahead.

"What's really hard is when people come in and say, 'I'm looking for a good wine,'" Jeff continued.

Peter nodded understandingly. "It's the same thing when people ask me what's a good movie. Especially since I have no idea what their taste is. I mean, their idea of a great movie could be *Big Momma's House Two*."

Except the first criterion for most people in buying a bottle of wine, unlike a movie, is price, I pointed out. That's a pretty critical difference. All movies cost the same. That's true, Peter conceded. Perhaps with that in mind Jeff could recommend three particularly good, reasonably priced wines—no more than $10 or $15 a bottle?

"Why don't we make it under twenty dollars? That would give me more options," Jeff said, turning to Peter. "What do you have in mind?"

Peter thought for a minute. "I'd like to see a good cheap Merlot just because the idea of a cheap Merlot is scary to me—and also because it's the wine that *Sideways* destroyed—and after that I'd like to have a great Riesling and a great Pinot Noir."

Jeff nodded. "You're really stacking the deck, aren't you? It's not easy to find good cheap versions of those grapes."

Peter nodded; he knew.

"The problem with Merlot is that it stopped being a wine and became a commodity," Jeff said. "It's hard to find something good that's cheap. And frankly, our Merlot selection is pretty dismal, but I'll see what I can find." He went off to search while Peter and I examined the selection of South African wines. "There's no Pinotage here," whispered Peter. "That's a good sign."

Jeff returned with three bottles: 2003 Selbach-Oster Spätlese

Riesling from the Mosel region of Germany; 2003 Falesco Vitiano, a Merlot blend from Umbria, Italy; and 2004 St. Innocent Oregon Pinot Noir. Total: $48. "The Riesling is a Spätlese, but it's drier than you might otherwise think," Jeff assured Peter, who asked about the Spätlese designation. (I was impressed that Peter remembered what it meant.)

"I'll let you know," Peter replied, a bit loftily. Peter added one more bottle: the 2004 Can Blau from Priorat, Spain ($17), which Jeff had described as "one of the best values" in the store.

Leaving Dobbs Ferry, both Peter and I agreed that Rochambeau had been a successful experience. "Even if I don't like the wines that Jeff picked, I liked his attitude," said Peter. "I felt like he was honest. Like when he admitted he didn't have Andrew Will Merlot right away." That, I told Peter, is exactly what a good retailer should do.

A SURPRISE AT STEW LEONARD'S

The first thing Peter and I saw upon walking into Stew Leonard's were giant stacks of cheap grocery-store wines. The loomed, they towered, they practically blocked the entrance to the store.

"What would Jeff say about this?" Peter asked, gesturing to the tower of $6.99 Stone Valley Cabernet. It didn't look promising, I admitted, but I knew there was more to the store. Peter looked skeptical. "I'm going to ask if they have Andrew Will Merlot." He bore down on a small blond woman wearing a nameplate that said PAIGE.

"Andrew Will Merlot!" Paige cried when Peter posed his question. "That's one of my all-time favorite wineries! Chris Camarda is one of my favorite winemakers!" For a moment it looked as if she was going to throw her arms around Peter in a hug. Instead, she led us past acres of cheap Australian wine, cheap Argentine wine, cheap Chilean wine, and a wide patch of South African wine. "Do you carry Pinotage?" Peter called to Paige as we passed this section. "We have a lot of Pinotage," Paige called back. "A lot of our customers really love it." Peter shot me a withering look.

Stew Leonard's not only stocked Andrew Will Merlot but even

had a Washington wine section (next door to magnums of Fontana Candida Frascati). "This is amazing!" Peter intoned, clutching the Andrew Will wine that Paige had handed him.

"We also have other Washington State wines," Paige said to Peter. "Do you know Rick Small of Woodward Canyon Winery?"

Peter shook his head.

"Do you know the winemaker Susana Balbo?" he countered. Paige did not. "You really should. Susana makes amazing wines. She's one of the top winemakers in Argentina."

Paige nodded and quickly said, "I feel like I've heard of her."

"Do you really sell a lot of Pinotage?" I could tell Peter wanted Paige to denounce it.

Paige nodded. "A ton of it." But did she like it? Peter pressed. "I hate it. It smells like fake lighter fluid."

"I do too," said Peter joyfully.

LAST CHANCE FOR CHARLIE

Our last stop was Charlie Rodriguez's store. "What's the actual name of the store?" I asked Peter.

"I don't know. I just know Charlie Rodriguez," Peter replied. This turned out to be just as well.

Charlie came rushing up to greet us as if it had been years since he'd last seen Peter. In fact, it had been a while since Peter had bought any fatty Chardonnay or, for that matter, Pinot Grigio from Charlie. "Are you going to ask Charlie for Andrew Will Merlot?" I asked Peter, who gave me a pointed stare.

"What are the wines in the front of the store?" Peter asked Charlie, pretending innocence.

"Oh, those are wines of the season." What did Charlie mean by that? "It means those are wines that are good to drink right now, in this season," Charlie replied helpfully. (As opposed to the rest of the wines in the store?)

Peter and I moved to the back of the store. Charlie stepped away and watched us go. Two other salespeople squeezed past us, on their way somewhere else, although no one was in the store but Peter and me.

"I don't think I would resent it if someone asked me what I wanted," Peter said aloud. "It's better than it seeming like we're just in their way." As Peter said that, the salesperson who had just passed us squeezed by once more.

We were standing in front of the California section, which featured largely commercial wines. Charlie suddenly materialized at Peter's side and said, "You know, Pinot Noir is the most versatile wine. It goes with everything."

"Is that so?" Peter replied skeptically. Whatever hold Charlie had once had over Peter was gone.

Charlie nodded vigorously. "It's true. Especially Oregon Pinot Noir. That's the best. It comes from a rain forest, you know." He gave us an affirming nod and went back to dusting bottles in the front of the store.

Peter was shaking his head when we left the store. "I just don't see how I couldn't have noticed all these years." Noticed what? "That I never had an actual conversation with anyone about wine in that store. Did you notice how many people just walked around us like we were in the way? That's just not right. I don't see how I can shop there anymore."

And so that day Charlie Rodriguez unwittingly lost his best fatty-Chardonnay customer ever.

THE ROCHAMBEAU CHALLENGE

A few weeks later Peter and I sat down to taste the three wines that Jeff at Rochambeau had chosen. The tasting didn't start off especially well. Peter immediately declared the Selbach-Oster Spätlese Riesling too sweet. "Jeff said it wasn't, but it is," Peter said. Strike one.

The Falesco Vitiano, a blend of Sangiovese, Merlot, and Cabernet from Umbria made by famed winemaking consultant Riccardo Cotarella, didn't fare much better. ("A blend? Couldn't he find something that was really Merlot?" Peter said.) And Peter didn't care for the label either. "There are too many names on this wine and not enough information: Falesco, Vitiano, Cotarella, and this guy Leonardo LoCascio, on the back. Who is this LoCascio guy? And why is his name so big?" Peter asked, turning the bottle around.

"I'm sure Riccardo Cotarella probably asked the same thing," I joked. In fact, LoCascio is the owner of Winebow, a company that imports some good Italian wines. LoCascio's name is a pretty solid indication that the wine will be good—maybe that's why his ego (and name on the label) was outsize.

Peter, examining the bottle, appeared not to hear. "Look here, it also says *vino tipico.* Doesn't that translate to 'cheap crap'?"

The Vitiano was soft and juicy, simple but appealing, with more in the middle than the beginning or end. "It doesn't have an end at all," Peter complained. You mean it lacks a finish, I corrected him. Peter waved one hand impatiently. "Completely." Was it possible Peter's expectations were too high for an $11 wine? He shook his head. "I don't understand why a wine under fifteen dollars can't have a finish. Or complexity." And Peter had a point. Strike two for Jeff. Things were looking grim.

I had higher hopes for the third wine, the 2004 St. Innocent Willamette Valley "Village Cuvée" Pinot Noir, made by one of the best winemakers in Oregon, Mark Vlossak. It's the most accessible of the five Pinots that Vlossak makes (therein the "Villages" designation, meant to invoke the idea of a Burgundian village wine).

"That's a little pretentious," Peter opined.

The wine was gorgeously rich and ripe, with a luxurious texture. "This is fantastic," Peter declared. At $20 a bottle, it was also the most expensive of the three wines. "But that's all right," Peter replied when I told him the price. "I'd rather spend more money and get something I'd really like. I'd buy this in a second."

Would Peter, having liked only one of the three wines Jeff had chosen, return to Rochambeau? Would he trust Jeff again? Peter decided he would. But he would also tell Jeff about his disappointments. "He succeeded so well with the Pinot Noir, I'd give him another chance. But I would also tell him the Falesco was a total washout. We'd have to talk about that."

But that, after all, I said to Peter, is what a good retailer is, some-one you can have a conversation with. "It's just like film," Peter said, nodding. "When I meet another film lover, I want to have a conversation. Wine is an art too and it deserves a conversation. Except that Vitiano. It deserves nothing but silence."

The fourth, extra-credit wine was the best value of all. In fact, Jeff scored a home run. The 2004 Can Blau (a blend of old-vine Syrah, Cariagne, and Grenache) from Priorat, Spain, was a great buy at $17 a bottle. Big, rich, and spicy, it was intense but not overwhelming. "The only problem is the name," Peter declared. "It's ugly. And so is the label. But Jeff gets major credit for choosing this wine."

FIVE FAVORITE RETAIL WINE SOURCES

Although Peter and I both prefer visiting wineshops in person, all of the stores listed below have websites.

Zachys—They may not have all of the wines Peter now loves (not much in the way of Finger Lakes Riesling or the wines of Susana Balbo), but if you're looking for Bordeaux, this supersize store in Scarsdale, New York, is a great place to go.

Rochambeau—The impassioned salesmanship of Jeff impressed Peter and me, as did the personal selections of Dieter. And if you love Sauvignon Blanc, this Dobbs Ferry, New York, retailer is your kind of store.

Stew Leonard's—This wine store is in Yonkers, New York (Peter's hometown), and while it has a lot of grocery-store wine (e.g., animal-label brands), it also holds a lot of surprises, such as Andrew Will Merlot, and a strong selection of Italian wines and Argentine Malbec.

Roots—This shop is located in Healdsburg, California, one of my favorite towns in Sonoma. It has a well-priced, eclectic selection of wines regularly described in the chatty, highly opinionated e-letter put out by proprietor Paul Root.

Sam's—This is the most famous wine retailer in Chicago, and by and large their reputation is justified. The selection is extraordinary and the prices quite reasonable (especially by New York standards). Their website is also good.

Lavinia (special overseas mention)—Although Peter and I haven't made a trip to France together (yet), I know he could spend days looking at the prodigious selection of wines in the Lavinia stores—there's one in Paris, one in Madrid, and one in Barcelona. Just about every imaginable wine, from the old and rare (1971 DRC) to *vin ordinaire*, can be found in Lavinia. I even found a bottle of Hermann Wiemer's Finger Lakes Riesling in the Paris store a short time ago.

THE FINAL EXAM

After months of lessons and many hundreds of glasses of wine, there was only one way to determine if Peter and I had truly accomplished what we'd set out to do: Peter would need to take a final exam.

"I really don't think that's necessary," Peter protested nervously when I broached the idea. "Can't you just take my word for it? Or maybe take me out to dinner again? I don't only drink fatty Chardonnay anymore, and I'm not scared of almost any red wine—including Cabernet. I know how to volatize my esters and I've got invitations to visit about a dozen winemakers and to stay at their homes—isn't that more than any final exam would tell you about the progress I've made?"

PETER'S WINE QUIZ

1. A slope-shouldered bottle indicates that
   A. The winemaker has bad posture
   B. The wine will contain sediment
   C. The wine is a Burgundy bottle

2. When a wine is called "hot," that means
   A. It's been approved by Paris Hilton
   B. It has too much alcohol
   C. It's been stored at Peter's house
   D. All of the above

3. Phylloxera is the name of a
   A. Vine-eating louse
   B. Bruce Willis movie
   C. Spanish grape

4. When a wine "shuts down," it becomes
   A. Tannic
   B. Quiet
   C. Flavorless

5. Wine auctions are most often attended by
   A. Lawyers
   B. Lawyers
   C. Lawyers

6. Noble rot refers to
   A. The decline of the House of Windsor
   B. A beneficial grape fungus
   C. The flavor of a type of Sherry

7. Which of these grapes is *not* grown in Bordeaux?
   A. Cabernet Sauvignon
   B. Semillon
   C. Gamay Noir
   D. Sauvignon Blanc

8. Which one of these wine regions does *not* have a major problem with hail?
   A. Mendoza, Argentina
   B. Burgundy, France
   C. Bordeaux, France

9. Swirling a glass of wine releases aromatic compounds called
   A. Esters
   B. Ethels
   C. Ernestos

10. Aroma is an important component in a wine's personality. Which of the following is the figure estimated as its importance?
    A. 50 percent
    B. 80 percent
    C. 95 percent

11. A corked wine can be said to smell like
    A. Wet newspapers
    B. Wet dogs
    C. Wet grass

12. Which of the following grapes (almost) never spends time in an oak barrel?
    A. Riesling
    B. Semillon
    C. Pinotage

13. Which grape is the most planted in the world?
    A. Chardonnay
    B. White Zinfandel
    C. Cabernet Sauvignon

14. *Barrique* is the name of a
    A. French oak barrel
    B. French card game
    C. French vineyard measurement

15. A "green" wine is one
    A. Made from underripe grapes
    B. Made from organic grapes
    C. Made in Ireland

16. Which of the following châteaux is *not* a first growth?
    A. Margaux
    B. Haut-Brion
    C. Pétrus

17. The wines of the Left Bank of Bordeaux are made predominantly from which grape?
    A. Cabernet Sauvignon
    B. Cabernet Franc
    C. Merlot

18 Which Médoc subregion, or "commune," has more second growths than any other?
    A. St. Julien
    B. Pauillac
    C. Margaux

19. The Côte d'Or is a
    A. Gated community in Beverly Hills
    B. Region in Burgundy
    C. Region in Champagne

20. The French use the term *manly* when describing
    A. Château Latour
    B. Hermitage
    C. Jerry Lewis

21. A négociant is a
    A. French movie agent
    B. French grape buyer
    C. French château broker

22. What is the biggest problem facing Alsace winemakers to date?
    A. An excess supply of Gewürztraminer grapes
    B. Wines that are considered too sweet
    C. An excess of German tourists on walking trips

23. The chief defining attribute of Loire Valley wines is
    A. Acidity
    B. Tannin
    C. Color

24. Marsanne and Roussanne are names of
    A. Vineyards in France's Rhône Valley
    B. Grape varieties cultivated in the Rhône Valley
    C. The fourth and fifth Musketeers

25. RD on the label of a bottle of Bollinger Champagne stands for
    A. Ready to drink
    B. Recently disgorged
    C. The real deal

26. Barolo and Barbaresco are the names of
    A. Italian towns
    B. Italian grapes
    C. Both

27. Falanghina is the name of
    A. A white grape grown in southern Italy
    B. A Roman emperor
    C. An Italian vine disease

28. There are good Italian Pinot Grigio producers. Where can some of
    the best examples be found?
    A. Tuscany
    B. Alto Adige
    C. New Jersey

29. Which of the following terms is used to describe a young Rioja wine?
    A. Infanta
    B. Crianza
    C. Niñera

30. Which man does not make a Spanish cult wine?
    A. Alvaro Palacios
    B. Peter Sisseck
    C. José Luís Rodríguez Zapatero

31. A port lodge is
    A. Where port is aged
    B. Where retired seamen congregate
    C. Where port is sold

32. The German wine classification system, known as the Prädikat sys-
    tem, ranks German wines according to
    A. Grape ripeness
    B. Bottle price
    C. Pronounceability

33. The most important grape in Germany is
    A. Riesling
    B. Müller-Thurgau
    C. Sylvaner

34. Blaufrankisch is a
    A. Red grape grown in Austria
    B. Two-door German sedan
    C. Red grape grown in Hungary

35. The Barossa Valley is
    A. A western epic colorized by Ted Turner
    B. A winemaking region in Australia
    C. Ted Turner's ranch in Montana

36. Pinotage is a
    A. Red grape native to South Africa
    B. Red grape native to Australia
    C. Car built by Ford in the seventies

37. One of the most famous Cabernets made in Chile is
    A. Don Melchor
    B. Don Ameche
    C. Don Pedro

38. Bonarda is
    A. A red grape grown in Argentina
    B. The head of a crime family in Brooklyn
    C. A red grape grown in Mendocino

39. Which grape is not successfully grown in Oregon?
    A. Pinot Noir
    B. Gamay
    C. Merlot

40. The father of New York State wine is considered to be
    A. Dr. Julius No
    B. Dr. Konstantin Frank
    C. Dr. John

41. Which of the following is a Napa Valley appellation?
    A. Mount Eden
    B. Mount Veeder
    C. Mount Napa

Extra-Credit Questions

42. Which of the following is the wine made by Francis Ford Coppola?
    A. Rubicon
    B. Opus One
    C. Don Corleone

43. Martin Scorsese's favorite wine is
    A. Chianti
    B. Barolo
    C. White Zinfandel

44. If movies were ranked according to the Bordeaux classification system, which movie would be a first growth?
    A. *Citizen Kane*
    B. *Basic Instinct*
    C. *South Park: The Movie*

45. James Bond's favorite Champagne is
    A. Cristal
    B. Dom Pérignon
    C. Bollinger
    D. All of the above
    E. B and C
    F. A and C

Extra credit: Write a one-paragraph description of your favorite wine.

Answers to the Wine Quiz

1.c; 2.b; 3.a; 4.c; 5.a,b,c; 6.b; 7.d; 8.c; 9.a; 10.b; 11.a; 12.a; 13.a; 14.a; 15.a; 16.c; 17.a; 18.a; 19.b; 20.b; 21.b; 22.b; 23.a; 24.b; 25.b; 26.a; 27.a; 28.b; 29.b; 30.c; 31.a; 32.a; 33.a; 34.a; 35.b; 36.a; 37.a; 38.a; 39.c; 40.b; 41.b; 42.a; 43.a; 44.a; 45.b

HOW DID PETER DO?

Quite respectably. Peter's score of 84 percent (answering 37 out of 45 questions correctly) meant he earned a solid B. "I don't feel bad about that," Peter said. "The only question I missed that really bothers me was the question on hail. Particularly since I spent so much time talking about it."

Meanwhile, Peter's description of his favorite wine earned him an A.

The Hermann Wiemer Riesling from the Finger Lakes region remains one of my earliest and most pleasurable experiences. To the nose, the wine provided a light, tickling sensation that promised great things to come. What it delivered on the palate was even better—a dry (not sweet or sickening as Riesling's reputation would have it) sense of dazzle with surprising fullness and flavor. It finished beautifully, leaving me with a feeling of celebration—the kind you get when you've sampled something extraordinary. A wine with a great start, middle, and ending struck me as exactly what a great movie should be as well—a completely satisfying experience.

THE FINAL WORD:
PETER

"This whole experience left me with an appetite to know more and to make wine as personal as I can," said Peter at the end of our last session. "Obviously, I learned how huge the wine world is, and yet despite that I feel like I actually retained a surprising amount of information, even if I only got a B on my quiz. I know how Bordeaux is organized and why the wines of Burgundy are so celebrated, and I think I understand why Italian wine is so confusing. I even learned to love Cabernet! It's not that there weren't some scary moments—like that South African Pinotage we tasted, and the night you made me order a bottle of wine at Cru. But in the end what I got was an emotional appreciation of wine. It was never just about facts and figures, but learning about the places and meeting the people who not only make wine their business and their life but turn it into an art form. And that's what will stay with me—always."

AN ADDENDUM FROM THE AUTHOR

I had a few reservations about Peter as an educational prospect. He was as confirmed a Chardonnay drinker as anyone I know (in fact, he remains the only man I've ever personally been acquainted with who really, truly, deeply, madly loves Chardonnay). But he's also one of the most passionately curious people I know. When Peter is interested in something, he immerses himself in the subject completely.

For example, I remember the day Peter bought his first digital camera. He was determined to master it—he took pictures incessantly (and still does), attended photography courses at night, enrolled in weekend seminars, until he was not only proficient but practically professional. He even began making cards and calendars from his photographs; he took a picture of my house that looked like a painting and turned it into a set of cards.

I witnessed this same intensity of focus when Peter undertook the study of wine—scribbling his notes into a series of impossibly tiny notebooks and calling to ask questions or relay a story about an encounter he'd had with a sommelier (sometimes he'd win, more often the sommelier did—at least according to Peter). And through the so-called education of Peter I was, in turn, reeducated to what I first loved about wine—amazing people like Bill Harlan, Naoko Dalla Valle, and Ed Sbragia, beautiful places like Napa and Burgundy, and wines as profound as Screaming Eagle and as unexpectedly good as a Finger Lakes Riesling. Each was, in its way, a revelation and an ongoing reminder of the joy that is wine.

How to Hold a Wine Tasting: The Director's Cut

There's no more inherently social beverage than wine. I know some beer drinkers who might disagree, but I don't know many who could (or would want to) debate the relative merits of pilsner versus lager for very long. Beer drinkers, in my experience, tend to prefer drinking to talking, while wine lovers tend to be quite fond of both. And of course, there's a much broader range of possible conversational topics when the subject is wine. For example, there are the wine's taste and aroma—which might resemble anything from berries to minerals to spices or slate. There are the place where it's made (e.g., the Languedoc of France, Chile's Rapel Valley, or Napa, California) and the grapes it's composed of (there are thousands of varietals in the world) and of course the vintage, the winery, the winemaker, and how much or how little the bottle cost. (My collector friends are particularly fond of discussing this last fact.)

And that's just the objective stuff. There's another, entirely much more subjective, side of wine tasting, where opinions are what matter and the metaphors flow: "This Chardonnay has the body of a seventeen-year-old cheerleader." For the record, this wasn't something Peter would say; he was more likely to compare wines to movie directors or vice versa. (Perhaps Alfred Hitchcock was Peter's beloved "fatty" Chardonnay?)

But wine certainly becomes more interesting to talk about when opinion and facts are combined. And that's what defines a good wine tasting to me: the conversation it inspires among friends.

WHAT MAKES A GOOD TASTING PARTNER

Just as my friend the Collector prefers to play golf with people whose skills are greater than his (never mind that they might feel the same way), I usually taste with collectors who, if they don't actually know more, usually have better wines than I do. They have cellars with tens of thousands of bottles (versus my mere hundreds) that are not only more expensive but also much older, and the historical perspective these wines provide is invaluable. It's one thing to know that, say, 1947 was a great vintage in Bordeaux, another thing to actually taste a wine made that year.

But I like to taste wine with less knowledgeable friends too. They might not have extensive collections or for that matter great tasting vocabularies (though like Peter they do manage to come up with some pretty creative, if unorthodox, ways to describe wine). Most important, they have great curiosity and a lot of enthusiasm, and therefore tasting with them is just as much fun as it is with my collector pals. In fact, I'd argue that anyone with an open mind, a spirit of adventure, and a flair for metaphor makes a good wine-tasting partner.

WHAT TO TASTE

What wines are a good focus for a tasting? It may sound simple, but the answer is: any of them. Save, perhaps, the grocery store labels that my sister buys—wines that cost $3 or $4 a bottle and are styled more for immediate consumption than for extended contemplation.

ONE WINERY/ONE REGION

Every wine tasting requires some sort of focus, unless the objective is just to get drunk. But the focus can be something as simple as a specific producer if there are enough people who like a particular winery's offerings. (There never seems to be a shortage, for example, of Silver Oak Cabernet fans.) This sort of tasting might include current vintages of the winery's entire range, from Cabernet to Chardonnay to Riesling, or maybe just the flagship bottling from a variety of vintages. While the former can give a complete picture of a winery's style (not to mention what the winemaker's talent may be with one grape or another) the latter can give tasters a sense of the history and evolution of the winery itself.

A single region, such as Napa or Bordeaux, is another good focus, as tasting several wines from the same region is a good way to understand the geography. Of course, Bordeaux, for example, is a very large region with a great deal of variation from one subregion to another, so it might be more useful to focus on wines from an even more particular place, such as St. Emilion or Margaux, both subregions of Bordeaux.

A tasting could also focus on a single grape, with examples from different places all over the world. When I was teaching Peter the six basic grapes, he developed a keen interest in Pinot Noir (along with the rest of the post-*Sideways* world) and wanted to taste Pinots from everywhere. So we tasted Pinots from California, Oregon, Burgundy in France (where it originated), parts of New Zealand, and even a few places where Pinot Noir has no business being grown (e.g., the Finger Lakes of New York).

In fact, Peter loved Pinot Noir so much I was surprised to hear that he'd recently staged a Sauvignon Blanc, not Pinot Noir, tasting. Sauvignon Blanc was one of the grapes Peter had liked the least. Had he been hoping to experience a conversion? Much the opposite, he replied. In fact, it seemed Peter wanted people to take his part, to tell him why they too hated the grape. Preferably in great detail. As Peter said, "No one gets away with telling me that they just loved or hated a movie. Now it's the same way with wine. I'll say, 'Oh, you like that Sauvignon Blanc. Why? Do you know why? Do you know its origins?'" (It sounded like the makings of a long night to me.)

THEME TASTING

Of course, tastings don't have to feature one type of wine, one producer, or a single region. They can also be arranged around an idea. I once put together a tasting for some friends that featured only bad vintages of Château Latour. This famous first-growth Bordeaux, according to legend, is always good even in the worst vintages, and I wanted to find out if that was true. So I bought a few wines (1984, 1991)—which were surprisingly expensive, considering how lousy those vintages were—and I got some others from my friend the Collector, including the truly lousy 1977 vintage. (What was he doing with that wine anyway?) In fact, the Collector said he couldn't remember how he'd acquired such a wine, except perhaps that it was to complete his collection of Latour. The enterprise turned out to be an interesting, if not particularly pleasurable endeavor (we found two of the eight wines to be actually drinkable), but I recommend trying it sometime, if only to test the conventional theory that a great producer can always make a great wine, regardless of the quality of the vintage.

VERTICAL OR HORIZONTAL

Although these may sound more like types of window blinds than wine tastings, they are two very basic ways to taste wine. *Vertical* refers to a single wine, tasted through a number of vintages, while *horizontal* refers to wines that are all from the same year. The latter might be a tasting of wines from several Bordeaux producers from a specific commune or subregion such as Pauillac or Margaux or of wines from Marlborough in New Zealand. A vertical tasting examines how a specific wine or producer fared through several years.

BLIND TASTINGS

Blind tastings are best regarded as recreational rather than informational pursuits. While they can be a good way to debunk preconceived notions about a winery, vintage, or place, they can be less than useful when it comes to accurately identifying a wine. This isn't just because it's a hard thing to do (and it is!) but also because, in this age of globalization, a lot of wines from all over the world taste much the same and it can be easy to stump even the most sophisticated palate with a wine served blind. I once gave Daniel Johnnes, wine director of all Daniel Boulud restaurants and a well-known wine importer, a fancy Argentine Malbec to taste with the bottle covered in a brown paper bag. (It was Cobos, made by Paul Hobbs, one of the first three-figure Malbecs to come from that country. It costs about $125 a bottle.) Daniel has one of the best palates of anyone I know, but he was unable to guess the wine's country of origin or even the grape. He did get around to guessing Argentina by his fourth or fifth try, but the wine was made in such a generic, modern New World style (big, ripe, forward fruit flavors, lots of new French oak) that it could have been from anywhere in the world.

A FINAL WORD ON THE PRACTICAL DETAILS OF WHAT YOU'LL NEED FOR A WINE TASTING

The physical requirements of a wine tasting are pretty straightforward: a clean, well-lit place and some decent wine glasses—preferably both Bordeaux and Burgundy stems (Bordeaux glasses have straight sides; Burgundy glasses are balloon shaped). Of course, I've been to tastings where everyone only gets one glass and others where each type of wine gets its own glass. (Riedel is famous for making a wine glass for just about every type of wine. I think they must produce dozens and dozens of different glasses by now—glasses for Chianti, glasses for Pinot Noir, glasses for Baco Noir, probably, too. I don't have the storage space, the fiscal wherewithal, or for that matter, the patience for that sort of thing.)

Nearly as important as good glassware is something into which tasters can dump the wine, e.g., a large bucket or spittoon. Although Peter hated the idea of spitting—and actually still does—it's an absolute necessity if you're going to keep track of what you're tasting. Everything else you might have at a wine tasting is an extra added attraction: notebooks or tasting sheets (Peter was partial to keeping track of the wines that he tasted in tiny ninety-nine-cent notebooks from CVS) and food such as crackers, cheese, or a good meal afterward. I believe in all of these, but it's up to the group.

THE LAST WORD ON TASTINGS: FROM PETER

For Peter, the best sort of tasting is one done at the wineries where the wines were made, as on our four-day trip to Napa. "Tasting helped me to focus and enjoy the experience more fully," he told me afterward, adding, "I'd encourage everyone to take wine-tasting expeditions. If you're traveling to France, Italy, Spain—take a day or two to just wrap yourself up in the wines of the region. Your memories of the wine and the place will be forever intertwined."

It was a beautiful sentiment. Had Peter actually said that to people? He had. "I just want to share all the wonder of what I experienced." And added in true Peter fashion, "I just hope I'm not being a jerk about it."